The Analytic Ambition

The Analytic Ambition

An Introduction to Philosophy

William Charlton

BLACKWELL
Oxford UK & Cambridge MA

First published 1991

Basil Blackwell Ltd
108 Cowley Road, Oxford, OX4 1JF, UK

Basil Blackwell, Inc.
3 Cambridge Center
Cambridge, Massachusetts 02142, USA

British Library Cataloguing in Publication Data
A CIP catalogue record for this book is available from the British Library.

Library of Congress Cataloging in Publication Data
Charlton, William
    The analytic ambition/by William Charlton.
        p.   cm.
    Includes bibliographical references and index.
    ISBN 0–631–16934–2   ISBN 0–631–16935–0 (pbk.)
    1. Analysis (Philosophy)   2. Philosophy – Introductions.
    I. Title.
    B808.5.C515   1991
    146'.4–dc20   90–27102
                                                                              CIP

Typeset in 11 on 13 pt Garamond (Stempel)
by Graphicraft Typesetters Ltd., Hong Kong
Printed in Great Britain by T.J. Press Ltd, Padstow, Cornwall

Contents

CONTENTS

Preface

This book is introductory in two ways. Instead of taking a single topic and going into it exhaustively I range over what I see as all the main issues philosophers have traditionally addressed. And I assume no previous acquaintance with philosophy in the reader. So far as I can, I dispense with technical terms and symbols. Those I have found indispensable I explain as I introduce them and the explanations are collected in a list at the end of the book (pp. 209–12).

But though it has these introductory features my book is not intended either to be uncontroversial or to be merely a description of what has been done by others. Philosophy is not a body of specialized knowledge which can be summarized. The topics philosophers discuss are of potential interest to everyone, and I have tried to find new arguments, analogies and other devices that will enable any intelligent person to see more deeply into them.

Gilbert Ryle read an early version of the book, made many suggestions and gave me extremely valuable encouragement. Others who read and commented helpfully on parts include Karl Britton, Norman Coles, Edmund Furlong, Jane Heal, Philip Percival, Richard Sorabji, Colin Strang and Christopher Williams. I also tried out all my ideas in lectures, tutorials and graduate seminars at the University of Newcastle-upon-Tyne. Since the department there has now been abolished I should like to record that the conditions it provided for philosophizing were excellent. The students were splendidly enthusiastic and stimulating. My colleagues exemplified a devoted and highly expert amateurism which is growing rare in British academic life but which greatly aids good philosophy. And thanks to the generosity of two of them who set up a fund to buy in replacement teaching, I had such a chance to think philosophical problems through as comes to few academics today in a six-month sabbatical in the Marquesas.

Material in chapters 3 to 7 and 10 has appeared in *Philosophy*, the *Philosophical Quarterly* and publications of the Aristotelian Society. I am grateful to the editors for permission to reuse it.

1
What is Analytical Philosophy?

1.1 What is philosophy?

Philosophy is the systematic applying of the resources of a civilization to the deepest problems that engage the human intellect.

These problems mostly concern the situation in which we find ourselves. We live in a world of changing objects; we are aware of what is going on and we act for purposes. Philosophy in a way peculiar to itself enables reflective people to understand the main features of this predicament: the nature of life, change, objects, awareness and purpose.

We may also wish to know whether any other kind of existence could be in store for us and whether the universe depends on a personal God. The resources of civilization for dealing with these religious problems are, in my opinion, limited; but such as they are, philosophy helps us to make the best use of them.

Today philosophy is taught and studied at universities as one particular discipline among others. You can get a degree in it or be a professor of it. This institutionalization has dangers as well as conveniences. For philosophy has no special subject-matter or field for research on a level with those of other disciplines like history, mathematics and biology; while to tackle the deepest problems philosophers must preserve the freedom of amateurs: they must not be bound intellectually by any terms of reference. If they become just another group of professional academics they cease to be of any use either as philosophers or as anything else: their philosophy turns into scholasticism.

Besides meaning what I have just said, the word 'philosophy' has other uses. It originally meant the pursuit of knowledge more extensive, more accurate or more profound than is needed for immediate practical purposes. This usage lingered on into the last century when physics was still sometimes called 'natural philosophy' and is preserved as a linguistic fossil in the names of some so-called 'philosophical societies'. In ordinary speech, if you bear misfortunes with equanimity, and not out of stark insensibility, but because you can see beyond the here and now, you are said to bear them 'with philosophy'. You may also, if you have general views on things which are thought out with care, call them 'my philosophy'. One might hope that acquaintance with academic philosophy would help people to be philosophical in adversity and to have a luminous philosophy of life; but I have to say that this cannot be guaranteed.

There is a more sombre warning I should add. The deepest questions that engage our minds are not easily answered and to gain any real insight into them one has to make a considerable effort. Philosophy is a hard subject. Some of the greatest philosophers have also had outstanding gifts for lucid exposition but even they, even Plato, Hume and Russell, are heavy going. If it is useless for philosophers to write only for philosophers it is equally unprofitable for a non-philosopher to take up a serious philosophical work without being prepared to invest much concentration in reading it.

1.2 Two kinds of philosophy

Analytical philosophy is the variety of philosophy favoured by the majority of philosophers working in English-speaking countries; those working on the Continent of Europe mostly practise a different variety sometimes called 'Continental'. Analytical philosophers do not differ from their Continental counterparts primarily in the positions they defend on disputed issues. They differ in how they conceive the subject and think it should be conducted. For part of their time they consider different questions altogether; when they converge on the same topics it is from different directions; and they have different methods of argument, different criteria for judging the merits of a piece of philosophizing.

This division hardly goes back beyond the beginning of the present century. English-speaking and Continental philosophers still acknowledge the same authorities down at least to Kant, and in the nineteenth century post-Kantian German philosophers were taken seriously in English-speaking universities: there was a British version of German Idealism. But then Russell and Moore, perhaps most strikingly the former in his *The Philosophy of Leibniz* (1900) and *The Principles of Mathematics* (1903), gave British philosophy a new orientation. Since their methods caught on, English-speaking and Continental philosophers have pursued their interests with very little regard for one another. The rise of Fascism probably contributed to this tendency. Some leading Continental philosophers like Heidegger compromised with the Nazis, and it is hard to doubt that some Nazis drew support for their ideas from writings which still strongly influence Continental philosophy, the writings of Nietszche; on the other hand, many of the German and Austrian philosophers who emigrated to English-speaking countries shared Russell's taste for empiricism and formal logic. But whatever the historical facts responsible, at the moment English-speaking and Continental philosophers neither read each other's journals nor attend each other's conferences.

In science or history that would be impossible. It can happen in philosophy only because of the nature of the subject. In many ways it is more like an art than a science, and painters and novelists are able to work away without heed to their contemporaries in other societies. Nevertheless it is nothing to be proud of that, while British philosophers are well informed about what is happening on the other side of the Atlantic and even in the Antipodes, they are ignorant of what is happening on the far side of the Channel.

That ignorance I shall not here try to dispel. There is no need, since analytical philosophy does not define itself in opposition to Continental philosophy any more than in opposition to Christian mysticism or to Buddhism.

In fact it hardly defines itself at all. As there is no set of doctrines analytical philosophers hold in opposition to Continental philosophers so there is no set they hold in unison with one another. They disagree obstinately, for example, about whether there is such a thing as objective truth on issues of good and evil and about whether or not states of mind can be identified with physical states of the brain. But they go to conferences together, read and write for the same journals and examine each other's pupils. As a result they have a consensus about what is and what is not a satisfactory treatment of a topic. They also have some agreement (though it falls short of perfect unanimity) about what topics are fit for philosophical treatment. Altogether they constitute not so much a school as a straggling, undisciplined movement. They pride themselves on their individualism, on each developing his own or her own views; but as one of them puts it, 'their work, together with that of their associates, disciples and critics, . . . constitutes a relatively well-bounded dialogue' (Cohen 1986, p. 5).

Because analytical philosophy has this character it is impossible to give the kind of descriptive account of it which would be appropriate for an articulated system or the work of a closely knit school. It is not impossible – John Hospers in his *Introduction to Philosophical Analysis* (1967) managed quite helpfully – to summarize arguments which prominent analytical philosophers have put forward on topics on which they disagree, but my purpose here is different. I believe that the questions analytical philosophers discuss have an interest and importance that match the time and care put into considering them, and that their methods have not yet yielded anything like the return of which they are capable. I doubt if I could convince anyone of that by exhibiting a picture of unresolved conflict. Anyhow my strategy will be to dive into the discussion myself and try to obtain some worthwhile results. Analytical philosophy has recently been the target of some severe criticism, not the least severe coming from within. I hope to vindicate it by showing that it works.

1.3 Topics and methods

The chief topics which analytical philosophers consider can be put into four or five groups:

1 things basic to logic and mathematics: existence, truth and number;
2 things basic to physical science: time, change and causation;
3 good and evil, the varieties of them (virtue, beauty etc.) and the nature of the difference between them;
4 mental processes, states and dispositions, especially the most general notions of belief, desire, skill, purpose and self-awareness or consciousness.

Some people would say that the philosophy of language is a branch of the subject distinct from the philosophies of logic and mind, and that the topics it considers, which include meaning and reference, form a fifth group. I have no objection: I am trying to make possible a conspectus of philosophy, not to impose a rigid compartmentalization on it.

Philosophers have sometimes used the word 'metaphysics' as a term of abuse for undisciplined speculations about things the existence of which they consider doubtful; but today it more commonly signifies the study of topics in groups other than group 3.

The ambition of analytical philosophers is to gain insight into the topics I have mentioned by logical, conceptual and linguistic analysis. The words 'logical', 'conceptual' and 'linguistic' are often used interchangeably but pick out different aspects of their method.

They are supposed to know enough formal logic to be able to tell whether an argument is valid and to put ordinary statements into a form in which the validity of inferences involving them can be ascertained. Peppering your papers with logical symbols, however, is considered uncouth, and the idea that all problems can be solved by turning them into algebra is described disdainfully as logicism. Respectable analytical philosophers use symbols only in so far as they can help to clarify conceptual points, only in the service of conceptual and linguistic analysis.

The phrase 'conceptual analysis' is new but what it applies to is as old as philosophy itself and analytical philosophers believe it to be the only satisfactory way of tackling philosophical topics. Aristotle defines anger as 'desire, accompanied by distress, for vengeance for an apparent slight to you or to your friends, by someone who has no business to be slighting' (*Rhetoric* II 1378ª30–2). How does he know that that is what anger is? Not by prolonged observations, complete with control groups, of baited psychology students, but by reflecting on how he and his friends conceive anger.

Some philosophers have thought that we can determine how we conceive things by a kind of introspection, by some process of looking into our minds. Unfortunately different people report different findings when they do this. Descartes says that when he examines his idea of a person or a thinker it turns out not to include the idea of a body (*Meditation VI, Reply to Objections IV* etc.). Other introspectors say their idea of a thinker is inseparable from the ideas of a brain or an agent that moves about. Analytical philosophers believe that how non-philosophers talk is a guide (though not an infallible guide) to how we think. They defend their own claims about how we conceive things, and attack the claims of their adversaries, by appealing to ordinary modes of speech; and linguistic analysis is pursued, not as it is by linguists, for its own sake, but as a means to analysing thought.

Linguistic analysis can take several forms. Sometimes it is just introspective conceptual analysis cast in terms of words. 'Awareness of an object as having the effect on our state of mind of tending to cause its prolongation', says Kant, 'is what, in general, we call "pleasure"' (*Critique of Judgement* s. 10). He is here saying how we conceive pleasure. Similarly, Aquinas is saying how our concept of beauty differs from our concept of goodness at *Summa Theologiae* Ia IIae 27. 1 ad 2: '"Beautiful" adds to "good" a certain ordination towards our powers of cognition, so that we call "good" whatever simply satisfies desire, but we call "beautiful" that the bare apprehension of which pleases.'

Aristotle recommends philosophers to distinguish different ways in which words are used, and gives as an example the use of 'good' for things good in themselves and for things which are good as means (*Topics* I 106ª4–8). At first that might seem mere lexicography; but it is directed only to words which, like 'good', express things of interest to philosophers, and it is guided by philosophical interest. Moreover the distinctions are often justified by appeals to grammar. Here is an example (slightly modified) from J. O. Urmson (1967). It is a philosophical problem how, when an image comes before the mind, we know whether we are remembering or imagining. To tackle it we must show that the verb 'to imagine' can mean two different things: to form a mental image and to believe. We can bring out the difference by observing that in the first case it takes a noun-phrase as object – 'He imagined the battlefield' – and in the second a 'that' clause – 'He imagined that he had been present on the battlefield.' In recent years philosophers have become aware that grammatical differences are a good guide to interesting conceptual differences. Jennifer Hornsby (1980) has gone so far as to base an entire new theory of the nature of human action on the distinction between transitive and intransitive uses of verbs.

Philosophers have also become aware that superficial similarities in grammar can conceal deep conceptual differences, and major philosophical errors have been traced to this source. I can say, 'I am in pain,' much as I can say, 'I am in Paris,' but Wittgenstein has argued at length (*Philosophical Investigations* I 246ff.) that whereas the second utterance expresses something I can properly be said to know about myself, the first does not. If you look at a circular tray from the side you may say 'It presents an oval appearance.' But this is only superficially like saying, 'The butler presented an oval tray', and failing to see the underlying difference can lead to rather deep confusion about our knowledge of the things around us. Ryle tried to refute certain initially attractive theories about the mind and its relation to the body by showing that attempts to formulate them produce sentences that are grammatical, indeed, but nonsensical. I once heard him say that the whole of his book *The Concept of Mind* (1949) is summarized in this piece of dialogue from one of P. G. Wodehouse's Jeeves stories:

'You mean the imagination boggles?'
'Yes, Sir.'
I inspected my imagination. He was right. It boggled.

Philosophers who use methods like this have to suppose that philosophical questions are at least partly conceptual; that they are in some way and to some extent about how we think about things; and they must suppose that we can learn something about how we think by considering how we speak. But that is all. They are not committed to any special theory of the subject-matter of philosophy like the theory Michael Dummett advances in this encomium of Frege:

Only with Frege was the proper object of philosophy finally established: namely, first that the goal of philosophy is the analysis of *thought*; secondly that the study of *thought* is to be sharply distinguished from the study of the psychological process of *thinking*; and finally, that the only proper method for analysing thought consists in the analysis of *language*. (1987, p. 215)

Still less do they have to hold any particular theory about what concepts or meanings are. To say that they analyse concepts is not to say (though this is not far from what some philosophers have believed) that there are non-physical entities called 'concepts' or 'ideas' which they can analyse in the way chemists analyse samples of suspicious liquid or powder: it is to use a metaphor for the kind of procedures I illustrated above.

Plato and Aristotle aimed at clarity and faulted their predecessors for talking in an excessively technical or oracular manner. Their ideal was that of Pope:

True wit is nature to advantage dressed,
What oft was thought, but ne'er so well expressed;
Something whose truth convinced at sight we find,
That gives us back the image of our mind.
(*An Essay on Criticism*, ll. 297–300)

The same ideal is shared by contemporary analytical philosophers and they sometimes write a little chauvinistically as if it distinguished them from their Continental confrères: 'Unlike Hegelians or Heideggerians they deliberately eshew tortuous syntax, elliptical exposition, and the replacement of plain statement by enigmatic hints, rhetorical paradoxes or woolly metaphor' (Cohen 1986, p. 42). The value they put on a clear, natural style is apparent in the work of some of the best-known English-speaking philosophers of this century, Russell, Austin, Ryle and Davidson.

1.4 A contentious discipline

Neither philosophy in general nor the analytical variety of it is without critics. Some criticisms can be ignored because they apply equally to all academic studies. It is not a peculiarity of philosophy that it does not immediately make the rich richer, reduce the numbers of the poor or promote other goals of enlightened government. But there are writers who say that analytical philosophy is played out, that it is coming to an end and that those of us who still practise it are like the fabled Japanese soldiers in the Melanesian jungles who believe that the Second World War is still going on. Salaried philosophers who do not want to find themselves out of a job should turn to fresh pursuits: to 'nurturing and making articulate' a 'faith in the power of intelligence to imagine a future which is a projection of the desirable in the present' (Dewey 1917, p. 69); to constructing and criticizing 'systems of ideals' (Kekes 1980); or to providing a package of literary criticism, the preaching of virtue and something called 'hermeneutics' (Rorty 1980, following Dewey and Heidegger 1967 and 1975).

According to these counsellors, higher education is here to stay and will soar from height to height but what analytical philosophers mean by 'philosophy' will cease to be a part of it. That is not a realistic forecast. Civilization might collapse altogether and pull philosophy down with it. But so long as it retains any relevant resources people will apply them to understanding what they are and how they stand.

Nevertheless philosophy is essentially self-critical and even self-doubting in a way other disciplines are not. I listed just now some leading topics philosophers discuss. Anyone who gives time to them is bound to wonder what they have in common and whether it is reasonable to think that they belong to a single study or will yield to treatment by a single method. Good and evil have not much to do with the nature of consciousness and still less with time or existence. Could the traditional topics of philosophy be just the contents of an intellectual lost property office, with nothing in common except that no one with a tried method of discovering truth is willing to claim them for his own?

This is a serious doubt which can be met only by a theory of the nature of philosophical enquiry. Such theories have been proposed in the past; indeed, any philosopher who has a distinctive set of philosophical views will have a distinctive position on the nature of philosophy. But I do not find that any of the theories on offer fully meets the problem. It is a principal aim of this book to provide a new one which does.

But philosophy's critics raise a number of specific objections besides the general one that the field of philosophy lacks unity, and before sketching my theory I wish to look at three of these.

Richard Rorty in *Philosophy and the Mirror of Nature* (1980) argues that the appearance of a set of perennial problems taxing the brains of philosophers in age after age is illusory. Each age has its own 'problematic', its own set of interests which is determined by the historical 'contingencies' of the time, that is, by developments in politics, science, religion or whatever happens to be on the move. In the Middle Ages philosophers wanted to reconcile Christian theology and the beginnings of natural science with a theory they supposed had been proved by Aristotle to the effect that material objects are composed of some sort of inert, featureless matter and substantial form. In the seventeenth century they wanted to free men's minds from the authority of theologians and were preoccupied with what is called 'epistemology', the theory of knowledge. The modern interest in language is something new again. It is a wild-goose chase, then, to seek knowledge of any kind of reality past philosophers were investigating; all we can do is see what contemporary 'contingencies' they were responding to.

This account would make philosophy subordinate in a way to history. But historical study itself tells against it. It shows that the topics I listed really were discussed by ancient, medieval and modern philosophers, and were understood in pretty much the same way. Take, for instance, time, space and change. Plato discusses these topics at length in two dialogues, the *Parmenides* and the *Timaeus*; so does Aristotle in two books of his *Physics* (books III and IV); and these texts were commented on and studied throughout the Middle Ages. Hume and Kant feel obliged to give sections to them (*Treatise* I ii; *Critique of Pure Reason*, Transcendental Aesthetic) before proceeding to the more congenial topics of causation and personal identity. They reappear in Hegel's *Science of Logic* and Russell's *Principles of Mathematics*. Where Rorty sees sporadic outbreaks of speculative conversation in different societies, history reveals a single philosophical tradition. There is no more reason to apprehend a radical breakdown in understanding between philosophers of different ages than between Homer, Virgil, Dante and Milton. The 'contingencies' of Homeric Greece must have been very different from those of nineteenth-century Russia and this must have affected people's conceptions of war, love and domestic life; but it is grotesque to say that the *Iliad* and the *Odyssey* are not about any of the same things as *War and Peace* or *Anna Karenina*.

A second line of criticism allows that successive ages addressed the same problems but brands these as pseudo-problems. One indication of something amiss is that after more than two thousand years of discussion none of them has yet received a definitive solution. People argue about time, about causation, about the nature of the mind, just as much now as in the days of Plato.

To this argument I reply that philosophical problems are not like problems in a mathematics examination, each of which has a unique answer that can be proved to be right. They are more like problems in the arts, which admit of good and bad solutions but which nevertheless present themselves over and over again to successive ages. The depiction of the human figure, of

trees, of the sea, presents problems to generation after generation of painters. A Giotto, a Turner, a Cézanne may solve
them very pleasingly within his own style; that does not make
it a waste of time for a Leonardo, a Hokusai or a Gauguin to
attempt them in a different one. Notre Dame of Chartres and
St Paul's of London are solutions are exactly the same problem: rebuilding a cathedral of national importance after a fire.
They are completely different, but neither invalidates the other.
As each epic poet or dramatist or novelist wants to give his
own delineation of the working of love or anger or ambition
or jealousy, so each philosopher wants to give his own account
of existence or causation or thought. The philosopher attains
truth in the way Michelangelo attains truth about the human
figure, not in the way in which a spy attains truth about a
country's military preparations.

Peter Unger has argued that philosophical problems are
spurious not because philosophical truth is of this insuffici-
ently hard-nosed character but because there is simply no truth
to be obtained at all. His argument is based on an alleged
systematic ambiguity in the words in which philosophical
questions are asked. Take the question which is oftenest on
the lips of philosophers from Descartes to Russell: 'Can we
know anything about the physical world around us?' This is
unanswerable (1984, pp. 3–5, 46–54) because 'to know' has no
determinate meaning. If we assign it a strict, invariant meaning
according to which knowledge excludes the faintest possibility
of error or uncertainty we can have no knowledge of anything
outside our own minds; if we allow the meaning of the word to
vary with the circumstances in which we use it, we can have
knowledge of the physical world. And the question 'What in
fact *is* the meaning of "to know"? Does it vary or not?' is not a
question of objective fact to which there can be a correct and
true answer.

I do not find this argument at all cogent. Why should we
conclude from it that 'Can we know anything about the
physical world?' has no answer rather than that it has two? Or
what does it matter if it has no answer provided that two other
questions, 'Can we know anything if "know" has a strict
invariant meaning?' and 'Can we know anything if the meaning
of "know" varies?' have the answers Unger provides?

A number of philosophers have argued that the traditional problems of philosophy are spurious because they rest upon or derive from philosophical mistakes. Dewey says the mistake is to think that we are non-material objects, souls or minds quite distinct from our bodies and the rest of the world (1917, pp. 30–1). According to Rorty (1980, p. 12 and *passim*) it is to conceive the mind as a sort of mirror or canvas, and knowledge as accurate reflection in this mirror or accurate representation on this canvas. Both critics complain that philosophers have traditionally been obsessed with problems about knowledge, and blame this obsession on their mistakes.

I agree that these views of human nature and the human mind are erroneous, that they were accepted by most philosophers from Descartes to Russell, that they give rise to insoluble problems about how we can know anything, and that much time has been wasted on those problems. I agree too that the philosophers of this period tended to approach all philosophical problems from the direction of the theory of knowledge, to concentrate on their epistemological aspect; and I share Dewey's and Rorty's dislike of this approach. But they do not show that all problems about the topics I listed, goodness and badness, time, causation and so forth, depend on mistakes about human nature and the mind. Although Dewey undertakes to question the genuineness of 'traditional problems' the only problems he mentions are epistemological ones. Even philosophers who are most wedded to an epistemological approach, like Locke and Hume, use it to discuss topics which have nothing to do with the nature and possibility of knowledge. And neither Dewey nor Rorty gives us any reason to think that we cannot be interested in these further topics without believing that we are non-physical beings or that thinking must be conceived on the model of mirroring or representing. They concentrate too exclusively on philosophers from Descartes to Russell. Dewey says nothing about ancient philosophy and his view of medieval philosophy seems to be distorted by some kind of religious hang-up. Rorty, as we have seen, denies that ancient and medieval philosophers are doing the same subject as Descartes and his successors; on that view their work can hardly be relevant to us. I shall argue, however, that an analytical philosopher has no need to conceive human nature and knowledge as Descartes, Locke, Kant or Russell did.

I think that some critics of analytical philosophy have been led astray by confusing belief in the methods of philosophical analysis I described above with belief in a particular theory of how reality, thought and language are interrelated. Since I want to dissociate analytical philosophy from this theory, let me try to explain what it is.

1.5   An atomistic theory

According to the latest version, the world ultimately consists of certain basic objects which are in themselves simple, which have certain simple properties and which stand to one another in simple relations. What are these objects? The theory leaves us a choice. We can have the most fundamental particles known to science, quarks or whatever now play the role once played by corpuscular atoms; or we can have more subjective phenomena such as after-images and bodily sensations. A basic property might be a shape, mass or colour, a basic relation between two objects might be being an inch apart. An object's having a basic property or standing in a basic relation is a basic fact. Corresponding to basic facts are basic propositions. If A is a simple object and the colour red a basic property, then A's being red would be a basic fact, and the utterance 'A is red', in which the colour is predicated of the object, would express a basic proposition.

Such propositions may be combined into complex propositions which are called 'truthfunctions' of them. What does that word mean? One proposition is a truthfunction of a second if its truth is a function of, if it depends solely upon, the truth of the second. The proposition that 5 is not the sum of 2 and 2 is a truthfunction of the proposition that 5 *is* the sum of 2 and 2: it is true if and only if that second proposition is false. Similarly the single complex proposition:

Either 2 + 2 = 5 or 2 + 2 = 4

is a truthfunction of the two propositions that 2 + 2 = 5 and that 2 + 2 = 4: it is false if both of them are false and otherwise true.

A truthfunction of simple propositions expresses a complex fact. We may call that fact a 'logical construct' out of the facts expressed by the simple propositions. The theory asserts that every actual fact in the world which is not a basic fact is a logical construct out of basic facts; we can express it in some proposition which is a truthfunction of basic propositions. That being so, the business of philosophy is to say what the simple elements of reality are and to analyse complex propositions and facts into simple ones. Susan Stebbing (1932/3, p. 65) summarized the theory as follows:

> Metaphysics is a systematic study to show what is the structure of the facts in the world to which reference is made, with various degrees of directness, whenever a true statement is made. Insofar as the aim of metaphysics were achieved it would enable us to know precisely what there is in the world. To know what precisely there is in the world is to know what the facts are which together make up, i.e. constitute, the world. To know precisely what a given fact is, is to know both the elements which make up the fact and the mode of their combination.

As I have stated it, this theory belongs to the first third of the twentieth century and is appropriately called 'logical atomism' (see Russell 1918–19; Wittgenstein 1922); but it is in a tradition which goes back to Descartes. In his *Rules for the Direction of the Mind* (1628) Descartes says that we must reduce 'involved and obscure propositions' such as the more advanced theorems of mathematics 'step by step to propositions which are simpler' (Rule 5), and that there are just a few 'pure and simple natures' (Rule 6). Locke thought that to every meaningful word (except particles like 'but') there corresponds an idea; and every idea is either simple and unanalysable or constructed out of simple ideas. If we want to give a philosophical account of something like time or human nature we take the word for it ('time', 'human being'), see what idea it expresses and analyse that idea into its simple constituents.

It can easily seem that the way to philosophize must be like this. Complex objects must be composed of simple objects, complex concepts or thoughts of simple ones, and philosophical understanding must come by identifying the basic

building blocks, so to speak, of reality and thought and describing the ways in which they are modified, shaped, fitted
together. Urmson (1956) gives the title *Philosophical Analysis*
to a book on twentieth-century attempts to carry out this programme. Still it is not necessary to see philosophy as analysis
of this kind to be an analytical philosopher. On the contrary,
the main attacks on this view of philosophy and on the atomistic theory which supports it have come from analytical philosophers: from Austin, Ryle, Quine and the later Wittgenstein.
The theories I myself shall develop in what follows are all
opposed to this atomism.

1.6 *The charge of triviality*

I return to the critics of philosophy. If they allow that there are
perennial problems and that these problems are not simply the
result of philosophical mistakes, a remaining theme of com-
plaint is that the problems are trivial, unworthy of the time
devoted to them; or at least that the methods of analytical
philosophy cannot yield any but trivial conclusions about
them. Unger says:

> First, it is assumed that the rather a priori, armchair methods of
> the subject are good for little other than the examination of our
> ordinary terms. But second it is assumed also that our ordinary
> common sense beliefs ... are ... correct almost without excep-
> tion. Thus philosophers are to be confined to almost nothing
> but a rather critical examination of our common sense beliefs
> ... No substantial result is to be expected from their examina-
> tion. Philosophy is to leave our view of the world unchanged.
> (1975, pp. 3–4)

Such criticisms are neither new nor confined to analytical
philosophy. In the time of Plato Isocrates warned young men
against 'wasting themselves away' on logic-chopping and 'getting stranded' on the arguments of thinkers of the past like
Parmenides and Anaxagoras who put the number of 'things
there are' at anything from one to infinity. Such 'fancy utterances are like conjuring tricks' and those who want to do

something worthwhile should write instead of matters of nationwide or political interest (*Antidosis* 262, 268–9). In the twelfth century that efficient administrator John of Salisbury revisited after twelve years those of his old companions whom 'dialectic', the analytical philosophy of the day, still detained in the schools of Paris. He reports that they had not advanced a step in solving old problems or added a single new proposition; and concludes that dialectic may help other disciplines but 'possessed by itself is bloodless and sterile' (*Metalogicon* II 10). No one ever put the case better than Hume:

> If we take in our hand any volume, of divinity or school metaphysics, for instance, let us ask, 'Does it contain any abstract reasoning concerning quantity or number?' 'No' 'Does it contain any experimental reasoning concerning matter of fact and existence?' 'No' 'Commit it then to the flames, for it can contain nothing but sophistry and illusion.' (1902A, p. 165)

Unger's remarks are far from being a correct representation of philosophical practice. Analytical philosophers do not study ordinary language in order to verify 'common sense beliefs': they aim at uncovering beliefs and ways of thinking which we do not know we have but which, they hope, are revealed by ordinary modes of speech. Do we think that time flows or passes? Common sense says, 'Ask a philosopher'; non-philosophers are happy to confess that they do not know what they think. The same is true of other typical philosophical problems like whether freedom is compatible with causal determination, whether a state of mind could possibly be identical with a state of the brain, whether when we disagree about the goodness or badness of an action there is a truth of the matter to be discovered. Common sense tells us that our thought on these topics is unclear; it can be clarified, I hope to demonstrate, by analysis of how we talk, not about these topics as such but about ordinary objects, occurrences and decisions.

It would be philistine to call these problems 'trivial' though it may be admitted that there is no air of urgency about them. Highbrows who are not trained philosophers feel inclined to contrast them with very big questions indeed which can seem to have an urgency for everyone, such as 'Has life a meaning?' 'What is the good for man?' 'What is justice?' No doubt these are questions of political or nationwide interest, but how are we supposed to have anything trustworthy to say about them? How are we to know whether life has a meaning or what justice is? By having the stars shine on our birth? By pulling answers out of the air? Poets and prophets may stand up in the marketplace and proclaim big answers, but philosophy was introduced by people who found this unsatisfying.

The great philosophers have had an influence on human history comparable with that of founders of religions. Plato and Aristotle may be said to have created the concept of an academic discipline. They set up two schools, the Academy and the Lyceum, from which all later institutions of higher education derive. They also introduced a certain view of human nature which now separates advanced from primitive societies. It is thanks to them that we today distinguish thinking from perceiving and feeling and conceive ourselves as intellectual beings with minds. This revolution was achieved precisely, as Isocrates complains, by logic-chopping and scrutinizing the speculations of past thinkers. In modern times Hegel and Marx have had no small responsibility for collectivist regimes in Germany, Italy, Russia and China; whereas opponents of collectivism have drawn ammunition from Hume and Mill. Of these four Marx was profoundly influenced not only by German Idealism but also (witness the Paris manuscripts) by Ancient Greek philosophy and the others were original academic philosophers who drew their moral and political ideas from roots that extend deep into metaphysics.

As for Hume's disloyal but eloquent outburst against metaphysics, anyone whose faith is shaken by it may find reassurance in the way in which the discipline still inspires fear and hostility in political and academic establishments alike. In the last ten years in which the British government has encouraged academics to close each other's departments Britain has lost a quarter of its university posts in philosophy. In less fortunate countries when the security police enter the universities it is the philosophers, not the pure mathematicians or the entomologists, who are the first to be arrested.

2
Outline of a Theory

2.1 Introduction

On p. 5 I ran over some topics philosophers discuss. A satisfactory theory of philosophy must show what those topics have in common and why we can hope to obtain insight into them by considering how we speak and think. Presumably this method works because they are things to enquire into which is at the same time to enquire into thought and speech; but how can such things be?

It seems that the central problems in philosophy have three dimensions. We can ask with crude directness what time or existence or consciousness is. Since the term 'ontology' is used for the study of reality or real things as such we may call this the 'ontological dimension'. Then there is a conceptual or epistemological dimension in which we ask how we conceive these things and how our concepts of them differ from concepts of things philosophers pass over in silence, such as oolite, finessing and bilharzia. And there is a linguistic dimension in which we consider how goodness, existence etc., are expressed in language and how the words which are most expressive of them have meaning. A good theory of philosophy should map out the isomorphism of reality, language and thought and explain why it exists.

The atomistic theory I described on pp. 14–16 goes some way to meeting this requirement. At the ontological level it puts objects which have properties and stand in relations; at the linguistic there are expressions which refer to objects and predicate-expressions which signify properties and relations; and at the conceptual, though we may not get exact correspondence, we are offered simple ideas of properties and simple thoughts which can be combined into complex thoughts that are truthfunctions of them.

The theory, however, has no chance of success. Its explanatory power lies entirely in a single, simple model, the relationship between the materials which a craftsman shapes or puts together and the shape or arrangement which gets imposed on these materials. I do not think that that model will enable us to understand any of the things philosophers discuss. Existence is not a property or relation; neither is time, change or number. There are some philosophical topics which are often referred to as properties such as wisdom, cowardice and beauty; but we shall never see deeply into them so long as we conceive them as analogous to the shape of a vase or the structure of a house. And it is a central task of philosophy to say how it is that our thoughts and speeches relate to the world and are true or false. Not only are truth and falsity nothing like shapes or spatial relations: there is no way in which they can attach to vases, houses, oil-paintings or any of the models which the atomistic theory proposes for thoughts and speeches.

The theory I wish to develop may be summarized in three theses:

1 Philosophers do not consider what objects exist, what changes occur or what properties are exemplified: their business is with the existence of objects, the occurrence of change and the exemplification of properties.

2 We can specify the things which come into our thought and we can describe the *ways in which* these things come in; a concept C is of philosophical interest if to say 'We apply concept C' is not to specify something which enters into our thought but to describe the *entry* into it of other unspecified things.

3 Words and constructions can have meaning in two ways: they can determine what things a speaker using them expresses and they can determine the way in which the

speaker expresses these things, the speaker's mode or form of linguistic expression. A linguistic item is of philosophical interest in so far as it has meaning in the second way, not the first.

These theses deal, respectively, with the ontological, the conceptual and the linguistic aspects of the problem 'What is philosophy?' If they are correct it will be easy to say where the isomorphism of language, thought and reality lies. Different forms of expression correspond to and reflect (sometimes insincerely or deceptively) different ways in which things enter into thought; and to describe how things do enter into thought is to say how we think they enter into reality.

In this chapter I concentrate on explaining what these theses mean. They will be found to entail definite and controversial views on the main topics of philosophy. In later chapters I develop and defend those views, and that constitutes my argument for this theory of philosophy: *probabitur philosophando*.

2.2 The ontological thesis

The ontological thesis was phrased in terms of objects, properties and changes. I am using these words in a technical way which I shall now explain.

By an 'object' I mean either an inanimate body composed of solid, liquid or gaseous material like a pebble, a cloud or a star; or an artifact like a chair; or a living organism like a tree, a tiger or a human being. I use the word not in contrast with 'person', as in 'Men should treat women as persons, not as objects' but in contrast with 'property' and 'change' as in 'Herpyllis is an object, magenta is a property, and apocolocyntosis is a change.'

I use 'property' to cover shapes, sizes, temperatures, colours and other physical properties and also spatial relations like being above and being a mile from. For reasons I indicate later I do not include relations like being larger than and being hotter than, though if anyone wants to I should not be dismayed. A more important exclusion is of temporal and causal relations and mental and moral qualities. These really are the

business of philosophers so if I included them the ontological
thesis would be false. I shall say later how I distinguish them
from physical properties and spatial relations.

Spatial relations which hold between two or more objects
seem very different from shapes and colours which an object
can exemplify all by itself. I group them together for two
reasons. First, they are all predicated of objects; the only
difference is that a shape or colour is predicated of objects
singly whereas being above or between is predicated of two or
more objects in a certain order. In 'Jupiter is between Mars and
Saturn' I predicate the relationship *being between* of Jupiter,
Mars and Saturn in that order. Secondly, relations, like shapes
and sizes, are exemplified by objects. A single object exemplifies any shape, length, surface area or volume it has; a pair of
objects exemplify the relation in which they stand and of which
they are terms.

Objects not only have or exemplify properties; they acquire
and lose them. Acquiring or losing a property is what I mean
by a 'change'.

The first moves a philosopher makes need to be scrutinized
with special care; the reader who lets them go by may find
himself caught by the philosophical equivalent of Fool's Mate
(the opening words of Hume's *Treatise* are a cautionary example). Let me dwell a bit longer, then, on these notions of an
object, a property and a change.

Why do I group together Socrates, my motorcar and the
planet Mars and call them all 'objects'? Not because there is
any physical resemblance between them; not because they have
any properties in common; but because we think and speak
about them in the same way. We say that they all *exist*, that
they all *have properties*, that they all *undergo changes* but not
that they *occur* or *are exemplified*. My reasons for grouping
together properties and changes are similar. The colour red, the
volume a gallon and the relationship being above are all, we
say, *predicated* and *exemplified*. Changes in colour, volume,
direction and distance all *occur*. We also speak of *reporting*
changes and *explaining* or *understanding* them, whereas we
describe objects and form *concepts* of them.

The difference between a rabbit and a hare exists in nature,

independently of us; so, in a way, does the difference between
a yard and a metre, though we select the objects, rods or
whatever they may be, that then serve to define these lengths;
and so too the difference between becoming brown and becoming white. But I have just said that the difference between a
hare, the colour white and the change to white that mountain
hares undergo in winter lies in the way we think and speak
about them, and it is doubtful if it exists apart from speech and
thought. When I say 'Hares become white' I use three distinct
words. We might say that these differentiate a sort of object, a
change and a colour *in my speech*. But it hardly makes sense to
ask if they are differentiated in reality as distinct from speech
and thought.

If this is how objects, properties and changes differ, two
further questions arise. First, does every language and every
thinker differentiate them? I am using these words as terms of
art to express technical concepts which I should not expect to
be current in a primitive society. I should not expect such a
society to have words with the technical meanings I have given
to 'object', 'property' and 'change'. But I should expect any
normal hunter-gatherer to have concepts of various sorts of
object, concepts of some properties and to think sometimes of
properties as being had, sometimes as being acquired or lost.
Still, I doubt if evidence of a tribe which lacked these intellectual resources would stymie my present project; it is enough if
they are shared by people interested in the traditional topics of
philosophy.

Secondly, might we distinguish other groups of things by the
way in which we talk about them? Might we use a different set
of categories? There are certainly things which cannot easily be
classified as objects, properties and changes. Among the more
interesting to philosophers are materials and states of mind. We
speak differently of blood and bronze and of tigers and spears,
differently of seeing and experiencing pleasure and of sweating
and turning green. I shall try, however, to explain how we
think about materials and mental states in terms of how we
think about objects, properties and changes. If others want to
use different categories, good luck to them: that is their style
of philosophizing. But objects, properties and changes are the

primary colours in which I personally shall endeavour to depict the traditional subjects for the philosopher's brush.

Saying that makes them sound analogous to each other, and so, perhaps, does saying that philosophy is concerned with the existence of objects, the exemplification of properties and the occurrence of change. In fact the lack of analogy between them is what accounts for their differing in the way I have just said and is one of the things that makes philosophy difficult. Objects which exist are particular individuals whereas properties and changes which take place are not. Changes which take place are things of which there are examples, whereas an object is itself an example of any properties it has. And it is not satisfactory to say that properties and changes are two different sorts of thing which are both exemplified, since we can equally say that things of a single sort, namely properties, are both exemplified or had and acquired or lost. The notions of an object, a property and a change are like eels that twist in the philosopher's hand; it is tempting to try to make them analogous, but yielding to the temptation results in losing touch with the realities of thought.

How contentious is my ontological thesis? It is clearly the business of scientists, not philosophers, to say what sorts of living organism, heavenly body etc., exist, what properties they have and what changes they undergo. Various non-philosophical experts have comparable knowledge about artifacts. It is for scientists too, and for social scientists, historians and so on, to explain the various changes that take place and the things people do. But no non-philosopher says what existing is, or taking place or exemplifying. Philosophers can have these topics to themselves without any competition.

But it looks at first as if only one of them, existence, is on my list of traditional topics. What about the other items on the list, truth, number, time, causation, consciousness, goodness and the rest?

The negative part of the thesis denies that any of these strictly speaking exists, occurs or is exemplified. To someone inexperienced in philosophy that may sound alarming. Does causation not occur? Do consciousness and goodness not exist? One had heard of philosophical scepticism but this surpasses one's worst imaginings. The seasoned metaphysician, in contrast, may hear a welcome explanation of the difficulties of trying to treat causing as a special process additional to change of properties or goodness as a property that can be exemplified in the same way as yellowness. The negative part of the ontological thesis is not sceptical in intent. I am not saying that the things philosophers discuss are one and all illusions. But the point of my denial must be gathered from my positive treatment of these topics.

I claim that some of these topics are simply modes of existence or occurrence. The notion of existence is closely connected with that of number. This is a commonplace of analytical philosophy. To say that tame tigers exist is to say that the number of tame tigers is greater than zero (so Moore 1936); up to a point existence can be explained as being many. Something which is not a commonplace but which I argue in chapter 5 is that time is the occurring or going on of change. We may distinguish between a change which takes place and a taking place of that change. This distinction is not, of course, between two different processes or changes; it is between two aspects of a change. I hope to show that the notion of a stretch of time is the notion of the second of these aspects. And in chapter 6 I advance a further contentious thesis. Considered in this second way, not as something which goes on but as a going on of something, a change is thought of as a cause, a bringing of something to pass. The ontological thesis, then, covers more of the traditional topics than a first glance might suggest.

It does not, however, claim that all these topics are modes of existence, occurrence or exemplification. It claims that all such modes are the business of the philosopher; but some things which philosophers consider are more easily brought under the epistemological thesis: to say that we apply concepts of them is to describe the role played in our thinking by other things.

2.3 The epistemological thesis

Macbeth wanted to become King of Scotland; Othello believed Desdemona loved Cassio. In saying this we attribute mental

states of belief and desire to these Shakespearean heroes. Descartes conceived beliefs and desires on the model of physical
properties: he thought that we have them in the way in which
things have shapes or colours (see, for instance, *Principles of
Philosophy* I 32). Some analytical philosophers today agree
(so P. F. Strawson, 1959, ch. 3; and, according to himself, J.
Fodor, 1981, pp. 228–33). But others make out that our concepts of belief and desire are primarily explanatory. Macbeth
wants to become king in that he acts *in order that he may*;
Othello believes that Desdemona is unfaithful in acting *for the
reason that she is*.

In chapter 7 I argue that this second view is right. If it is,
then mental states can be brought under the epistemological
thesis. It will be true to say 'Iago thinks Othello believes
something about Desdemona' or 'Iago applies the concept of
belief to Othello' if Iago thinks that it is for the reason that
Desdemona is sleeping with Cassio that Othello smothers her.
But for Iago to think this is not for him to make use of a
special concept of belief over and above the concepts of various
parts of the human body, various spatial relations, a pillow etc.
It is for him to use these other concepts in a special way.
Equally it is true to say 'Othello applies the concept of desire
to Desdemona' if Othello thinks that it was in order that she
might sleep with Cassio that she gave him the handkerchief.
But for him to think this is not for the concept of desire to
come into his mind in addition to the concepts of a handkerchief, limb positions etc.; it is for those unproblematic concepts
to come into his mind in a special way. The concepts of
belief and desire are concepts, we might say, of roles which
circumstances and events can play in the explanation of human
behaviour.

Our basic notions of good and evil are very closely related to
the notions of desire and aversion. The good (as Aristotle says
in the first sentence of the *Nicomachean Ethics*) is what is
aimed at. It is that to secure which we act, that lest we prevent
which we refrain from doing things we might otherwise have
done. The bad is the opposite: that to prevent which we act
and that lest we cause which we keep quiet. If desire and
aversion are explanatory notions so are good and evil. To say 'I

thought something good' or 'I applied the concept of goodness'
is to specify not a concept I applied but a role something
unspecified played in my thinking.

Similarly with causation. If I think that a branch is becoming
bent because a squirrel is moving along it I may be said to
apply the concept of a cause. But that is not a concept I apply
in addition to those of a squirrel, a branch and certain shapes
and positions. To say I apply it is rather to say how I apply
those other concepts. As Rorty complains, philosophers tend
to conceive thought simply as a kind of forming of images or
likenesses of things. But intelligence or intellect is the ability
not to form likenesses but to understand. Understanding is a
matter of relating or connecting things. We understand purposive action in relating real or fancied circumstances and possible
events to it as the agent's reasons and purposes. We understand
a physical change in a thing by relating objects and changes to
it as the agents and the causal action responsible. To say that
I apply the notion of a reason or a cause is to describe the
character of my understanding.

My epistemological thesis points to a prime source of error
and confusion in philosophy. We are conscious (at least sometimes) of our thought. We can say what things come into it,
and we can describe their coming in. That is to describe two
aspects of a single piece of thinking. But if I say 'I wondered
if there was a causal connection' or 'I wondered if there was
an aeroplane' there is no sure way of telling from my words
whether I am specifying the first of these aspects, the second or
a complete piece of thinking in which these two aspects may
be distinguished. I may myself be unsure whether what I am
conscious of is what is entering my thought, or its mode of
entry or both. Here is an example.

If I see an ordinary ripe tomato under good viewing conditions I think it is red. If I reflect, I know this; that is, I know,
and know pretty well infallibly, what colour I think the tomato
is. But I could misconstrue my certainty that red is the colour I
am attributing to the tomato as an incorrigible belief that there
is something red before me. Many philosophers have done this.
Since no belief about a material object can be incorrigible in
this way they have been led to imagine that these beliefs are

about non-physical entities which they call 'appearances' or 'sense data'. Misinterpretation of our awareness of the concepts we apply conjures up a whole world of fictitious entities.

I know that red and not blue is the colour I think the tomato is; I also know that I rather *think* it is red than think it is not, or wonder if it is, or wish it were. So I may say 'I believe that the object *has* a property' or 'I have a positive belief.' These remarks really describe the way the property comes into my thought. But they may be misconstrued as specifying something further that comes in, namely belief. The question then arises 'What is belief?' and all sorts of answers have been proposed. Descartes says it is a kind of mental act of acceptance or assent; Hume that it is a certain brightness or vivacity in our mental images; modern philosophers describe belief, incredulity, wishing and so on as mental attitudes which we adopt towards propositions. Utterances of assent, degrees of brightness and bodily attitudes are things which come into our thought, but believing that red is the colour of a certain object, wondering if it is and wishing it were are ways in which that colour comes in. The question 'What is belief?' as understood by the philosophers I have mentioned is a spurious one.

Perhaps it will be replied: 'The ideas of belief, wondering etc., may well be ideas of how things come into our thought. But why should they not also be ideas of things that come in? Cannot the entry of things into thought itself enter in? If not, what are we thinking about here and now?'

Breathing and perspiring coming into our thought and we really do have ideas of them. We have ideas (accurate or inaccurate) of *how* we breathe, of *how* perspiring occurs. If believing and desiring come into our thought in the same way, ideas of them will be ideas of how we believe, of how desire occurs. They will be ideas of processes by executing which or by undergoing which we believe or desire. My idea of how to divide an orange is an idea of the movement by causing which in a knife I divide oranges. My idea of bisecting a line is an idea of the arcs by drawing which I bisect lines. If I have a comparable idea of belief or desire it is almost bound to be the idea of a physical process in the brain the occurrence of which is

believing or desiring; though philosophers who feel nostalgia
for Cartesian dualism may hope there are mental processes by
which we accomplish these mental acts. But if that hope is
incoherent the belief that it makes sense to ask how we believe
or desire leads straight to physicalism.

There are some things, at least, of which this question cannot
intelligibly be asked. One is causing. There is a movement by
causing which in a knife I effect a change in an orange. There
can be no movement by causing which I effect the *causing* of
the movement in the knife. Another is following a procedure
or using an object. I *use* a knife if I not only cause a movement
in it but do so *in order to* effect some further purpose. I follow
a procedure if I not only do something prescribed but do it
because it is prescribed, for example if I draw intersecting arcs
because that is the procedure for bisecting lines. It is obvious
that there can be no procedure for following a procedure, no
change by causing which I can bring it about that my causal
action is for a reason or a purpose. Believing things and wanting things are involved in using objects and following procedures, and I think there can be no further procedures for them.

Many analytical philosophers would agree that the search for
such procedures is misconceived and that the notions of belief
and desire are explanatory. But they make the explanation
involved causal. It is part of their general view of life that there
are no non-physical objects or states and that human behaviour
is woven into a seamless physical order of things. So if they do
not jettison the whole notion of a mental state as confused and
pre-scientific they say we must understand a mental state to be
a physical state of an organism which plays a special causal
role. A simple suggestion would be that my belief that there is
a glass of wine before me is a state of my brain which is partly
caused by light from the glass stimulating my optic nerve and
which in turn causes me to reach for the glass. In recent years
great technical ingenuity has gone into arguing that we can give
satisfactory analyses of various psychological phenomena without invoking any non-causal notions. I hope to show that this
is wasted effort and that our notions of belief and desire are
irredeemably teleological.

2.4   The linguistic thesis

Speech or language is the expressing of things in words. The
same things come into our speech as come into our thought,
and the different ways in which they come into speech are
expressive of different ways in which they can come into
thought.

Objects of various sorts and properties come into thought
and speech, and if I am right they are the only things which
come into ordinary thought and speech about the world. Individual objects come into speech by being referred to. In the
utterances 'Mars is red' and 'Odysseus built a raft' I bring in an
individual planet and a (perhaps fictitious) individual human
being. In the first of these utterances I also bring in a property,
and in the second a sort of artifact. I cannot be said to express
Mars or Odysseus – it does not make sense to talk of expressing an individual – but in bringing in properties and sorts we
may be said to express them.

My linguistic thesis is that existence, time, belief and so on,
do not strictly speaking enter into our speech or get expressed
in words. Something is of philosophical interest in so far as to
say I expressed it is to describe my expressing of properties or
sorts or my referring to individuals – and referring to individuals is not something we can do independently of expressing
properties and sorts.

What things enter into our discourse and the ways in which
they enter depend partly, at least, on the words and constructions we use. As philosophers go wrong through interpreting
descriptions of applyings of concepts as specifications of fancy
concepts we apply, so they go wrong through supposing that
words or constructions signify special things we express when
they really determine our expressing of other things. Let me
try to say what I mean here by 'words' and 'constructions'.

We express things linguistically by constructing sentences
out of words. (We also construct longer speeches out of sentences, but that does not involve any further complications.)
We construct a sentence by producing words in sequence
(sometimes a single word is enough), inserting particles like 'if'

and 'not', and, in some languages, doing what is called 'inflecting' the words, that is, modifying them in certain ways. 'Sits' and 'sat' are inflected forms of the English verb 'to sit'. Latin is a highly inflected language the verbs of which have inflections of voice, mood, tense, number and person. Polynesian languages are more or less uninflected, and the work done in Latin by the mood-inflection of 'ama' or the tense-inflection of 'amabo' would be done in Marquesan by putting a particle, ''a' or ''e', at the beginning of the sentence. In general the grammar of a language is an account of the ways in which sentences in it can be constructed.

I am not sure that philosophers have, or need, any very precise notion of a word; but they are happiest to call something a word if it satisfies two conditions: (1) it is something out of which a sentence is constructed according to grammatical rules, and which therefore belongs to a grammatical category; (2) it belongs to the vocabulary of a language. Proper names like 'Paris' satisfy the first condition but not, I think, the second. By 'a construction' I mean something like the word order in 'Is Mars red?', the tense-inflection in 'Lalagen amabo', the insertion of 'not' after 'is' in 'The Moon is not blue.' I shall use the awkward phrase 'linguistic item' to cover both words and constructions. The distinction between a word and a construction is not in itself philosophically important; what is important is a distinction between two ways in which a linguistic item can have meaning.

It is obvious that constructions are significant or meaningful but it is not so obvious how they have meaning. We are inclined to think an item can have meaning only through signifying a property like 'spherical' or a sort of object like 'alligator', or perhaps by being the name of some person or thing like 'Paris'. People sometimes oppose syntax to semantics in a way which suggests that constructions, things specified in the syntax of a language, have no semantics or meaning at all. I hold that they have meaning in that what construction we use determines the way in which we express the properties and sorts we express. We express properties by predicating them of objects and the simplest way of expressing a sort is to refer to an object as an object of that sort (as in 'A mosquito bit me').

How we predicate properties and refer to objects is determined by the constructions we use.

We all know the significance of the constructions we use but when we try to explain this kind of meaning we often use words which can suggest that we are specifying further things we express. We might say 'The inflection of "became" in "His face became red" expresses past time', as if past time or pastness were something we express. Or we say 'In "The candle melted because it was on top of the stove" "because" expresses a causal relationship', as if causal relationships came into speech in the same way as spatial relationships. In fact 'because' belongs to the construction of the sentence. Inserting it makes a difference to how the spatial relationship between the candle and the stove is brought into the speech. According to my linguistic thesis a linguistic item is the business of the philosopher, it falls to the philosopher to explain its meaning, just in so far as it has the kind of meaning that attaches to constructions.

My linguistic thesis is highly contentious. So far as I am aware, nobody recognizes the kind of meaning which I say attaches to constructions. People may distinguish between what a speaker expresses and his expressing of this; but they take what he expresses to include statements, questions, orders, facts or at least propositions – they do not see why it should be limited to properties and sorts of object – and by his 'expressing' they mean his style and such things as whether his speech is clear or obscure, impassioned or flat. They do not have the notion of expression as the linguistic counterpart to the actual entry of things into thought and reality.

Because my linguistic thesis is so contentious, and also because it is, I hope, easier to explain and establish than the other two, I shall proceed to develop it in the next two chapters. I shall try to show that the theory of meaning on which it depends is superior to existing theories, and that developing it gives us insight into philosophical topics in the first group I distinguished, the topics existence, being as contrasted with not-being, number and truth.

3
Meaning

3.1   The three-tier and Frege-Austin theories

Why do philosophers discuss meaning? Because it's there?
They have at least two further reasons.

First, philosophical enquiries are apt to take a linguistic turn.
Questions like 'What is existence?' and 'What is time?' sound
extremely odd. They would never be asked except in a philosophical discussion. It can seem more realistic to ask 'What
is the meaning of the verb "to exist"?' or even 'What is the
meaning of the tense-inflection of "peccavi"?' But once an
enquiry is transferred to the linguistic dimension it must be
prosecuted in the light of some theory of meaning. We must
have some idea of how words have meaning and what sorts
of thing they can mean. It is sensible to examine these ideas
because errors in them will lead to philosophical mistakes
about anything we discuss in this way.

Secondly, a satisfactory theory of meaning will explain how
words can relate to things and how speakers can make true or
false statements. A non-philosopher might wonder why that
needs explaining. A system of symbols which did not enable us
to say anything true or false would not be a language at all.
These features of language, however, that is relates to things
and admits of truth, also characterize thought. They seem to be
an important part of what makes psychological states psychological. And the relation in which language and thought stand
to the world seems quite different from any ordinary spatial or

causal relation. To be able to analyse it is to have insight into a problem than which none deeper engages the human intellect.

If both language and thought have this mysterious character (technically known as 'intentionality') which should we tackle first? Some philosophers seem to hope to explain it by the representative power of pictures. They see language as a form of representation and thought as internal representing or as a silent discourse we hold with ourselves. Others see language rather as the voicing of thoughts and go straight for mental states. In this chapter I shall argue that the notion of representation will not do the work asked of it but that a correct theory of meaning does shed light on intentionality. Mental states as distinct from language I defer to chapter 7.

The history of philosophy contains two main theories of meaning. Until recently most philosophers accepted a three-tier theory. Words signify objects and properties, but we know what they signify, and this grasp of their meaning is something intellectual – it is not a matter of grasping anything in the hand. So it appears that between the word and the object there is something mental, perhaps a kind of mental likeness of the object. The word does not simply mean the thing; it expresses a concept of the thing.

Natural as it may be to say this, there are difficulties. These mental intermediaries are not accessible to observation in the same way as words, which are studied by linguists, and things, which are studied by science. What, exactly, are they like? Can we really be sure they exist? And if they do, will they not breed a regress? If the word 'tiger' cannot mean a sort of animal without first meaning a sort of likeness of an animal, how can it signify an animal-likeness without first signifying a likeness of an animal-likeness?

The philosophy of language was inaugurated by Aristotle's *De Interpretatione* and readers have found the three-tier picture suggested by its opening sentences. That explains the hold it had on philosophers until the seventeenth century. The authority of Aristotle was then thrown off, but this theory of meaning was saved from the general smash by a new theory of perception according to which our senses give us access not directly to physical objects but only to mental representations of them. Instead of seeing roses and hearing nightingales we are presented with mental pictures of roses and mental tape-recordings of nightingales. If these mental items are the only things with which (as Russell liked to say) we are directly 'acquainted' it seems to follow that they are what words signify in the first instance. This theory of perception has been seriously assailed only in this century. We can now say that while we have words for things and ideas of them, things, ideas and words need not be viewed as forming a kind of meta-physical sandwich.

Today most philosophers use a theory of meaning which derives from Frege (especially 1952 and 1956) and Austin (1962, 1961). It has two advantages over the three-tier theory. It dispenses with mental intermediaries; and whereas the three-tier theory assigns meaning to words as they sit in the lexicon, independently of their work in sentences, on the Frege-Austin theory to grasp the meaning of a word is precisely to know what difference it makes to the meaning of sentences in which it is used. That general account of word-meaning I take to be wholly sound.

The theory goes on to distinguish three main ways in which a word can contribute to the meaning of a sentence, and hence three kinds of meaning it can have:

1 It can help determine what proposition the speaker expresses. By a 'proposition' is here meant something which is true or false and which is also expressible in words. That there really are propositions in this sense is the foundation of the Frege-Austin theory.
2 A word can indicate the force of the utterance in which it is used. Utterances can have various forces including those of a statement, a command, a promise and a warning. Which they have is not absolutely fixed by the words or construction. 'If you don't stop he'll give you one' might have any of the forces I have mentioned. But mood-inflections, particles etc., can give an indication of force.
3 An item can contribute to the aptitude of the utterance to affect a hearer's state of mind: it can help to make an utterance convincing, alarming, amusing or bewildering.

English-speaking followers of Frege use the word 'tone' for a speech's aptitude to affect states of mind. So the third way of having meaning is by imparting or modifying tone. 'Your tears are womanish' Friar Laurence says to Romeo; he chooses 'womanish' instead of 'feminine' because he thinks it more apt to brace Romeo up.

Of these ways of having meaning the most important for our purposes is the first. When we enquire into the meaning of a word like 'exist', 'cause' or 'future' we surely hope to see what difference it makes to the propositions we express when we use it. But the ways in which the Frege-Austin theory allows a linguistic item to determine what proposition a speaker expresses are severely limited. (1) It can determine what is predicated. If I say 'Mars is red' the significance of 'red' is that by using it I predicate the colour red and not, say, the colour green or spherical shape. (2) It can determine what sort of object is referred to. 'Python' does that in 'A python squeezed me': it ensures that the speaker refers to a python and not, say, to a bear or a Japanese wrestler. (3) Words like 'all', 'some' and 'no' (sometimes called 'quantifiers') determine the number of things the speaker refers to and predicates things of. (4) 'If', 'and' and 'not' determine what truthfunctions of simpler propositions (see p. 14 above) we express when we use them. Suppose that instead of saying '7 + 5 = 12' and also saying '7 + 6 = 13' I say 'If 7 + 5 = 12 then 7 + 6 = 13.' I here express a proposition the truth of which is a definite function of the truth of the two simpler propositions. Logicians would call it the truth function 'if p then q' (or '$p \rightarrow q$'). The conjunction 'if', which is called on this account a 'truthfunctional connective', enables me to do this.

How good a theory is this? The notion of tone is sound but of marginal importance to our present enquiry. I think that the Frege-Austin notions of force and a proposition are both irremediably faulty and the theory fails to do the two jobs for which we want it.

The first job is to cover the meaning of philosophically interesting words and constructions. The Frege-Austin theory cannot say how any of these items has meaning with the exception of quantifiers and truthfunctional connectives; and these are of interest only to philosophers of logic and mathematics. (In fairness to Frege it should be said that the philosophy of logic and mathematics was all he was interested in; but it is a narrow strip of the subject.)

Adjectives like 'good', 'bad', 'honest' and 'beautiful' may look grammatically similar to 'red' and 'spherical' but they do not signify properties which everything good or everything bad exemplifies because there are no such properties. They do not determine what we predicate when we use them. Neither do verbs like 'to believe' and 'to want': believing is not something of which credulous people are instances, nor is wanting a drink a property exemplified by the thirsty. Unlike 'if' and 'and', conjunctions which express temporal relations or which introduce explanations are not truthfunctional. The truth of 'Caesar died *because* Brutus stabbed him' does not depend simply on the truth of 'Caesar died' and 'Brutus stabbed him'; neither does the truth of 'Caesar died *before* Brutus stabbed him.' But propositions are bearers of truth and falsity and to know what proposition a speaker expresses is to know under what conditions it is true. Adherents to the Frege-Austin theory have difficulty in seeing how a connective I use can determine what proposition I express except by determining how its truth depends on the truth of the propositions connected: they have no place for non-truthfunctional connectives. It is also quite unclear how tense-inflections or words like 'has', 'will', 'may' and 'must' could determine what proposition a person using them expresses. So none of these items seems to have meaning in the first of the Frege-Austin ways.

Have they meaning, then, in the second or third? Does the inflection of 'came' indicate a special force, or the conjunction 'in order that' impart a special tone? That sounds ridiculous. We should not be far wrong in saying that a linguistic item is of philosophical interest precisely when it has meaning in none of the ways allowed by the Frege-Austin theory.

Faced by this mismatch we can either scrap the theory or force the recalcitrant items somehow or other through the slots it provides. Much twentieth-century philosophy consists of attempts to carry out the second policy.

Moore said that 'good' does after all signify a property, but a strange, 'non-natural' one (1903). Others claim that it has meaning in the second or third way. When you say euthanasia is good and I say it is bad we do not express different propositions, but either your utterance has the force of a command and mine that of a prohibition (so Hare 1952) or yours has the aptitude to make hearers keen on euthanasia and mine the aptitude to make them averse to it (so Stevenson 1937). McTaggart (1927, pp. 10, 19) says that (at least in popular thinking) the words 'past', 'present' and 'future' signify properties of events or states of affairs. On that view we might explain the meaning of the tense-inflection of 'I came' by saying that the speaker predicates pastness of his coming. Davidson would shrink from counting pastness, presentness and futurity as properties; but he thinks events do have properties, and for him 'is earlier than', 'is a cause of' etc., appear to have meaning through signifying relational properties of events (1980, essays 6–9). All these questionable doctrines are inspired or supported by the Frege-Austin theory of meaning.

The second job of a theory of meaning is to explain how language can relate to reality and accommodate truth and falsity. I shall show the failure of the Frege-Austin theory to do this when I criticize the notion of a proposition, but first some words on force.

3.2 Force

The Frege-Austin notion of force depends on a distinction between acts *of* speaking and acts performed *in* speaking. Referring to objects, predicating and expressing propositions are supposed to be acts of speaking. Asserting, asking, ordering, warning and promising are supposed to be acts performed in speaking: in referring to the bull and predicating rage of it I ask a question, make an assertion, issue a warning or perform some combination of these acts. This distinction between acts of speaking and acts we perform in speaking is unsound and the whole Frege-Austin conception of a linguistic act performed in speaking is confused.

Austin himself confused acts and expressions for acts: he made out that asserting, warning, announcing and replying are different acts (1962, ch. 12). The verbs 'to assert', 'to warn' etc., are different verbs with different meanings but they do not signify different acts. 'To assert' signifies simply a kind of act; the others signify in addition a way in which or a purpose for which an act is performed. I warn you that the bull is enraged if I assert that it is for the purpose of putting you on your guard; I reply that it is if I assert that it is because you have asked me about it; I announce that it is if I assert that it is in a public or authoritative manner. Obviously doing something for a particular purpose or in a particular way is not a different act from doing it. You can say that *in* speaking I warned or announced; but that is as much as to say that *in* speaking I had the purpose of instilling caution or that in speaking I acted authoritatively. Having this purpose and behaving in this way do not constitute a pair of acts additional to speaking, and neither do warning and announcing.

John Searle (1979, ch. 1) avoids this confusion but persists in another: he assimilates genuinely linguistic acts to social acts for which the procedure is linguistic. A genuinely linguistic act is one we do in a language by complying with grammatical rules of the language. Asserting and ordering are genuinely linguistic acts: we perform them in English or French, and learning Turkish is learning how to perform them in Turkish. By 'a social act' I mean one performed in a society by carrying out a procedure which is customary in that society or laid down in its rules or laws. Naming a child, finding an accused person guilty and promising, that is, putting yourself under an obligation to do something, are social acts. I marry a lady (put myself under an obligation to cherish her etc.) in Spain in accordance with the laws of Spain. In most societies the procedures for performing these acts are at least partly verbal. I marry Dolores by uttering some words. The words may be Spanish; still, I marry her in Spain, not in Spanish, in accordance with Spanish law rather than in accordance with Spanish grammar.

It might be objected that all linguistic acts are social, that language is a social institution. Certainly languages could not exist without at least rudimentary societies, and a society without a language would be brutish indeed. Still there is a difference between acts like asserting and ordering and acts like promising and naming, just as there is a difference between both and acts like serving and trumping. We serve and trump in games, in accordance with the rules of those games. Games too are a social institution. Nonetheless, games, societies and languages are different. They differ in their aims or purposes. The purpose of a game (which need not be the purpose of a particular player) is to win: not, that is, to gain a stake, but to vanquish the opposition by checkmating your opponent's king, getting out your patience or what not. The rules of the game lay down what counts as winning as well as the procedures to be followed in progressing towards that goal. The purpose of a society may be either a particular project (a company formed to denude Honduras of mahogany) or a kind of communal life. The purpose is often spelt out in the rules; in any case they say how it is to be reached. The purpose of a language is neither some kind of winning nor some kind of communal life. Its rules enable us to express things in words in various ways and that, I think, is what languages are systems for.

Asserting, denying, asking, ordering, forbidding and expressing wishes are genuinely linguistic acts. The Frege-Austin theory says they are acts we perform in speaking. Rather, they are acts *of* speaking: we have no concept of an act of speaking which does not presuppose the notion of asserting or ordering or something of that kind. The Frege-Austin theory counts referring and predicating as acts of speaking. But to refer to Caesar it is not enough to utter the name 'Caesar'; for predicating it is not sufficient merely to utter the syllables 'spherical' or 'under'. To refer to an object I must say something about it and to predicate a property I must say something has it; or else I must ask if something has it, or express the wish that something did not have it, or perform some other act which the Frege-Austin theory would class as an act performed in speaking.

Searle admits this: 'One cannot *just* refer and predicate without making an assertion or asking a question or performing some other illocutionary act' (1969, p. 25). But he fails to see

that this invalidates the distinction he wants to maintain between acts of speaking and acts performed in speaking. He
suggests that these are related 'as making an "X" on a ballot
paper stands to voting' (p. 24). But causing an 'X' to appear on
a piece of paper is a purely physical act and we *can* just do it
without voting or performing any other social or conventional
act. Referring and predicating do not stand to asserting, ordering etc., as a physical act stands to the conventional act it
constitutes. The relationship is more like that of being coloured
to being red, being blue etc.

Some philosophers may have been led astray because if I say
to you 'Your tie is crooked' my purpose might be to get you to
straighten it; and if I am a person in authority you might say
that my utterance 'has the force' of a command. I agree that it
may have the same practical effect as a command, and that my
purpose in speaking was to encompass that effect. Still, what
has and is intended to have the force of a command is my
assertion or *statement* that your tie is crooked. The grammar of
my utterance does not determine its purpose; but neither does
its purpose determine whether in fact I give an order or make a
statement.

Defenders of the Frege-Austin theory could, no doubt,
define stating or ordering as speaking with certain purposes.
That is not, however, how 'state' and 'order' are used at present; and if the new definitions are to be intelligible we must
have some conception of speaking which is independent of all
notions like stating and ordering in the way in which the
notion of stating is independent of those of replying and warning, and the notion of cutting flesh is independent of those of
wounding and surgery. Adherents to the Frege-Austin theory
think they are in possession of just such a notion: it is that of
proposition-expressing. I shall now argue that the Frege-Austin
notion of a proposition is incoherent.

3.3 *Propositions*

A proposition is supposed to be something which is true or
false, which can be expressed in words and which we can

believe to be true or otherwise entertain in thought. Are there
really any such things as propositions so conceived? If there
are, they will be worth their weight in gold to the philosopher.
Asked 'How is it that we are able to speak about the world and
say what is true or false?' he can reply 'There are propositions
which are about the world and true or false, and we can express
them in words'; asked 'How can our thoughts have a relation
to something outside them? How can we think about the
world?' he can say 'We entertain propositions and believe they
are true or wonder if they are.' But the very facility of these
answers should put us on our guard. How can propositions be
about the world? How can they refer to things in it, as they
must if they are to be true or false? If I contrive to say
something about Mars by expressing the proposition that Mars
is red, will not the proposition have to say something about
Mars? And if it is mysterious how our thoughts can relate to
objects like Mars, will it not also be mysterious how they can
relate to propositions like the proposition that Mars is red, as
they must if we are to wonder whether these propositions are
true?

But could there be such wonder-entities as propositions
are claimed to be? What could a thing be like which is both
expressible in words and true or false? And how are we to
conceive expressing it?

On the Frege-Austin theory I express the same proposition
(provided, at least, that I refer to the same individual and the
same time) in the following utterances:

1   Theaetetus is seated.
2   Be seated, O Theaetetus!
3   If only Theaetetus were seated!
4   Is Theaetetus seated?

(I take the example from Plato's seminal discussion, *Sophist*
263.) The same proposition will be present to my mind if I
believe that Theaetetus is seated, wonder if he is or wish he
were. The difference between these mental states, allegedly, lies
in the attitude I adopt towards the proposition; believing it is
taking up one such attitude.

The model we are invited to use in conceiving these mental states is that of entertaining a visitor. The expression 'entertaining a proposition' is frequently used, and the attitudes we can adopt towards visitors – welcome, hostility, suspicion etc. – are natural models for attitudes towards propositions. Believing that Theaetetus is seated is welcoming the proposition with a broad smile and stretching out our arms to embrace it; wondering if he is seated is maintaining a more cautious or suspicious stance. That being so, a proposition must be analogous to something which can be presented to us, and the model to which philosophers are drawn, as much today as in the time of Locke (so Fodor 1981, p. 26), is a picture: for the present example, a picture of a seated figure like Theaetetus. Expressing a proposition can then be conceived on the model of exhibiting a picture, showing it to people, or perhaps (since the picture itself is locked up in the private safe of the individual's mind) showing a reproduction of it.

But pictures and picture-showing cannot provide a model for saying anything true or false. To make the true or false assertion that Theaetetus is seated it is not enough to produce a picture of a seated figure with Theaetetus' features. We must also (as Plato recognizes in *Cratylus* 430) *say* something; we must say 'This is a picture of Theaetetus, and this is how he is' or 'This is not how he is.'

We may think that pictures will provide a model because we speak of true and false pictures. But we must distinguish two uses of the words 'true' and 'false'. I can say that something is true *of* something: 'It is true of Theaetetus that he is seated.' Or I can use the words by themselves, 'absolutely' as grammarians say: 'That Theaetetus is seated is true.' When we say that a picture is true we mean that it is a true picture *of* something. That, in turn, means that the properties depicted or shown in it are true of or had by the thing. But the picture is not true absolutely. It does not in itself refer to any object, even though the artist may have had some particular object in mind when producing it; still less does it assert or deny that any object has the properties depicted.

But may not Theaetetus be the subject of the picture, and does it not represent its subject as having the properties depicted? If I paint Theaetetus as seated, do I not assert that he is seated? Seated when? At the time when I paint, at some time or other, at any time at which the picture exists? I make no such assertions. I represent Theaetetus as seated only in the way in which I speak of him as seated in all four of the utterances we are considering. A picture is not like a complete sentence but like a predicate-expression: it is like 'a seated Theaetetus' or 'a seated, snub-nosed, pop-eyed mathematics student'. We can use a picture instead of a predicate-expression to assert something or to ask something. But it does not in itself assert anything or ask anything. Hence it will not serve as a model for anything which is true or false absolutely or which is about anything; and neither will painting a picture or exhibiting one.

Wittgenstein makes a suggestion in the *Tractatus* (2.15, 3.1432) which might seem to show how a picture can be true. In a picture of his room Van Gogh depicts his chair as being to the left of his bed. A patch of paint *A* represents the chair, a patch *B* the bed, and *A* stands to *B* in the relation *being to the left of*. Wittgenstein suggests that the *standing* of *A* to *B* in this relation *asserts* that the chair stands to the bed in the same relation. Similarly with the sentence 'The chair is to the left of the bed.' Here the words 'the chair' stand to the words 'the bed' in the relation *preceding and being separated by 'is to the left of' from*. Their standing in this relation makes the sentence the true or false assertion that the chair and the bed stand in the relation signified by 'is to the left of'.

This is a subtle suggestion but it will work only for simple assertions. For consider 'The chair is not to the left of the bed.' It is absurd to say that the *not* standing of 'the chair' to 'the bed' in the relation *preceding and being separated by 'is to the left of' from* asserts the not standing of the objects in the relation signified, for there are infinitely many relations in which 'the chair' does not stand to 'the bed'. And what of 'Is the chair to the left of the bed?'

My argument may be summarized as follows. Propositions are supposed to be both expressible in words and true or false absolutely. But what is expressible in words must be conceived on the model of spatial relations or other things that can be exemplified by likenesses; and no such thing can be true or false absolutely. Absolute truth and falsity, I shall argue below, attach only to acts of using words or applying concepts in certain ways.

I have to recognize, however, that the notion of something which is both linguistically expressible and true or false is tenaciously rooted in the philosophical mind. Let me expose three of the roots and try to sever them.

1   We say things like 'What I say is true; the thoughts you express are false.' Do not such remarks show straight off that truth and falsity attach to things we express?

They do not. It does not immediately follow, if I say something true, that there is something which is both true and said by me; any more than it follows, if a stick partly immersed in water presents a crooked appearance, that there is something which is an appearance, and crooked, and presented by the stick. 'I said something true' is not like 'I dropped something blue' where this inference would hold. It is like 'I did something clever.' I do something clever not if there is something which is clever and which I come along and do, but if I act in a clever way. One way of acting cleverly is to effect some change in circumstances in which doing that is clever. To sell my shares when the market is high is thought clever; doing the same thing, giving the same instructions to my stockbroker, when the market is low may be silly. Saying something true is like that. If I say, 'Your face is red' at a time when the face of the person I address is red I say something true. If I say, 'Your face is red' when it is not I say something false. As doing something clever is acting cleverly so saying something true is speaking truly – which is not the same as speaking truthfully. If I say, 'Eleanor is in Paris,' while believing her to be in Los Angeles I do not speak truthfully; but I speak truly if Paris is where she is.

The Greeks would have found it hard even to formulate argument (1). Greek has single verbs, *alêtheuein* and *pseudein*, for saying something true and saying something false. Modern philosophers, in contrast, have probably found it natural to believe in propositions because modern philosophy of language started with the study of mathematical utterances like 'The sum of 2 and 3 is 5.' These contain no reference to particular objects

or times. Hence if anyone ever in saying '2 + 3 = 5' says
something true, so does anyone else uttering the same sentence
at any time. Someone might therefore think that there is something which is true and said by anyone uttering '2 + 3 = 5',
whereas no one imagines that there is something which is true
and said by anyone uttering the words 'Your face is red.'

2   Suppose I say, 'If Icarus is spherical it is a planet.' I do
not assert that Icarus is a planet; but surely I express the
proposition that it is. Similarly if I say, 'Icarus is not spherical'
or 'Suppose Icarus were spherical.'

I agree that in these utterances I refer to Icarus and express
spherical shape. But I do not see why I should agree that I
express the proposition that Icarus is spherical, at least if by 'a
proposition' is meant something true or false. In saying 'Suppose Icarus were spherical' surely I do not say anything true or
false at all. And in 'If Icarus is spherical it is a planet' I say
something which is true not if Icarus is spherical but if Icarus'
being spherical is a sufficient condition for its being a planet.

We should think of utterances as constructed progressively.
If I say, 'Icarus is spherical,' I do say something which is true if
the property I predicate is had by the object I refer to. If I
insert a 'not' the effect is that I say something which is true if a
related but different condition is fulfilled, if the object does *not*
have the property. And if, instead of 'Icarus is spherical and it
is a planet' I say, 'If Icarus is spherical it is a planet,' the effect
of my using this construction is that I say something true if
either the object is of the sort specified or it lacks the property
signified. Each grammatical transformation results in a different
bearer of truth or falsity. And it will not do to say that the
proposition that Icarus is spherical is expressed not by the
whole sentence 'If Icarus is spherical it is a planet' but only by
'If Icarus is spherical'. I say something true or false if I say,
'Icarus is spherical'; but if I add a word, if I say, 'If Icarus is
spherical' or 'Icarus is spherical if', and leave it at that, not
only do I no longer say anything true or false but I no longer
even refer to anything.

Anyone who feels that I express the proposition that Icarus
is spherical in saying 'Icarus is not spherical' must, I think, be
conceiving proposition-expressing on the model of picture-

exhibiting and expressing the negation of a proposition on the model of exhibiting a picture with a sticker on it containing a cross or the words 'not like this'. It is enough for my present purposes if it is clear that this model will not do; I offer a positive account of denial in chapter 4.

3   Logic is about propositions. It studies arguments the premises and conclusions of which are propositions, and complex propositions like 'If no asteroid is spherical nothing spherical is an asteroid' which are true by virtue of their form. If, then, we deny that there are propositions, do we not abolish logic? Or at least degrade it to the status of the zoology of unicorns and centaurs?

Logicians certainly deal with bearers of truth and falsity and call them 'propositions'. But they do not have to suppose they are propositions of the kind required by the Frege-Austin theory, that they are expressed in words. A logician might say, 'The proposition that if Icarus is a planet it is spherical is a truthfunction of the two other propositions that Icarus is a planet and that it is spherical; it has the logical form "If p then q".' But nothing in logic requires this to mean 'Whether what is expressed by a person saying, "If Icarus is a planet it is spherical," is true depends on whether the things expressed by people saying, "Icarus is a planet" and "Icarus is spherical" are true.' Nothing stops us from interpreting the logican's claim as 'Whether someone saying, "If Icarus is a planet it is spherical" *speaks truly* depends on whether people saying, "Icarus is a planet" and "Icarus is spherical" *speak truly*.' The choice between these interpretations does not belong to logic; it belongs to the philosophy of language. Logicians are respectable people and no doubt supporters of the Frege-Austin theory would like to have them on their side; but in this debate they must be neutral.

3.4   A new theory of meaning

On the Frege-Austin theory a linguistic item can have meaning through indicating force or through determining the proposition a person using it expresses. If we reject the notions of

force and a proposition we must construct a complete new
theory of meaning.

Language is the expressing of things in words. So much is
uncontroversial but also unilluminating because there are so
many things we can be said to express. We express statements,
questions and orders; we express feelings and thoughts; and we
express properties and sorts of object. I suggest that language
should be viewed by philosophers who want to be clear about
meaning as the expressing in words of properties and sorts. We
can then distinguish two main ways in which linguistic items
can have meaning: they can determine what properties and
sorts the speaker using them expresses; or they can determine
the way in which the speaker expresses these things. That is the
theory. I shall proceed to say which items have meaning in
which of these ways, how my distinction between expressings
and things expressed differs from others, and how this theory
compares with the Frege-Austin theory.

There are certain words or phrases of which we say that they
are expressions *for* things, are others of which we do not say
this. In the first category go common nouns for sorts of object
like 'cat', 'planet' and 'washing-up machine'; adjectives for
non-relational properties like 'spherical', 'crimson' and 'litre'
(as in 'a litre bottle'); and prepositions like 'under', 'to the left
of'. In the second category are what Locke (*Essay* III vii) called
'particles' – words like 'the', 'for' and 'than' – and constructions. I claim that items in the first category have meaning in
the first way: they determine what properties and what sorts
of object the speaker expresses in words. Items in the second
have meaning in the second and determine ways in which the
speaker expresses these things. I do not mean that items in
the first group do not also determine the speaker's form of
expression; I think every item does this to some extent. But
items in the first group do determine what is expressed,
whereas items like 'as' and the subjunctive mood have meaning
only in the second way.

There are various items which we refer to as if they had
meaning in the first way: expressions for sorts of material like
'gold', 'air' and 'wine', and expressions for mental and moral
qualities like 'wise', 'ignorant' and 'generous'. For the present I

wish to leave these aside; later I shall argue that though they appear to determine what a speaker expresses really they have meaning more in the second way and describe ways in which other things are expressed in words or enter into thought. Nouns like 'gorilla' and 'chair' besides determining what speakers express also have meaning in this more complicated fashion, but that too I shall argue only in later chapters.

A further class of linguistic items comprises technical terms like 'subjunctive', 'hypothetical' and, though we may not normally think of them as technical in this way, 'object', 'property', 'change', 'shape' and 'size'. I shall not discuss these formally but the reader may be able to surmise how I should wish them to be handled.

But words like 'green' and 'man' are paradigms of expressions for things and determine what speakers using them express. How do they do that? Words for properties determine what properties the speaker predicates. Using these words is predicating and for properties, to be expressed is to be predicated. One and the same property can be predicated in various ways, and exactly how it is predicated will be determined by the construction of the sentence and by words which have meaning in the second of our two ways.

Words for sorts of object determine what sorts of object the speaker refers to. What do I mean here by 'refer'? In ordinary speech 'to refer' is a transitive verb which can signify directing ('I referred him to the encyclopedia') or connecting ('He referred my poor health to my diet'). The main idea behind the use of the word in the philosophy of language is, I think, predication: to refer to an object is primarily to refer to relate some predicate to it. If I say 'Mars is red' I refer the colour red to the planet Mars. We can also refer some effect or causal action to an object. If I ask, 'Does the Moon cause the sea to rise?', I refer a change in the level of the sea to the Moon – in this example, of course, my reference is interrogative, not affirmative or declarative.

In order to refer to an object we must, as I noted on p. 40, say something about it in a broad sense of 'say'. But there are two ways of doing this. We can refer definitely to a definite object, using a name, a demonstrative like 'that tree' or the definite article 'the salmon I lost yesterday'. Or we can refer to objects indefinitely. Examples of indefinite reference are: 'A wasp stung me'; 'There is no burglar under the bed'; and 'How many of the sheep in your flock are not black?' In the first I say that there is (or was) some wasp which stung me, but I do not say which wasp it was. In the second I say that there is no burglar which stands to the bed in the relation of being under it. In the third I ask how many sheep there are in your flock which are not a certain colour.

Any object must be an object of some sort, and to bring it into our speech we must refer to it explicitly or implicitly as an object of some sort. In 'A wasp stung me' I refer to something explicitly as a wasp: indefinite reference is usually explicit. In 'Paris was delightful' I do not refer to Paris explicitly either as a city or as a Trojan hero; but I must intend, at least, to refer either to the city Paris or to the hero Paris or to an individual of some other definite sort which bears the name 'Paris'. A word expresses a sort, then, in that using it is referring to an object as an object of that sort: and sorts are expressed in language in that speakers refer to objects in this way.

It is often supposed that words like 'man' are typically used not just to refer to objects but to predicate. 'Socrates is a man' is a favourite philosophical example. Surely in uttering that sentence I predicate of Socrates what is signified by 'man'? Natural as this view seems I shall argue that it is erroneous: nouns like 'man' have predicative uses, but such uses are rare. On reflection we realize that utterances like 'Socrates is a man' are quite exceptional and that much more usual would be 'I met a man' or 'A man came to see me.' Sorts are expressed typically in using such nouns referentially. What sort we express depends on the noun we use; how we express it depends on how we refer, which in turn depends on the construction and on words which have meaning in the same way as constructions, like the English definite and indefinite articles.

I shall develop these points in chapter 4; for the moment I wish to compare my notion of expression with others that are current.

Besides properties and sorts we express on the one hand feelings and thoughts; on the other, statements, questions and commands. In each case we can distinguish what is expressed from the mode of expression. In the case of feelings we sometimes distinguish between merely giving way to a feeling and expressing it in words as a poet might express love or grief. The pursuit of that distinction belongs really to aesthetics. But why not say that a linguistic item can have meaning either by making a difference to the thought, statement or question which a speaker expresses or by making a difference to the expressing of this?

This is not a genuine alternative to my distinction; rather it is a distinction between both of my ways of having meaning and making a contribution to 'tone'. My distinction is between two ways in which an item can determine what thought, statement or question a speaker expresses. An item determines the expressing of this in so far as it determine the aptitude of the speech to affect people's states of mind.

Literary critics when they distinguish expression from what is expressed usually have in mind this aptitude and the choice of words on which it depends. But for the purposes of the philosopher of language I think my usage is preferable. For expressing a statement is simply making it; expressing a question is asking it; expressing an order is giving it. I perform these acts in utterances (1), (2) and (4) concerning Theaetetus (above p. 42). The difference between those utterances is not that in each I express something different, a statement, an order and a question. In each I express the same thing, the attitude of being seated. It is my expressing of this which is now indicative, now imperative, now interrogative. To suppose that we express statements as well as properties and sorts is to slide back into belief in propositions.

It is true that whether I say, 'You are smoking', 'Are you smoking?' or 'Don't smoke!' may affect the aptitude of my speech to get you to put out your cigarette. The choice between these constructions, therefore, may belong to what the literary critic would call 'expression'. It does not follow that there is no firm distinction between expression in his sense and in mine: it follows only that a construction can make a difference to both. Something similar goes for words like 'red'. 'The poet said his mistress had red lips' tells us a couple of things –

the colour red and lips – the poet brings into his poem, but it also tells us something about his style and the way in which he expresses the thought that his mistress is attractive. The choice between mentioning the colour of a lady's lips, the shape of her thighs or the size of her feet is stylistic and has practical as well as semantic implications.

My distinction between determining what things are expressed and determining the speaker's mode of expression may not at first seem very different from the Frege-Austin distinction between determining what proposition is expressed and indicating force. Let me, then, spell out some differences.

First, on my theory whether a speaker asserts, asks or orders is determined, and not just indicated, by the construction used.

Next, on the Frege-Austin theory proposition-expressing is logically prior to asserting, ordering etc.; in principle it should be possible to express a proposition without doing any of these things. I say asserting, asking etc., are *species* of linguistic expression and we cannot express anything without performing one of these acts.

This difference has implications for the philosophy of mind. Bare proposition-expressing is the linguistic counterpart of entertaining propositions. Once we see the impossibility of expressing a proposition without asserting, ordering or doing anything like that we shall be less inclined to think we can just contemplate a proposition without thinking it is true or wishing it were false or having any other definite thought. We might imagine this is possible because I might see a sentence written up somewhere ('No eagles are promiscuous' for example) and know what it means but not think that what it says is true or false or even wonder if it is. Am I not then just entertaining the proposition that no eagles are promiscuous? No: I have the definite thought that this is what the graffito says.

Third, the Frege-Austin theory leaves it unclear how language relates to the world. Philosophers sometimes ask how language 'hooks onto' reality or 'reaches up' to it. These metaphors are taken from Wittgenstein but since the time of Descartes philosophers have tended to think that each of us lives in the solitary confinement of his own or her own mind and that we try to reach out from this internal space to an external world. I should prefer to say that we move freely through the world but construct languages that we bring things into. Language relates to the world through having objects and properties brought into it. But that is for the properties and the sorts to which the objects belong to be expressed in words. Since, according to me, philosophers are concerned precisely with our expressing of the things we express, with modes of reference and predication, how language relates to the world is just what philosophy in its linguistic persona tells us. In saying how items like tense-inflections and 'because' contribute to our expressing we say how we are able to ask questions, give orders and make true statements about the world.

A fourth difference between the Frege-Austin distinction and mine is that they fall in difference places. On the Frege-Austin theory 'if', 'not', 'all' and 'some' are grouped separately from imperative mood-inflections and the interrogative word-order, and together with 'red', 'spherical' and 'planet'. On my theory it is the other way round: 'if', 'all' etc., go with the mood-inflections. Consequently I conceive the class of acts which includes asserting, asking and ordering as having a larger membership than the Frege-Austin theory would allow. I include saying that things exist or do not exist, speaking of one thing as conditional on another or as an alternative to another and denying as distinct from asserting. This more liberal policy will be defended in chapter 4.

Finally my theory covers items which the Frege-Austin theory cannot reach. Moral terms, tense-inflections and non-truthfunctional connectives can all be said to contribute to our expressing of the things we express. That is the linguistic dimension of the theories of time, change, causation and mental states I develop in later chapters. There is no need to say that these items signify properties exemplified by changes; still less that they have meaning chiefly through imparting tone.

A general picture of how the theory I propose relates to the theories of Austin, Searle and Frege is set out in figure 1.

Figure 1

<table>
<tr><td>Austin/Searle speech acts</td><td colspan="3">locutionary or propositional</td><td colspan="2">illocutionary (in speaking)
asserting   promising</td><td>perlocutionary (by speaking)
convincing</td></tr>
<tr><td rowspan="2">Austin: kinds of meaning</td><td colspan="3">sense, reference</td><td colspan="2" rowspan="2">force</td><td rowspan="2"></td></tr>
<tr><td colspan="2">content</td><td>form</td></tr>
<tr><td rowspan="2">Frege: kinds of meaning</td><td colspan="3">sense or thought</td><td colspan="2" rowspan="2">force</td><td rowspan="2">tone</td></tr>
<tr><td colspan="2">content</td><td>form</td></tr>
<tr><td rowspan="2">Proposed acts</td><td colspan="4" rowspan="2">linguistic
(of saying)</td><td colspan="2">practical</td></tr>
<tr><td>institutional</td><td>psychological</td></tr>
<tr><td rowspan="2">Proposed kinds of meaning</td><td colspan="4">linguistic</td><td colspan="2">practical</td></tr>
<tr><td>content</td><td colspan="3">form</td><td>conventional</td><td>psychological</td></tr>
<tr><td>linguistic items</td><td>red
cat</td><td>wise
true</td><td>not
all</td><td>O that
good
mood-inflections</td><td>I promise
Two no trump</td><td>you scum
you angel</td></tr>
</table>

4
Being, Existence and Truth

4.1 Being and not-being

Properties are expressed in language by being predicated. What
is predication? We considered the sentences:

1 Theaetetus is seated.
2 Theaetetus, be seated!
3 If only Theaetetus were seated!
4 Is Theaetetus seated?

Most philosophers would agree that the same property, the
seated position, is predicated in all these utterances. But what
about the following:

5 Theaetetus is not seated.
6 Theaetetus is coming to be seated.
7 Theaetetus was seated.

Is the same property predicated here too, or are different
properties predicated? Is there such a property as not being
seated? Is there a property of becoming seated distinct from
that of being seated? Is there a property of past seatedness,
of being seated in the past, different from that of present
seatedness?

Asking such questions is one way in which analytical philosophers approach the notion of being. It is well known that
philosophers talk a lot about being, and non-philosophers find

this confusing. A collection of papers by Heidegger was published in English under the title *The Question of Being*. When a philosopher asked for a copy at a shop, the shop girl said, 'The question of being what?' Ryle on being told of this incident said, 'That girl should be found and given a Ph.D.'

Some languages have no verb 'to be' or 'to have'. Marquesan is an example (which makes it hard to explain in Marquesan what many philosophical problems are about). Things which we say with their aid in utterances like 'There are mangoes on that tree', 'This mango is sweet', 'I have a canoe' 'Have you been to France?' a Marquesan says with the aid of particles and word-order. But in languages like Greek, Latin and English which have verbs of being they are used in two principal ways: to express existence as in 'Is there any wine in the cellar?' and to predicate as in 'This wine is red.' In the latter case we can ask what the speaker says about the wine in saying it is *red*, but not what he says in saying that it *is*. In its predicative use 'to be' does not itself signify anything predicated; it is the word which complements it that does that. But it is still possible for philosophers to consider being as distinct from existence. Considering being as distinct from existence is considering being as contrasted with not being, being as contrasted with becoming, being as contrasted with having been or being about to be – and perhaps there are other philosophically interesting contrasts too. The contrast between being and having been is a way into the notion of time, and the contrast between being and becoming is a way into the notion of change. I shall discuss these contrasts in chapters 5 and 6. But the contrast between being and not being provides an approach to the notion of truth, and I shall discuss it now.

I suggest that the same property is predicated in sentence (5) about Theaetetus as in sentences (1)–(4). The difference in meaning between (5) and (1) lies not in what is predicated or expressed but in the mode of expression. In (1) it is affirmative: the property is asserted of Theaetetus; it is said to be exemplified by him. In (5) the mode of expression is negative: the property is denied of Theaetetus or said not to be exemplified by him. The notions of assertion and denial are notions of two alternative modes of expression, one of which we may call 'expressing being' and the other 'expressing not being'. The particle 'not' gives the utterance of (5) this form.

Perhaps everyone would agree that 'not' is a negative particle, that it is somehow expressive of denial; but what does this mean? Not that it is an expression for denial: 'denial' is the English word for denial. 'Not' is expressive of denial in that using it in an utterance like (5) is denying. It is expressive of not being, not in that not being is something we can express, but in that inserting it gives the speaker's expressing of something else, in this case the property signified by 'seated', a particular form: it gives it the form *saying that the property is not exemplified by something*.

This account contrasts sharply with current orthodoxy. Most philosophers (a possible exception is Ramsey 1990, p. 43) accept one or both of two very different theories of the meaning of 'not'. The simpler and more popular is that 'not' combines with the rest of the clause in which it is used to express the negation of the proposition expressed without it. This theory, of course, rests on the Frege-Austin conception of a proposition which I have argued to be unsound.

The second theory is that in (5) 'not' combines not with all the other words but just with 'seated'; it forms with 'seated' a complex predicate-expression which signifies a property related in a definite way to the property signified by 'seated'. 'Not seated' signifies a property which belongs to all the objects in the universe to which the property signified by 'seated' does not belong, and to none of those to which it does: to all the objects which are not seated and to none of those which are.

One objection to this theory is that it is unrealistic. There is in reality no property which belongs to all those objects, and only to those objects, which are not seated. Another is that it is circular or regressive. This fancy property is supposed to belong to objects to which the seated position does not belong. What do we mean when we say that a property does *not* belong to an object? Take the remark: 'The seated position does not belong to Theodorus.' Does 'not' combine with 'belong to Theodorus' to signify an ultra-fancy property which belongs to all properties to which the property of belonging to Theodorus does not belong? Or perhaps an ultra-fancy relation which is stood in to Theodorus by all properties which do not stand to him in the relation signified by 'belongs to'? The same question arises about these ultra-fancy entities – what do we mean when we say that the property of belonging to Theodorus does not belong to a property? – and we shall have an endless multiplication of them.

4.2   Existence and number

Nouns like 'elephant' and 'theodolite' signify sorts of object: what sort of meaning is that?

We can say, 'Barbar is an elephant', 'That instrument is a theodolite.' Do these nouns, then, signify things we predicate, perhaps sets of properties? Locke thought so (*Essay* III vi 3–8) but there are difficulties.

First, the utterances I have just given as examples can most easily be interpreted as remarks not about objects but about words. If you hear us using the name 'Barbar' and ask, 'Who is Barbar', I reply, 'Barbar is an elephant', meaning we are using the name to refer to an elephant. If you ask 'What is a theodolite?', I might say, 'That instrument there is a theodolite', meaning that the word 'theodolite' signifies instruments like that. It is hard to think of circumstances in which I might say, 'Socrates is a man', without intending to say anything about the name 'Socrates' or the word 'man'. Is he suspected of being an android?

Secondly, to refer to an individual we must refer to it explicitly or implicitly as a member of a sort. If in saying 'Socrates is lazy' I make a genuine statement I must be referring either to the man Socrates or to my bloodhound Socrates or to some other namesake of a definite species. If I want to say that an individual is a man I clearly cannot refer to it either as a man or as a member of a different species. 'That man is a man' is vacuous; 'That tree-stump is a man' is self-contradictory (though it might, in some circumstances, serve my practical purpose well). I must say something like 'That dark object' or 'That rustling object'. But it is only in exceptional circumstances that we identify individuals as dark objects or noisemakers. Normally we identify them as men or trees. Our concepts of sorts and species are primary for purposes of identification.

Some philosophers, notably Hilary Putnam (1975) and Saul Kripke (1980, ch. 3), say that to know what a word like 'elephant' means we must know not just what properties speakers using it have in mind but what the objects are to which it in fact applies or which the people who first introduced it wanted a word for. These philosophers sometimes say that for such words 'sense' depends (at least partly) on 'reference'. (The terms 'sense' and 'reference' were introduced to distinguish two things non-philosophers call 'meaning'. We can say 'The phrase "the morning star" means "the bright heavenly body you sometimes see just before sunrise"' or 'It means the planet Venus.' In the first case we give the sense of the phrase and in the second its reference.) I wish to develop a suggestion which may sound similar but which is quite different. Putnam and Kripke do not distinguish sharply between referential and predicative uses of words like 'elephant'; indeed, they concentrate on predicative uses like 'Is that an elephant?' My suggestion is that the primary use of such words is not predicative but referential: they are used not to predicate properties but to refer to objects. Putnam and Kripke have no need to deny this. They can say that to grasp the meaning of 'elephant' is to know what species it is of which I refer to something as a member when I say, 'The elephant trumpeted,' and this is in fact the species to which those animals belonged which 'elephant' (or its ancestor in some other language) was introduced to refer to. I shall say something against this general theory in chapter 6 and something in favour of a different account in chapter 9. My concern here, however, is to explain how words for species, and also words for sorts of inanimate object, mean whatever it is they mean; and for this it is enough to consider how they refer or what referring is.

I noted earlier that reference can be either definite or indefinite. In 'Jemima mewed' or 'The cat mewed' I refer definitely. The English definite article is an indicator of direct reference though not an infallible one – consider 'The hand that rocks the cradle rules the world.' Here I start with indefinite reference, of which the following are examples:

1   Did a cat mew?
2   Two cats mewed.
3   If only there were not so many cats in my garden.
4   Shoot every cat you see.

Indefinite reference, it will be noticed, is not exclusive of definite and may require it. In (3) I refer definitely to a garden and in (4) to a person (you); and in the first two there is probably implicit reference to a particular region of the world and a particular time.

In these examples I bring a sort of object, cats, into my discourse. How do I do that? In (1) I ask if there was a cat that mewed; in (2) I say that there were two that mewed; in (3) I wish there were not so many standing in a certain relation to my garden; and (4) is more or less equivalent to 'Let there not be one single cat seen by you at which you refrain from shooting.' I suggest, then, that 'cat' signifies a sort of object in that using it is saying that there is some definite or indefinite number of objects of that sort, or asking if there is, or in some other way enumerating cats or expressing number.

Indefinite referring is expressing numbers of objects somewhat as predicating is expressing properties. As expressing a property may be saying that it is had, or asking if it is, or wishing it were, so expressing a number may be saying that there is that number of objects of some sort, or asking if there is, or ordering someone to make sure there is. But this resemblance goes with an important difference. Different properties are different things we express. If you express one colour and I another we express different things. I suggest that if you express one number and I another our *forms* of expression differ: the linguistic item which would most naturally be said to determine the number I express makes a difference to the way in which I express something else, a sort of object.

Up to a point that would be widely agreed. The words 'all', 'some' and 'no', which are sometimes called 'quantifiers', clearly have meaning in a different way from 'red' and 'spherical'; and if I say, 'Some cats are blue,' and you say, 'No cats are blue,' our statements differ in logical form. But if 'My aunt has some cats' and 'My aunt has no cats' differ in form, so, surely, do 'My aunt has many cats' and 'My aunt has few' or 'My aunt has ten' and 'She has two.' I suggest that all these words have meaning through determining the way in which we express sorts in indirect reference.

It might seem an objection to this that there are infinitely many finite numbers. So if expressing each is a different form of expression there will be infinitely many forms of expression.

I think the objection fails. There do not actually exist infinitely many expressions for integers; it is merely possible to go on constructing new ones; and I do not see why it should not be possible to go on constructing new forms of expression. It is significant that the rules for constructing numerals and the numerals themselves which we use over and over again in the process are included in the grammar of a language. Words like 'fifteen' do not appear only or primarily in the vocabulary. If a word is discussed in the grammar of a language it generally has meaning chiefly in the same way as constructions.

Philosophers sometimes say that words like 'few' and even words like 'fifteen' signify properties of a special sort. This claim is important because it bears on existence. Saying that there are some tame tigers or even that tame tigers are few is surely saying that tame tigers exist; whereas saying that the number of tame tigers in the world is zero is saying they do not exist. If quantifiers signify properties will not the same be true of 'exist'?

The case for saying that words like 'fifteen' signify properties is this. We are sometimes able to put all the members of one set of things into one-to-one correlation with all the members of another. That happens when I join my hands: each finger of my right hand comes into contact with a different finger of my left, and conversely. When laying for a frugal meal I put knives, forks, plates and glasses into one-to-one correlation. We can say that all sets which can be put into this correlation with one another have something in common or form a distinct class. The set of eyes in my head would go into one such class, the set of fingers on each hand into another, the set of hairs in my moustache into a third. Evidently there are just as many possible classes like these as there are integers. Why not say, then, that the word 'five', for example, signifies a property which many familiar sets, including the set of fingers on my right hand, have in common?

Certainly if a set is a five its members are one-to-one corre-latable with members of other sets in this class, and we can say that this is a kind of property of the set. But it is one thing to say that the set of toes on my left foot has this property, another to say that being a toe on my left foot is a kind of property which is exemplified by five objects, and therefore has the special, second-order property of being exemplified by five objects. It is this further suggestion which leads to the dubious theory of existence. If being exemplified by five objects is a property of properties so, surely, is being exemplified by some objects, and for elephants to exist is for the property of being an elephant to have just that second-order property.

This theory was originally proposed as an alternative to the idea that existence is a first-order or ordinary property, a property which is had by objects. Grappling with the problem of what it is to believe something to be the case, Locke sug-gested that as we have ideas of whiteness and sphericality so we have an idea of real existence. When I believe that Theaetetus is seated I have a mental picture of a seated Theaetetus and I connect this (somehow) with real existence: I think that some-thing of which the picture is a likeness really exists (see *Essay* IV i 7). Hume (*Treatise* I ii 7) rightly rejected this naive idea, and analytical philosophers on the positive side have empha-sized that existence and non-existence are expressed by quan-tifiers like 'some' and 'no'.

But to go on and say that being exemplified by a definite or indefinite number of objects is a property of properties is to relapse into the original error. If existence is not a property of objects still less is exemplification a property of properties. So linguistic items which are expressive of number do not have meaning by signifying properties of properties.

We may say that they are expressive of existence in a way. For they contribute to our expressing of sorts in indefinite reference; indefinite referring is saying that there are numbers of objects or asking if there are or wishing there were; and these may be reckoned as ways of expressing existence. But we should distinguish these ways from the way in which we express existence when we refer to an object definitely or by name.

If I say, 'Was the King of France beheaded?' or 'Was Louis beheaded?' I do not ask if there was a King of France or bearer of the name 'Louis'. I say that there was and ask if he was beheaded. Referring definitely is bringing a particular individual into discourse, and doing that is always saying that the individual exists. Betsy Prig could not ask if Mrs Harris existed or say that she did not; she could say only that there was 'no such person', no person such as to bear the name 'Mrs Harris' and be always extolling the virtues of Mrs Gamp.

Because of this difference between expressing the existence of numbers of objects and expressing the existence of particular objects it is a little misleading to use the single word 'existence' in characterizing both modes of expression. We may prefer to say that only definite referring is strictly speaking expressing existence, and indefinite referring is primarily expressing number, though to express a number is to say that there is that number of objects, or ask if there is, or the like.

In general, then, a word for a sort of object *means* that sort in that using it is either referring to some number of objects of that sort or (as in the famous 'The cat is on the mat') expressing the existence of particular objects of the sort. But to complete this account I should say that these words can be used predicatively: not to predicate properties they signify, but to predicate properties typical, or supposed to be typical, of objects of the sorts they signify.

'Arthur's head', I say, 'is the shape of an egg; it is the size of a pumpkin.' Here I use 'egg' and 'pumpkin' to predicate a size and a shape. I accomplish this by replacing 'is' by 'is the size of', 'is the shape of', and the words 'shape' and 'size' determine the character of my predication: 'shape' makes it an act of shape-expressing, 'size' an act of size-expressing.

Let me dwell for a moment on these modes of speech. First, they could be used for relational properties. Instead of saying, 'Achilles is to the right of Odysseus', Helen could say, 'Achilles stands to Odysseus as the hand with which you usually eat stands to your other hand.' We could, though it would be inconvenient, make do with a vocabulary consisting only of common nouns, words like 'shape' and 'relation' and syntactic words.

Next, 'His head was the size of a pumpkin' and 'His head was the shape of a pumpkin' seem to differ only in form. In both utterances a head is referred to and pumpkins are brought in. The difference is that in one the speaker predicates the size commonly associated with pumpkins and in the other the shape; these seem to be formally different ways of bringing in pumpkins.

If that is correct, size-expressing and shape-expressing are different kinds of linguistic act. Hence 'gallon' and 'spherical', in so far as the first is a size-word and the second a shape-word, will make a difference to the form of the speaker's expression. That is why I said that all words have meaning in this way, though some ('spherical' and 'gallon' are examples) also determine what is expressed.

Finally, it is obvious that 'His head was the size of a pumpkin' is not a relational statement in the same way as 'His head was to the left of mine.' The speaker does not say that there was a pumpkin to which the man's head was equal in size. Neither is 'His head was larger than a pumpkin' relational. What about 'His head was larger than mine'? Certainly in this utterance I refer to my head as well as the other man's. But if 'larger than' signified a relation in this utterance it should signify a relation in 'His head was larger than a pumpkin' and in saying that I *would* be saying that there is a pumpkin to which his head stands (or perhaps that there is no pumpkin to which his head does not stand) in the expressed relation.

As 'His head is larger than a pumpkin' differs in form from 'His head is rounder (a more perfect sphere) than a pumpkin' so, I suggest, 'His head is larger than mine' differs in form from 'His head is equal in size to mine' and 'His nose is redder than mine' differs in form from 'His nose is just as red as mine.' At first this suggestion may seem to threaten us with an unwelcome new proliferation of forms of linguistic expression. But we should reflect that being larger than, being redder than etc., are expressed not by items which belong to the vocabulary of a language, not by prepositions like 'over', but by inflections of the positive adjectives. The procedure for making these comparisons is laid down in the grammar of a language, and grammatical rules tend to determine forms of linguistic expression. That is why, though items like 'larger than' can be used as two-place predicate-expressions, I do not count being larger than, being twice the size of etc., as relational properties in my sense of 'property'.

To return to common nouns, I shall say more later about the concepts they express and their meaning in utterances like 'He thought there were crocodiles in the pool'; but the present discussion may be summarized as follows. These words are chiefly used referentially. Expressing a sort is usually referring to some number of objects of it or saying that some particular object belonging to it exists. But the words can be used predicatively, in which case expressing the sort is not saying that something belongs to it but predicating properties associated with it.

4.3   Truth and falsity

Against the Frege-Austin conception of a proposition I argued that truth and falsity (that is, 'absolute' truth and falsity) attach not to things we express but to acts of expressing. Saying 'Theaetetus is seated' is speaking truly if the position expressed *is* exemplified by Theaetetus, and it is speaking falsely if the position *is not*. The difference between truth and falsity in language (and, no doubt, in thought) is explained by what appears to be an ontological difference, the difference between being and not being. In section 4.1 I then argued that grasping the difference between being and not being is grasping the difference between two forms of expression. Does that invalidate my account of truth or make it circular? No, because I am not saying that speaking truly and speaking falsely are themselves two different forms of expression. I say only that grasping the difference between them depends on grasping the difference between two forms of expression; and that seems to me to strengthen my account.

Any satisfactory account of truth and falsity should show how we grasp the opposition between them, how we understand that the same thing cannot be both true and false. On the Frege-Austin theory when I say something true and you say something false the opposition lies in what we say: our modes of expression are or can be identical, but we express contradictory things. I think we shall never understand our grasp of the difference between truth and falsity like this. According to me, when you say, 'Theaetetus is seated', and I say, 'Theaetetus is not seated', we express the same things, but our expressing of them is contradictory. Your expressing of the sitting position is asserting, mine is denying. It is because we grasp the contradictory character of these acts of predication that we understand that truth and falsity are incompatible.

One difficulty concerning truth is to see how it gets a foothold at all; a second is to give a non-circular account of how it is incompatible with falsity; and a third is to justify the idea that it consists in some kind of correspondence with reality, that I speak truly if and only if things are as I say. The distinction between expressing and what is expressed enables us at least to make a start at this third task.

The 'is' and 'is not' in 'Mars is red' and 'Mars is not red' are expressive of being and not being or exemplification and non-exemplification; the quantifiers and other referential devices are expressive of existence and non-existence. If the colour red is in fact exemplified by Mars then the mode of exemplification of which 'Mars is red' is expressive is identical with the mode of exemplification of the colour expressed. If there are in fact a lot of cats in my garden, the mode of existence of which 'There are a lot of cats in my garden' is expressive is identical with the mode of existence of the sort of animal expressed. Or suppose that there does not exist one single object of the planetary sort which does not exemplify spherical shape. Then the modes of existence and exemplification of which 'All planets are spherical' is expressive coincide with those of the sort of object and the property expressed in that utterance. Suppose, in contrast, both that Icarus is a planet and that it does not have spherical shape; then the modes of existence and exemplification of which 'If Icarus is a planet it is spherical' are expressive are non-identical with those of things expressed.

These examples suggest the following general account:

A speaks truly (*A*'s utterance corresponds to reality; things are as *A* says) = the modes of existence and exemplification of the things *A* expresses are identical with the modes of existence and exemplification of which A's utterance is expressive.

If this account, or something like it, is correct, what sort of meaning attaches to the words 'true' and 'false' when used 'absolutely'? Do they signify relations between linguistic acts and reality? There is no harm in saying that so long as it is understood that these relations are second-order properties, properties expressed in talk not about things but about language or thought. But if I say, 'That Icarus is spherical is false', am I not talking about Icarus? Do I mention any utterance? Perhaps I make some implicit reference to my utterance itself; it may be like saying 'Icarus is spherical – no – that is false' (compare Davidson 1984). It should be recognized, however, that words which have a primary use in second-order discourse in *describing* the forms of ordinary speeches are often used also to *give* a certain form to an ordinary speech. In 'Is it true that Mars is red?' 'true' combines with 'is it ... that' to do the work of an interrogative particle (the second 'est' works similarly in 'est-ce que c'est que'). In 'That Icarus is spherical is false', 'false' can be treated as forming part of an emphatic negative.

My account of correspondence holds only for declarative utterances; if an utterance is interrogative or imperative we may have to say that there cannot be an identity between the modes of existence and exemplification of which it is expressive and those of the things expressed. Whether this is a serious flaw I shall not consider because for my present purposes it is less important to defend the possibility of a correspondence theory of truth than to maintain the impossibility of Frege-Austin propositions. To that end I add some further remarks about negation; the reader who is already satisfied could proceed safely to the next chapter.

4.4   Appendix on 'not'

On the Frege-Austin theory when we insert 'not' into a sentence we express a proposition which is a truthfunction of the proposition we should have expressed otherwise. I deny that there is anything which is expressed in words and true or false but agree that 'not' is a truthfunctional operator. Nothing we express is a truthfunction of anything else but one expressing can be a truthfunction of another. In 'Theaetetus is not seated' the effect of saying 'not' is precisely that the speaker's expressing is a truthfunction of the expressing in 'Theaetetus is seated.' Uttering the negative sentence is saying something true if and only if uttering the affirmative is saying something false (I here ignore the difference between 'Theaetetus is not seated' and 'It is false that Theaetetus is seated').

'If Theaetetus is wrestling Theaetetus is not seated' is not a truthfunction of 'If Theaetetus is wrestling he is seated' and the 'not', therefore, does not make it one. It is a truthfunction of the two utterances 'Theaetetus is wrestling' and 'Theaetetus is seated' and 'not' makes it the truthfunction 'If p not q' as contrasted with 'If p, q'. Similarly, in 'If Theaetetus is not wrestling Theaetetus is seated' putting in 'not' makes the utterance the truthfunction 'If not p, q' instead of 'If p, q'.

Saying what truthfunction an utterance is of some other utterance or utterances is saying all that a logician needs to know about its meaning, but the philosopher of language may seek a further account of how 'not' contributes to our expressing.

Inserting it into the main clause of a declarative sentence makes the speaker's act denying. When I say, 'Theaetetus is not seated', the denial is categorical. In 'If Theaetetus is wrestling he is not seated' it is conditional: the speaker denies on the condition that Theaetetus is wrestling. I do not mean that if Theaetetus is wrestling the speaker's mode of expression is denial and otherwise it is something else, but that it is conditional denial. What kind of expressing is that? It is expressing a property as one which is not, if a certain condition is fulfilled, exemplified by something. 'Not' in the apodosis of a conditional is expressive of conditional non-exemplification. Similarly in 'Either Theaetetus is not wrestling or he is not seated' the speaker denies disjunctively. The sitting position is expressed as something the non-exemplification of which is an alternative to not wrestling.

In all these cases 'not' plays the same role: it turns an assertion, categorical, conditional or disjunctive, into a denial. In 'If Theaetetus is not seated he is wrestling' its role is slightly different. The speaker does not deny the seated position of Theaetetus: he expresses it as something the non-exemplifying of which is a condition of something else. That 'not' has a different function here is shown by the fact that in Greek a different particle would be used, *mê* instead of *ou*. Similarly in 'There is not one thing which is a planet and which is not spherical' the first 'not' is expressive of denial but the second is like 'not' in a conditional clause: it enables spherical shape to be expressed as something the not exemplifying of which is sufficient for not being of a sort.

It might be argued that 'not' must have the same meaning in conditional clauses and in main clauses because the inference from 'If Theaetetus is not seated he is wrestling' and 'Theaetetus is not seated' to 'He is wrestling' is valid. But all that is necessary for the validity of this inference is that the first utterance should be the truthfunction 'If not *p*, *q*' of 'Theaetetus is seated' and 'Theaetetus is wrestling' and I have agreed that 'not' in a conditional clause has that effect. I am now saying that this does not exhaust the way in which it affects the speaker's mode of expression. The fact that there is only one negative particle in English has probably supported the belief of many philosophers in propositions. On the Frege-Austin theory I express a proposition which is true if Theaetetus is not seated when I say 'Theaetetus! Be not seated!' or 'If only Theaetetus were not seated' – which might have alerted more people to the theory's unsoundness. In fact 'not' makes one of these utterances a prohibition and the other a negative wish; in Greek *mê* would again be used instead of *ou* and in Latin *ne* instead of *non*.

Besides arguing from its use in complex sentences that 'not' does not make an utterance a denial, Frege and his followers have some arguments to show that asserting and denying cannot be coordinate alternatives. None of these succeed.

Frege thought that anyone who makes denying an alternative to asserting must say that asserting and denying are, respectively, joining a predicate to a subject and separating it from one. I agree with him that this is not an acceptable account of these acts but I am not proposing it. On my view asserting and denying are both ways of relating a predicate to a subject but they are different ways. Asserting of Icarus that it is spherical is relating spherical shape to it as something it exemplifies; denying is relating the shape as something not exemplified.

Michael Dummett (1973, p. 317) is afraid that if we allow denying to be a form of linguistic act distinct from asserting we open the floodgates. We shall have to say forbidding is an alternative to ordering, lamenting to rejoicing, declaring on a negative condition to declaring on a positive and so on. Why not? There may be some awkwardness in finding names for the more complicated varieties of expression, but it is nothing to the awkwardness of assimilating the difference in meaning between 'Theaetetus is seated' and 'Theaetetus is not seated' to that between 'Theaetetus is seated' and 'Theaetetus is snub-nosed'.

Finally, Frege (1952, p. 125) argues that if denial were an alternative to asserting it should be possible to determine whether a given declaration is negative or affirmative. But that is impossible. We cannot go by whether it contains a negative particle because a sentence with a negative particle can have exactly the same meaning as one without. 'Caesar did not have hair on the top of his head' means the same as 'Caesar was bald'. If we say that 'bald' expresses something negative, what about the words 'die', 'mortal' and 'immortal'? The question whether a predicate-term expresses something negative or positive is sterile and, in some cases at least, wholly undecidable.

Frege is here challenging a way of thinking which is not peculiar to philosophers who make denying an alternative to asserting. We recognize a class of expressions the meaning of which can be explained ostensively. To explain the meaning of a term ostensively is to point out an object that exemplifies it, so what is meant by such a word should be positive. Can I not point to some Micawber-like figure and say, 'He exemplifies what I mean by "bald"'? It seems to me obvious that grasping the meaning of 'bald' depends on possessing the concept of hair. Whether a word expresses something positive or negative may be difficult to prove but that does not show that the question is spurious, and where proof is lacking at least we can offer argument. To take up the challenge of Frege's example, surely dying is ceasing to be able to do certain things. Hence 'Socrates is mortal' is a denial that he will always be able to eat, converse etc., not an assertion that he will do something called 'dying' or acquire a property signified by 'dead'. And 'Socrates is immortal' is a denial of this denial, a double negative, which I take to be a different form of expression from an assertion even if the two are logically equivalent. A stiffer challenge is provided by 'open' and 'shut' as applied to doors. I suggest that the positive notion is movement from place to place. This is impeded by things like walls. The impediment is partially removed by an opening. The impediment is restored by a movable object called a 'door' which turns the opening into a doorway. And the door impedes when shut and does not impede when open.

5
Time

5.1 Introduction

We live in a temporal world. When we reflect on its temporal character our first instinct, I think, is to try to conceive time on a spatial model. A stretch of time seems analogous to a line. As a line begins and ends and is divisible at points which have no extension at all so we think of time-stretches as being bounded by and divisible at completely durationless instants. As I can jump onto a bicycle and go from one spatial location to another so H. G. Wells imagines someone mounting a time machine and travelling from one time to another. There are, or seem to be, regions of empty space where nothing material extends, and we think there could be stretches of time in which nothing whatever happens.

This way of thinking builds up into a metaphysical picture. If we take a particular occurrence as a reference item – Bede introduced using the birth of Christ in Bethlehem – then any other event can be located relatively to that by means of four measurements or coordinates: it is, so to speak, x miles north or south, y miles east or west, z miles above or below, and t years earlier or later. Physicists often treat the phenomena they study in this way, viewing three-dimensional space and time as a unified four-dimensional continuum. It is enough for them if this helps them to understand or explain physical events, and they are not competent to say whether or not time really is a fourth dimension analogous to latitude, longitude and altitude.

But philosophers who are already conceiving time on a spatial model incline to that opinion. In the way in which things to the north and things to the south are equally real they think that past and future events are equally real. If I face north I can see what is north of me but only guess what is south; they suggest that the difference between the past and the future is like that. We can find out for certain what *has* happened and only conjecture what *will* happen; but this difference lies not in the past and future events themselves but in our orientation towards them.

If the past and the future are there in the same way as the poles and the tropics what becomes of change? The view of change which goes with this view of time (and the discussion of which I defer to chapter 6) is that it reduces to being different at different times. I move if I am at different places at different times; I blush if I exemplify different shades of pink at different times.

This theory of time is pretty much the current orthodoxy. The only alternative to it which analytical philosophers discuss is a theory that time also has a dynamic aspect in which it somehow passes or flows. Continental philosophers consider that whatever there is to time besides a one-dimensional series of instants is a product of human consciousness. Time, says Heidegger on the last page of *Being and Time* (1967), is 'that which makes possible the being-ahead-of-itself-in-already-being-involved-in, that is, which makes possible the being of care'; similarly Merleau-Ponty (1962, pp. 412, 420).

I believe that the spatializing view of time is wrong and there is a better alternative to it than supposing that it is a thing which somehow passes or flows – a supposition I find incoherent. I shall first expound what I take to be the correct theory and then criticize current orthodoxy.

5.2   *Time as an aspect of change*

Neither time nor anything else of philosophical interest can be defined in the rigorous way in which geometers define plane figures and scientists elements. But philosophers who reduce change to being different at different times think time is indefinable in a special way: time and space are supposed to be primitive notions out of which we construct the notions of movement and change (so, Gale 1968, p. 4). It seems to me, in contrast, that the notions of time and space are both logically and psychologically posterior to that of change. We are confronted with changes of various kinds, we obtain opaque ideas of them, and we arrive at the notions of time and distance by trying to analyse and clarify these ideas. Distance and time are aspects of motion and change.

I speak here, as usual, of physical change, not of psychological or legal occurrences like getting angry, acquiring a belief or ceasing to be the owner of something. Physical change is in respect either of intrinsic properties like temperature, shape and volume or of relational properties. Movement from place to place, rotation and acceleration are changes of the latter kind. I shall concentrate on movements from place to place but what I say should be easily applicable to other varieties of change.

Suppose that a body A moves from a place P_1 to a place a mile away P_2 in ten minutes; and suppose it moves continuously, that is, without stopping en route. Then we can say two things:

1   A moves a mile.
2   A moves for ten minutes.

We cannot, however, put these remarks together and say:

3   A moves a mile for ten minutes.

We can say that a traveller travelled on for miles or that he travelled on for hours, but not that he travelled on for miles and hours. A movement may be reckoned in units of distance: (1) says that A's movement is a one-mile movement. It may also be reckoned in units of time; (2) says that A's movement is a ten-minute movement. But it cannot be reckoned in both ways at once.

A material object which can be seen from two different positions, as my house can be seen from the north and from the south, literally has two aspects. It is a natural metaphor to say that a movement has two aspects in that it can be thought of and spoken of in these two distinct ways, but not in both at once. A linguistic obstacle of speaking of A's movement in both ways at once is that instead of (2) we can say 'A is in motion for ten minutes' whereas it is incorrect to say 'A is in motion a mile' or even 'A is in motion for a mile.'

In one aspect a movement is measured in units of distance, in another it is measured in units of time. What is measurable in units of time surely *is* a time, that is, a time-stretch; and what is measurable in units of distance surely is a distance. So it looks as if our notions of a time-stretch and a distance are notions of these two aspects of a movement. A movement, in so far as it is a number of miles long, is a distance, and any change, in so far as it is a number of hours or minutes long, is a time. If that is right we can say that the generic notions of distance and time, as distinct from the notions of *a* distance and *a* time, are notions of these aspects.

This programme for explaining distance as an aspect of movement and time as an aspect of change generally depends, of course, on finding some way of characterizing these aspects which is not in terms of distance-units and time-units. For to say 'A time-stretch is a movement in its temporal aspect' or 'considered as measured in time-units' would be too grossly circular.

When we think of A's movement as a one-mile movement we think of it as a movement which is made, which takes place, which goes on. When we think of it as a ten-minute movement we think of it as a making or a taking place or a going on of a movement. It is obvious that A's making of the movement from P_1 to P_2 is not something over and above the movement made. It is not a further movement. But when A moves from P_1 to P_2 we can consider, specify or describe the movement made and we can describe A's making of this movement. These are two aspects of a single thing. The relationship between them is that of a possibility which is fulfilled to a fulfilment of that possibility.

This relationship is not peculiar to motion or change. It is the relationship between properties which are instantiated or exemplified and instances or examples of them. Spherical shape is a possible shape for objects and examples of this shape, that is, spherical objects, are fulfilments of this possibility. The relationship of examples to that of which they are examples is traditionally known as the relationship of particulars to universals. It is best understood as the relationship of fulfilments of a possibility to the possibility fulfilled (so my 1989). And it holds not only between objects and properties but between changes measured in time-units and changes measured in other ways.

I claim, then, that A's movement is a mile long considered as a movement which is or can be made, and ten minutes long considered as a making of a movement. The following considerations support this claim. (1) The first minute of A's movement is the first minute of travel; the first furlong is not a furlong of travel but a furlong travelled. (2) We can say 'A made a one-mile movement in ten minutes' but not 'A made a ten-minute movement in one mile.' It is, then, as a one-mile movement, not as a ten-minute movement, that A's movement is *made*. (3) We can say 'A's making of the movement was a ten-minute making of a one-mile movement'; it is incorrect to say 'It was a one-mile making of a ten-minute movement.' (4) There can be many makings of the same movement. Now there can be many travellings of the same mile but there cannot, surely, be many travellings of the same ten minutes.

Some philosophers (e.g. Putnam 1962; Harrison 1971) think time-travel might be possible. If it is, there really can be many travellings of the same ten minutes: we can travel for or live through the same ten minutes many times. Most people feel that time-travel is logically impossible but find it hard to say why. One suggestion is that if I could live through the same month twice I could do different things each time and it could be both true and false that I was in Crete throughout March 1978. But why (as Putnam asks) should I not be both in Crete and in the Marquesas? If sea-serpents can do this, why not time-worms? My theory of time provides a more direct argument. Unlike a distance, a time-stretch cannot be travelled because the notion of a time-stretch is already the notion of a travelling. If we cannot think of something both as travellable and as a travelling at the same time, and thought of as ten

minutes long a movement is thought of as a travelling, we
cannot think that a time-stretch is travellable. We may imagine
that time-travel is conceivable but it is not.

A couple of objections could be made to my thesis but I do
not think they will stand. First, we can say 'The flight to New
York is five hours long; zealous businessmen make that five-
hour flight several times a week.' Here, however, by 'a five-
hour flight' we simply mean a distance which a modern airliner
can fly in five hours. Secondly, a keep-fit fanatic might say
'Running for an hour is something which I do every day'; does
that not show that he conceives running for an hour as something which is done, as a feat which is repeatable daily? In
'Every day he runs a mile' we can construe the words 'a mile'
with 'runs' to express a feat, running a mile. But it does not
follow that in 'Every day he runs for an hour' we can take 'for
an hour' with 'runs'. For instead of 'Every day he runs for an
hour' we could say 'For an hour every day he runs' whereas it
would be incorrect to say 'For a mile every day he runs.'
Running a mile is a feat. Running is not so much a feat as a
skill. We can learn to run as we can learn to write or knit, and
we can exercise any of these skills for a time. But there is no
such skill as running for an hour or knitting for ten minutes. If
there were, these skills too could be exercised for periods of
time. For how long today, then, does the fanatic exercise the
art of running for an hour?

I conclude that it is makings of movements and goings on of
changes that we measure in time-units. Goings on of changes,
then, are stretches of time.

It might be objected that two different changes can go on
contemporaneously or even that two different makings of the
same movement (your going from London to Paris and mine)
can be contemporaneous; but it sounds odd to say that two
time-stretches can be contemporaneous. If your making of the
journey to Paris is contemporary with mine, surely the time
for which we travel is something distinct both from your
travelling and from mine? We are being asked to choose
between saying that the hour for which we travel is something
over and above your travelling and mine, and saying that the
hour for which you travel is contemporaneous with the hour

for which I travel. The first option seems to me extremely unattractive. What could this additional hour be? 'Absolute, true and mathematical time,' says Newton in the famous scholium to Definition 8 of *Principia Mathematica*, 'of its own nature and without relation to anything else, flows equally.' If the hour for which we travel is something over and above your travelling and mine, it must be an hour of this legendary fluid. The second option may sound a little awkward at first, but I have already pointed out that it is quite natural to identify the first hour of your journey with the first hour of travel, and we can say that an hour of travel by you is contemporaneous with an hour of travel by me if we start and stop simultaneously. We can define contemporaneousness of time-stretches in terms of simultaneity of startings and stoppings. Startings and stoppings are events of a sort but they are not changes; they are beginnings and finishings of changes; and unlike changes they neither occur in times nor go on for times. I shall return to them and to the simultaneity that can hold between them shortly, but I may say here that this simultaneity does not have to be defined in terms of contemporaneousness of time-stretches.

If the notion of a time-stretch is the notion of a going on or taking place of a change we can complete our theory of time by saying that time in general is the going on of change. Time is said to bring things to pass. Shakespeare in his sonnets writes as if were a causal agent, as if it makes us old and ugly in the way in which plastic surgeons make us young and beautiful. But that is just poetry. Years make us old in the way in which beauty makes people beautiful. Time produces change in that it is the actual coming about of change; it is not the efficient but the formal cause of passage.

5.3   Time-travel, empty time and distance

One way of testing a philosophical theory is to examine its consequences. If these are unacceptable the theory must be rejected; if they are welcome, though the theory is not thereby proved we obtain a fresh motive to adopt it. One consequence of my theory of time has already been noted: it rules out time-travel. A second is that it rules out empty time, time in which no change is going on.

Perhaps that needs proving. If we can say that changes go on, why not say states of peace, quiet and immobility go on too? In the past children were required to do something called 'resting': perhaps to rest for an hour or two in the afternoon (such hours passed slowly). We can speak of inanimate objects as being at rest for periods of time; so it looks as if there are hours of rest or immobility as well as of change or motion, and as if time is the going on not only of change but also of staying unchanged.

I can certainly say of a particular object like that chair that it remained motionless and unchanged for an hour. But when I say this I assume that other things like clock-hands and the Earth continue to change. The chair stays unchanged for an hour if its ceasing to change is simultaneous with the Earth's starting, and its beginning to change again with the Earth's finishing, a rotation through 15°. There is nothing problematic here; what is doubtful is whether there could be a time-stretch during which nothing in the universe was changing in any way at all.

We can imagine a universe parts of which appear to freeze into changelessness at regular intervals (so Shoemaker 1969). Perhaps one part freezes up for every third year, one for every fourth and one for every fifth. In that case we may calculate that everything will be frozen up for every sixtieth year. But if things start to change again in the sixty-first year, then, during that sixtieth year when everything appeared to be locked in changelessness, surely there were some hidden processes going on. Otherwise why should changes start up again in the sixty-first year? Why does the universe not start to change earlier, during the sixtieth year, or else like Theseus in the Underworld stay unchanged for ever?

We could say that the starting up again of change is totally inexplicable: it just happens. But this would be very hard to believe; for reasons I shall indicate later our conviction that changes need some kind of explanation is not easily shed. Philosophers, therefore, who want to leave open the possibility

of time without change suggest that we could assign a certain
causal power to time-stretches themselves (so Newton-Smith
1980, ch. 2). We could say that the mere lapse of time throughout the sixtieth year causes change to start up in the sixty-first.
This is Shakespeare's metaphor of time as an efficient cause
presented as cold cosmic fact. The cost of the presentation is
accepting Newton's absolute, true and mathematical time. The
passage of the sixtieth year must be a year of this absolute time.

Newton thought that time is something which goes on in
addition to change, and space something which extends in
addition to matter. He conceived time and space as physical
realities. But he also thought that they differ in an important
way from other things that exist or go on like air or rotation.
He thought that they have no power to affect other things, and
other things have no power to affect them. The objection to
this way of thinking is that it is incoherent: there could not be
a physical reality without powers to affect or be affected. This
objection, however, is not disposed of by endowing absolute
time with the power to start up change in the universe after an
interval. For anything which had that power would not longer
be absolute time: it would be some ordinary physical process
of change which takes time or goes on for time. The idea of
absolute time equipped with causal powers is as incoherent as
the idea of absolute time without causal powers.

This argument against time without change depends on ideas
about causation: that changes need explanation and that any
genuine mode of causal action must be the going on of some
ordinary physical process like pushing, pulling or heating. It
might be replied that the fundamental forces of nature, gravitation, electromagnetism and so on, do not work by means of
such processes. Although it seems to me bizarre to attribute
such a fundamental force to absolute time, a second argument,
independent of causal considerations, can be drawn from a
comparison with the notion of an empty space.

If *A* is at a distance of a mile from *B*, and there is nothing
material between them, then between them there is an empty
space or gap: a space of a mile or one-mile gap. Although we
may speak here of a mile of emptiness, a one-mile gap is not
a mile of something called 'emptiness'. We can have a mile of

string or sand, or, indeed, an acre of sand or a billion gallons of water, but not a mile, an acre or a gallon of emptiness or nothing. A mile, an acre and a gallon are units of extension in one, two or three dimentions. They are units for which the materials of material objects extend, and what is measured in them must be material. A gallon, acre or mile of nothing would be one for which sand, water and the rest do not extend. But it does not follow, because we can have miles for which sand extends that we can miles for it does not extend or miles of non-sand. Miles for which nothing extends, miles of non-matter, are rather non-miles than miles.

But if a one-mile gap is not a mile of nothing, what is it? If *A* and *B* are a mile apart and there is nothing material between them, no doubt there *could* be a mile of something between them. A mile of string would just reach from *A* to *B*; a mile-long rigid rod could be put between them without dis-placing either. There is *room* in the gap for a one-mile object and in general the magnitude of an empty space is the magni-tude of any object which would exactly fill it. But if we wish to understand what an empty space is, saying this will not help. It merely introduces another puzzling entity, the possible filler of the gap. Are we to suppose that this is some real object existing elsewhere or something imaginary? The gap, at least, seems to be not merely imaginary but real.

If *A* and *B* are a mile apart the movement from *A* to *B* is a one-mile movement. If what is measured in time-units is a time-stretch, what is measured in units of distance should be a distance or stretch of space. I have argued that a movement is measurable in distance-units when it is considered as something which is made or which goes on; so the notion of a stretch of space is that of a makable movement.

We use the same words ('yard', 'metre' etc.) for units of distance and for units of length, but the notions of distance and length are different. We move distances, whereas we move *over* lengths: I run a mile, but I run over or across a mile of sand. The mile of sand exists independently of runners: there it is beside the sea and I come along and run over it. But when I run a mile the mile does not exist in the same way unrun. In 'I ran a mile' 'a mile' is a so-called internal object, like 'a race' in

'I ran a race'; indeed, when I run a race, the race is simply a distance I run competitively. Similarly, when I jump six feet the six feet I jump are simply the jump I jump.

If movements and lengths are so different, why do we use the same words for units in which we measure them? Perhaps because the same material object can be used to define both the length a yard and the distance a yard. The length is the length it exemplifies, and the distance is the movement it would be necessary to make to get from one end to the other. The distance between you and me is three yards if the movement is thrice the movement from one end to the other of the Standard Yard; and if that is the case an object thrice the length of the Standard Yard will just fit between us. But although it is possible to define distance-units and length-units together like this, for some purposes it may be better to define distance-units by means of some natural causal process. A light year is the distance a light particle travels in the time it takes the Earth to revolve round the Sun.

The stretch of space, then, between A and B is the movement we make if we go from one to the other. Movements are neither full nor empty, so we are not using 'empty' in quite the same way when we say 'There is an empty space between A and B' and when we say 'There is an empty bucket between A and B.' There is an empty space between them if there is a distance between them and there is no object or stuff between them. We can say with perfect correctness that empty spaces exist; but they exist rather as possibilities than as fulfilments of possibilities or as positive realities additional to expanses of water, air etc. A one-mile gap really exists between A and B if there is in truth nothing material between them and if it is really possible to get to B by moving a mile in some direction from A.

If there were to be an empty time, an hour during which nothing whatever happens, it would have to be analogous either to a mile for which nothing whatever extends or to a one-mile gap. The notion of a mile for which nothing extends is, I have argued, incoherent. Any actual mile must be a mile of string, sand or something like that, and by the same reasoning any actual hour should be an hour of rotation, alteration or the like. An empty hour, then, would have to be a kind of temporal gap analogous to the one-mile spatial gap. But a one-mile spatial gap is a mile that *might* be moved or travelled, as contrasted with a moving or a travelling. A stretch of time, in contrast, is not something that might be travelled but precisely a travelling. Either way, then, an empty time is impossible. The spatial model which is a genuine analogue, the mile of non-material, is incoherent, and the model which is coherent, a mile of motion, is not a genuine analogue.

5.4 Are there durationless instants?

If my theory of time and distance is correct, a stretch of time and a line are as far from being analogous as any two things could be. A going on of one change might be analogous to a going on of another, but nothing could be less analogous than a going on of a change and the change of which it is a going on. Other philosophers pay no attention to any distinction between changes and goings on of changes and think that the analogy of time-stretches to lines is fundamentally sound. My criticism of them will be in three parts. First I question whether anything stands to a time-stretch as a point stands to a line. Then (section 5.5) I sketch a couple of objections to holding that time really is a fourth dimension coordinate with the three dimensions of space. Finally (section 5.6) I attack the view that only alternative to understanding time as a linear system for ordering events is to say that it flows or passes.

A line begins, ends and is divisible at points which have no spatial extent at all. If a time-stretch were analogous to a line it would be bounded by and divisible at durationless instants. But whereas there are physical procedures for dividing objects and geometrical procedures (involving rulers and compasses) for dividing lines, we have no procedure for dividing time-stretches. There is, perhaps, a sense in which we can divide movement. If I am travelling from Paris to Constantinople by train I can break my journey at Trieste. A movement is divided in this way by the moving body's stopping, and if there are to be durationless instants they will be temporal items at which objects start to change or stop changing. Starting and stopping are not temporally extended. An object takes time to undergo a change in velocity by a given amount, for example, to acquire a speed of 6 m.p.h. from nothing; but the 'switch', as Colin Strang has called it (1974) between being in motion and being at rest takes no time at all.

But there is no need for things to start or stop at temporal items. If (relatively, as usual, to a frame of reference) *A* starts to move, there must be a *place* at which it starts. It starts somewhere. But we can say when it starts without supposing that there is also a time at which it starts. Things start and stop before and after time-stretches. *A* stops after ten minutes; perhaps it started an hour ago, that is, before the last hour.

Startings and stoppings can be simultaneous with other events which like them have no temporal extension. When I say 'The train started to move at noon', I say that its starting was simultaneous with the passage of clock-hands through the noon position (or with the beginning to be displayed of numbers on a digital clock). To say this, however, I do not have to suppose that the train starts at the same instant as that at which the hands pass through the noon position, or that there is an instant, distinct from both events, at which they both occur. For what would it mean to say that the events occur *at* this instant? Presumably that they occur simultaneously with it. But if two events cannot occur simultaneously with one another without occurring simultaneously with an instant distinct from both, surely they cannot occur simultaneously with that instant unless there is a second instant that they and the first instant occur at; and that opens up a regress.

What, then, is it for events to occur simultaneously? There are several possibilities. When clock-hands pass through the noon position without stopping, their reaching that position is simultaneous with their leaving it because their reaching it and their leaving it are one and the same event under two descriptions. 'They reached it' and 'They left it' report one event, not two. Similarly the death of Tully occurred at the same time as the slaying of Cicero because it was the same event. Sometimes two events can be held to be simultaneous because they are parts of the same event. Suppose that Einstein's train is travelling from London to Edinburgh when it is struck by lightning (Einstein 1920, p. 25). Then the departure of a light particle in the direction of Edinburgh is simultaneous with the departure of a light particle in the direction of London because these are parts of the same event.

But when events are far removed from one another in space it is not too clear what a person who does not believe in absolute time would be asking if he asked whether they were simultaneous. According to the Special Theory of Relativity they are simultaneous if we have to suppose them simultaneous for either of two purposes: to explain some third event as the effect of both or to explain them both as the effects of some third event. For example, suppose that part of each event is the emission of a light particle. The meeting of the particles will be an effect of both the original events. Since the speed of light is constant, if the particles meet at a place exactly halfway between the places where the original events occurred, the original events must have been simultaneous. To put it another way, they are simultaneous if equal time-stretches separate them from an event which is the effect of both or the cause of both.

We do not need durationless instants, then, for starting, stopping or simultaneity. But that they are unnecessary is not my only objection to them; like time-travel and empty times they are ruled out by my theory of time.

If they exist at all they must be boundaries of time-stretches; they must be what periods of change begin and end at. If the ten minutes for which A is in motion between P_1 and P_2 do not begin or end at instants, we may cross instants off our list of things there are. But a period of change is a going on of a change, and while changes start, stop and go on, goings on of changes do none of these things. If they did any they ought to do all. A's movement starts at P_1, stops at a place a mile away, and goes on for ten minutes between these places. If the going on of A's movement starts at an instant T_1 and ends at an instant T_2 ten minutes later, it ought to go on between those instants, presumably for a supertime of some sort. There will then be a going on of a going on, and the way will be open for a going on of that, and for endless goings on, something deeply distasteful at least to the strait-laced compatriots of William of Ockham. To prevent this scandal we should say that just as there is no time-stretch for which starting or stopping goes on, so there is no instant at which going on starts or stops.

It will not follow that changes go on for ever. A mathematical model for the going on of A's movement would be the series of vulgar but rational fractions the squares of which are greater than 2 and less than 3. For every fraction in this series there is a larger in the series and a smaller in the series. But there are fractions outside the series, greater or less than all within it, like $\frac{3}{2}$ and $\frac{5}{4}$. And there are no fractions bounding the series, since there is no fraction the square of which is exactly 2 or 3. The fractions divide without remainder into those the squares of which are greater than 2 and those the squares of which are less, into those larger than $\sqrt{3}$ and those smaller. In a similar way if A starts from P_1 at noon there is no first time at which A is in motion; but there are times before all times at which it is in motion; and its existence can be divided without remainder into times at which it is still at rest and times at which it is already in motion. (By 'a time' here we may understand a time-stretch as short as we please.)

5.5   Is time a fourth dimension?

Many philosophers wish to do in metaphysics what their scientific colleagues do in physics and conceive time and space as forming a single four-dimensional (4-d) continuum. If time really is a fourth dimension coordinate with latitude, longitude and altitude durationless instants and empty times ought to be just as possible as points and empty spaces. That, however, is not my only objection to this theory of time. I shall now sketch a couple of others which are independent of my positive views. (The reader who is already satisfied that time is what I say and also pressed for it may proceed at once to the next section.)

To evaluate the 4-d theory of time we must first study a possible way of conceiving 3-d objects. A tower is such an object, whereas its sides and base are 2-d. A round tower has a circular base, and if some giant with a gigantic breadknife were to slice through the tower making his cut parallel to the ground the bottom face of the upper part and the top face of the lower would be circles. Or they would if the tower stood up straight, at right angles to the ground. If it leans like the Tower of Pisa slicing it parallel to the ground would produce elliptical faces, and furthermore higher cuts would produce faces which were not directly above lower, but displaced in the direction in which the tower was leaning. If the tower was square and did not lean, the faces produced would be square; but if the tower tapered as it rose, higher squares would be smaller than lower ones. Evidently it would be possible to describe a tower in terms of the 2-d objects, the faces, produced by cuts at different points in its height, and such a description would give the same information as one in which we spoke of the tower as changing throughout its height or as it gets higher. We could say either 'Each face is circular, and higher circles are one foot smaller in diameter than circles five feet lower' or 'It is a decapitated cone, and gets smaller by one foot in diameter in each five feet of its height.'

Have we now accustomed ourselves to the idea of a 3-d object divisible at different points in its height, which changes in size and shape and even inclines to different points of the compass throughout its height? Then we move up a dimension. The tower is a 3-d object, one dimension of which is its height or extension from the ground upwards; now we think of a 4-d object one dimension of which is its *age* or extension from its coming into being (or some reference-event) onwards. As we can describe the 2-d objects (faces) at different points in a 3-d object's height, so we can describe the 3-d objects (solid bodies) at earlier and later points in a 4-d object's temporal extension. Cuts through a 3-d object produce objects with outline shape, area, latitude and longitude; cuts through a 4-d objects produce objects with 3-d shape, volume, latitude, longitude and altitude. We can describe a 4-d object either by describing the 3-d objects at different points in its age or by speaking of it as changing and staying unchanged throughout its age.

All this is, as Edwin Abbott says in his pioneering work *Flatland* (1926, p. 94), 'strictly according to analogy'. The metaphysical theory is that our notion of a 3-d object at a time is a notion of what there is at a point in the temporal extension of a 4-d object, and our notion of an object which persists through time like Caesar or the Parthenon is the notion of a 4-d object. The belief that Caesar crossed the Rubicon is the belief that there is a point in Caesar's age such that cuts before that give us 3-d human figures on one side of a 3-d watery expanse, and cuts after it gives us 3-d figures on the other. Caesar lived for about 70 years; so he is a 4-d object extending 70 years through time, small and infantile at one end and big and dictatorial at the other. This 4-d object does not change in size or shape or spatial location; but the 3-d objects at different points in the 70 years differ in these respects, and also in mental state. A crucial difference here is that mental states at later times can partly mirror (in the form of so-called 'memory') mental states at earlier, but not the other way round.

According to this theory an entity that really has only three dimensions exists only at a single durationless instant. That sounds strange because we think material objects must persist for periods of time. But the claim is that our notion of a persisting 3-d object is either identical with, or an opaque alternative to, the notion of a 4-d object which is different in three of its dimensions at points on its fourth.

The 2-d faces at different points in the height of the tower never change their height: higher slices are always higher. But they are all equally real. Partly for this reason we are inclined to say that any change the tower undergoes in the course of its height, such as starting to lean to the north after 12 feet, is not a real change. Similarly a 3-d object at a later point in the temporal extension of a 4-d object is always later; they do not exist at the same instant; but both are equally real. It seems, then, that changes taking time which we ascribe to Caesar or the Parthenon are not real changes, that the temporally extended objects are unchanging. Some people may feel that this constitutes an objection to the theory we are considering: it appears to entail fatalism. The friends of the theory, however, do not think this a blemish; they mostly like the idea of fatalism; or at least they like to tease libertarians. A more promising line of objection insists that the theory need not be fatalistic.

The theory claims that changes which take time like my going to Madrid and a tomato's getting larger and turning red can be understood without loss or embarrassment as changes which a 4-d object undergoes through one of its dimensions; the model for this way of thinking being our thought of a tower as getting narrower throughout its height (or, for that matter, our thought of a road as getting higher throughout its length). This is not a claim about physics or about the practice of physicists; it is a claim in metaphysics and concerns our ordinary thinking. My first objection is that thinking in the proposed way does involve embarrassment: we allow questions to be raised which cannot be answered.

Not only do towers change in width as they get higher; they can also change in height. What is on Monday morning the top face of a tower, with no feet of tower above it, on Friday evening has a further 3 feet above it. If our 4-d Caesar is really to be analogous to a tower it must at least be possible for him to increase in temporal extent, for more years to be added to him. Perhaps we shall have to postulate a fifth dimension for this to happen in. But then at one point in the fifth dimension Caesar will have only, say, 50 years: there will simply not be any 3-d human figures 51 years after his birth. And in that case not only does the theory not entail fatalism; it is consistent with any kind of libertarianism that takes our fancy. But *do* these 4-d objects change in temporal extent? The question cannot be ruled illicit because 3-d objects change in all their dimensions; but neither can it be answered.

Next, objects change through causal action. As I shall argue in chapter 6, we have no idea of a coming about of change which is not an idea of its being brought about and we think a change genuine only in so far as it is due to causal action. A road really changes in getting wider not just if it widens as it nears the capital but if it widens thanks to workmen with bulldozers. The fourth-dimension theory shows change coming about but not being brought about. It allows the 4-d Caesar to have months (especially early in its temporal extent) of getting

larger, but this is not a real change in the 4-d Caesar. To be a
real change it would have to be due to action over the months
by other 4-d objects, as a real change in the width of the road is
due to action over a length of it by workmen. But we cannot
even make a start at conceiving the action by which one 4-d
object could cause a change in another. From what deep quar-
ries of being are the metres[4] obtained that add years to Caesar's
age?

A final objection is this. We can think that what we are
inclined to call a persistent 3-d object is a kind of 3-d slice or
extremity of a 4-d object analogous to the 2-d faces at which
we divide 3-d objects without identifying the fourth dimension
with time. That is shown by Abbott's story. The hero is a
square (prophetically well-named) living in a 2-d space, a plane.
He is convinced that there are 3-d objects by seeing an intelligent, loquacious circle shrink and vanish into nothing in one
place, and then grow again from nothing in a place a short way
off. The best way of explaining this is to suppose he is seeing
slices of a sphere that moves out of his 2-d space and back into
it. Here the third dimension is plainly spatial. We can imagine
something similar in our space. An articulate adult shrinks to a
baby and vanishes, and then a few feet to the north a baby, or,
better, a shrivelled nonagenarian, appears and fills out into a
similar-looking adult chatting about the same things. If this
happened (I have never heard of it happening) we might decide
that what seemed to be an ordinary 3-d object was really a slice
of a 4-d object; but again the fourth dimension would be
spatial.

It looks as if any empirical evidence we could have that what
we see is a 3-d slice of a 4-d object would be evidence for a 4-d
object all four dimensions of which are spatial. The only justification for saying we are seeing a 3-d slice of an object the
fourth dimension of which is temporal would be that though
this sounds different from saying it is a 3-d object which exists
for a time, there could be no empirical grounds for deciding
between these statements. But if the claim 'This is a 3-d slice of
a thing with three spatial dimensions and one temporal one'
differs in this way from 'This is a 3-d slice of a thing with four
spatial dimensions' it surely follows that we do *not* conceive

time as analogous to or coordinate with the three dimensions of space.

5.6 The reality of time

Some philosophers who are reserved about four-dimensional continua nevertheless hold that time is nothing but a linear system of ordering events. Every such event (relatively to some frame of reference) is earlier than, later than or simultaneous with every other. Time is real in that the events really stand in these relations, and differs from space only in so far as these relationships differ from relations like being north of, being south of , and being on the same latitude as. This view differs from mine in that I would prefer to say that time is *the taking place* of the events which stand in these relations. So far as I can see, it differs from the fourth-dimension theory only in that the notion of a dimension in which things are earlier or later is not brought to life by analogies with leaning towers or rising roads.

It is sometimes thought that the only alternative to this view is to accept the reality of some kind of temporal process, property or position the concept of which is irredeemably incoherent. The most famous of these dubious entities were all, as it happens, thought up in the University of Cambridge. We have already seen that Newton says absolute time 'flows equably'. He means not only that time goes on as well as motion, alteration etc., but that whereas a gallon of water can take longer or shorter to drip away through a hole in a bucket, an hour of absolute time always takes the same time to elapse. McTaggart (1927, ch. 33) said that ordinary people believe that events undergo changes from being future to being present and from being present to being past; that they imagine events have properties of being past, present or future which they acquire and lose. In our own time Hugh Mellor (1981) has made out that the only alternative to his version of the fourth-dimension theory of time is that there really exist entities he calls 'tenses'.

The supposedly aseptic view of time as a system of relations between events is associated with conjunctions like 'before', 'after' and 'while' and the corresponding prepositions: these linguistic items express the unproblematic temporal relations. Less healthy views are associated with inflections of tense and equivalent devices like temporal auxiliaries and particles. Since these items are not in themselves improper it must be wrong to say that anything incoherent is actually expressed by them; but philosophers do say or think that incoherent views of time are somehow begotten by misunderstanding them. It seems to me that any misunderstanding lies not in the thinking of ordinary people who use these items, but in the Cambridge philosophers' interpretation of this thinking.

In ordinary thinking people distinguish between changes which occur and their occurring; for they think changes occur which might not have occurred, and that changes which might have occurred do not. They need, then, the notion of the actual occurring or going on of change. But although people often speak of time as going on, there is no evidence that they really, like Newton, think time is something over and above movement, alteration and the rest which goes on in addition to them. I have argued that they conceive time as the going on of change. I do not believe that ordinary people would say that the going on of something is another thing that can go on, and therefore when they talk of the passage of time I take them to mean the passage or going on of change. The popular idea to which justice is not done by saying time is a system of relations between events is the idea that change really occurs. Time is not thought of as a reality additional to change: it is thought of as *the reality of* change, as *what it is* for change to come to pass.

Some philosophers would concede that all that non-philosophers want is for change really to occur; but they imagine that people conceive the occurring of change as a further change which befalls change. According to McTaggart they believe that for an event to occur is for it to lose the property of futurity and acquire that of being present; they take futurity, presentness and pastness to be properties of events.

Why should they think anything of the kind? An occurring of a change is a fulfilment of a possibility and being fulfilled is not a change that a possibility undergoes. People would think that taking place is something which happens to changes only if they thought that being actual is a property. But that is not something any non-philosopher ever thought: it is a peculiarly philosophical error.

And if people do not think actuality is a property, why should they think pastness, presentness and futurity are properties? The word 'future' comes from the future participle of the Latin verb 'to be'. What is future is what will be, that is, what will exist or will occur; whereas what is not future is what will not be. Similarly the present is simply what is and the past is what has been. If non-philosophers do not think that to be actual is to have a property, actuality, it is indeed capricious to suppose they think that to be going to be actual is to have another property, futurity. For even if to be actual were to have the property of actuality, the inference would be that to be going to be actual is to be going to have that same property, not that it is to have already a different property, futurity.

McTaggart would dispute that. He believed in what we may call 'dated properties'. In his view to say that the poker (thanks, no doubt, to being stuck in the fire) is red on Monday 12th, is to attribute to it the property called 'being red on Monday 12th,' the property of Monday 12th redness, which is sharply to be distinguished from the property of Tuesday 13th redness which I attribute to the poker in saying 'It was red on Tuesday 13th.' If this were right, to be going in the future to be actual would be to have the property of future actuality.

But McTaggart's analysis is arbitrary and absurd. There are no such properties as Monday redness or Tuesday redness; and grammar and common sense alike point to a different analysis. Grammarians say that in 'It was red on Monday' the phrase 'on Monday' is an adverbial phrase modifying the verb, not the adjective. It is not like 'dark' in 'It was dark red' which combines with the adjective 'red' to express a sort of function of the colour expressed by 'red'. In 'It was red on Monday' 'on Monday' goes with 'was'. We could say 'Red is the colour it was on Monday' (whereas we cannot say 'Red is the colour it was dark').

David Lewis (1986, pp. 203–4) avoids construing temporal

phrases with predicate expressions only to construe them with
subjects. Believing that objects are four-dimensional entities
with temporal extent he would take 'on Monday' in 'The poker
was red on Monday' with 'the poker' and say the the speaker
predicates redness of the Monday part of the poker. I have
already given philosophical reasons for rejecting the notion of a
four-dimensional object with temporal parts, and from a grammatical point of view taking 'on Monday' with 'the poker' is
even more perverse than taking it with 'red'.

Properties which are predicated of objects are properties that
can be exemplified by objects. They are exemplified at times,
and when we predicate them we speak of them more or less
precisely as exemplified at times. As predication involves reference to objects so it involves explicit or implicit reference to
times. As I assert that *this* poker is red or ask if *any* pokers are,
so I ask if there was *any time* when this poker was red or assert
that there *was on Sunday* at least one poker which *will on
Wednesday* be red.

What I mean by 'a time' is not, of course, a durationless
instant or a bit of absolute time but a process or event: this
Monday is the second rotation of the Earth this week. And
when I say that we refer to times I do not mean that what we
predicate is predicated of times or that all predicates have, as
it were, an extra space for a time. In 'The poker was red on
Monday' 'red' does not signify a relation, being red on it, in
which I say the poker stands to a particular terrestrial rotation.
The sentence is like 'The poker was red when Nero fiddled.'
Saying this I refer to Nero but I do not say the poker stood in
any relation to him; rather it is part of my saying that red was
exemplified by the poker to say it was exemplified simultaneously with Nero's fiddling.

We can refer to an object by using a so-called indexical word
like 'this' – 'This poker is red' – and perhaps in order to refer
to anything we must be able to relate it somehow or other
to something we can indicate. If I say 'The man who stole
George's spoons ...' and you interrupt 'Who is George?' I
reply 'The husband of that woman over there.' We can also
refer to times by using indexicals and tense-inflections are such
means of reference. In 'The poker *is* red' the significance of the

present tense is that I refer to the time of my utterance: I predicate red of the poker as something it exemplifies even as I speak. In 'Was the poker red?' I (interrogatively) predicate the colour as something exemplified before my utterance.

McTaggart says that people are inclined to believe that pastness, presentness and futurity are properties of events; Mellor that they believe in the reality of certain entities which he sometimes calls 'temporal positions' (so 1986, p. 167), and more often 'tenses' (confusingly, since this use of the word is unknown to lexicographers). These entities appear to be things signified by at least some tense-inflections and by such expressions as 'past', 'future', 'last century', 'this month', 'tomorrow' (1981, p. 16). I am not quite sure whether he thinks (1) that these linguistic items do signify positions in time, and people go wrong in taking these positions to be objectively real independently of our thought, or (2) that people go wrong in imagining they signify positions in time when really they have meaning in other ways. If he thinks the second it is a pity he does not give us the correct account of their meaning and I should like to know what non-philosopher ever made the howler of imagining them to signify temporal positions. If, on the other hand, he believes that the linguistic items do all signify temporal positions, but these positions are somehow second-class citizens of the real world, I object that the linguistic items are a mixed bunch and have meaning in different ways.

'Tomorrow' means 'the day after the day of this utterance'. It is an indexical term for referring to days or rotations of the Earth. Rotations of the Earth are first-class citizens of reality, completely independent of our thought; and I should not call them 'positions in time'. We can say when something will happen by referring to the rotation with which it will be contemporaneous – 'The Moon will be eclipsed tomorrow' – but that hardly makes the next rotation after this a position. What goes for 'tomorrow' goes for 'last year' and 'this month'. These are locutions for referring to particular occurrings of definite physical processes.

That being so, they have meaning by determining what is expressed in speeches in which they are used. They bring rotation, revolution, the Earth and the Moon into those speeches. It is different with tense-inflections and 'past', 'present' and 'future'. If I refer to anything in using a tense-inflection it is to the utterance in which I use it. Hence the inflection does not add to what I express. An utterance cannot be part of what is expressed in itself. The tense in 'The poker is red' no more determines what I express than does 'true' in 'That the poker is red is true.' The difference in meaning between 'Theaetetus is seated' and 'Theaetetus was seated' lies in the way in which the posture signified by 'seated' is predicated of Theaetetus; it lies in the way in which the speaker relates it to him.

The adjectives 'past', 'present' and 'future' have meaning in the same way as tense-inflections. 'Our wedding is future' is an awkward way of saying 'We shall be wed', and 'Our wedding is not future' means 'The wedding's off.' If that seems doubtful, consider the particles which replace inflections in some languages. The Marquesan sentence "e kai au' might be translated 'I'll eat' or 'It is future that, it will be that, I eat.' We now take "e' to be a tense-marker, but the first student of the language interpreted it as the future tense of the verb 'to be' (Dordillon 1931, pp. 27–44).

As for the phrases 'the future' and 'the past', rather than positions in time I should say that they designate all times or time-stretches, all goings on of changes, which are, respectively, before or after the utterances in which they are used.

It may be asked whether on my view all events are equally real. Are future events just as real as past ones? If by 'future events' we mean events which will occur as distinct from events which will not, and analogously with past events, presumably what will occur will occur as truly as what has occurred. But that does not entail fatalism. To say that I will be in Paris tomorrow is to say that I will tomorrow have the location Paris, not that I now have the dated location Paris-tomorrow. For fatalism we need dated properties. Neither does my analysis call into question the reality of occurring. To deny the reality of occurring would be to say that nothing really has happened or really will happen.

I agree, then, that events may be ordered in a linear way. If we take any two events then (relatively to a frame of reference) either they are simultaneous or one is earlier than the other. But what needs to be added in order to obtain a satisfactory analysis of the concept of time is not the notion of some special process, property or position but the distinction between a change and a going on of that change.

6

Change and Causation

6.1 Introduction

The main thesis of chapter 5 is that time is the going on of change. What, then, is change? That is the philosophical question which naturally presents itself next; let me say why I wish to treat it along with questions about causation.

Change does not occur in pure mathematics; numbers do not change and neither do the properties of triangles and circles. But all physical objects change and we try to understand the changes they undergo. Change is the target of understanding; understanding, moreover, of a particular sort. We can understand things in mathematics, for instance why the angle in a semicircle is a right angle or why, if a number is divisible by three, the sum of the digits in which we express it is also divisible by three. Understanding things like this, however, is seeing that they are logically necessary, that they follow from premises which are the definitions and axioms of mathematics. I do not think any non-philosopher ever supposed that when an object moves a distance or changes shape or colour this change is logically necessary or deducible simply from the first principles and definitions of science. At most we think these changes are causally necessary and we aim at understanding them in the way we call 'causally'.

We also think that many of the changes which occur are caused by people and that sometimes, at least, people cause changes intentionally. When that happens we try to explain the causal action by giving the agents' reasons and purposes; and at first sight this seems different both from mathematical and from causal explanation.

That is how the situation presents itself before we start doing philosophy: change is a feature of the physical world and the object of a kind of explanation different from that appropriate to the timeless truths of mathematics and perhaps also from that appropriate to human action. But is this really how things are? Do objects really undergo change in addition to existing and having properties? Are there really three realms, so to speak, the realm of mathematics, the realm of caused changes and the realm of human action, or can the picture be simplified? To maintain the distinctness of these three realms, the mathematical, the physical and the psychological, we must at least maintain that there are these three kinds of understanding and explanation: might one kind be basic and the others reducible to it? Might it be a sheer illusion to think we can understand actions in a different way from caused changes or changes in a different way from mathematical truths? Big questions, these, which will dominate the rest of this book.

Most philosophers today think we should try to understand actions in the same kind of way as other events, that is, causally. They think that understanding an event causally consists in seeing, not that it is in any way necessary – they are reluctant to recognize any kind of necessity other than logical necessity – but that it is regular, that it accords with the usual course of nature: in the circumstances in which it occurs it was predictable. And few acknowledge any need to say that objects undergo change besides having properties. Russell offers a definition of change according to which acquiring a property is having it after not having it; a satisfactory explanation, then, of Theaetetus' coming to be seated would explain his being seated after not being seated.

Of this current orthodoxy the doctrine that human actions are to be explained in the same way as caused physical events is the most dramatic: it seems to commit us to a radically physicalist view of human beings. But the spectacular, meaty theories of philosophy spring from decisions which seem purely academic and technical. Causal explanation seems applicable to human action because it is conceived as showing events to be, not necessary, but merely regular or predictable. And that conception of causal explanation is forced on us if for a change to occur is simply for a property to be exemplified and not to be exemplified at different times. The history of the world then dissolves into a lot of atoms of occurrence or, as they are called in the theory described in chapter 1, atomic facts. Instead of connections between these atoms we can find only further atoms, and the only kind of understanding we can envisage is detecting patterns and regularities (so Mackie 1974, p. 217). I shall start, then, with this view of change and propose an alternative. The rest of the chapter is an analysis of causal explanation and I defer to chapter 7 the question whether purposive action has to be explained differently.

6.2   Being and becoming

Change, says Russell, is 'the difference in respect of truth and falsity between a proposition concerning an entity and a time T and a proposition concerning the same entity and a time T′ provided that the two propositions differ only by the fact that T occurs in one where T′ occurs in the other' (1903, s. 442). What he means may be illustrated by the propositions 'The tomato was red on Sunday' and 'The tomato was red on Wednesday.' If the first is false and the second true the tomato becomes red and this, Russell suggests, is just about all there is to its becoming red. His account is meant to do away with change altogether and replace it with momentary states of affairs. 'We must', he continues, 'entirely reject the notion of a *state* of motion. Motion consists *merely* of the occupation of different places at different times' (s. 447) – and what goes for motion goes for other kinds of change as well.

This account ignores the distinction between a movement and a making of a movement but Russell might, I suppose, accommodate it by saying that a movement made is a set of places occupied and a making of it a set of occupyings.

Offered this reduction of movement to being at different places at different times we may ask: 'How many places?'

Suppose I go from London to Paris. If I occupy only a finite number of intervening places there will be intervals between them and I shall have to leap those intervals in no time at all. My movement will therefore be jerky. The jerks may be so small that no one notices them but the world will still be like a cinematograph film in which a series of still shots of figures in slightly different positions is projected in quick succession.

Russell prefers to say that the intervening places are infinite in number. If motion is conceived as continuous and he wants to analyse the concept of it he must say that. But motion is being *reduced* to place-occupation. My going to Paris, then, must depend unilaterally on my being at the intervening places at intervening times. So each place-occupation must be logically independent of every other. So continuous change is possible only if there can be infinitely many logically independent occurrences or existences.

Is that really possible? Mathematicians have to suppose that there are infinitely many finite numbers, but it is far from clear that 22914895 or even 3 is an actual thing that exists. It is at least arguable (though I shall not argue it here) that any number there can be of actual things, things like hydrogen atoms or rotations of the Earth, must be finite. If that is right Russell's analysis makes continuous movement impossible.

Is there any alternative to Russell's account? Far from reducing change to being different at different times Davidson (1980, essay 6) suggests that objects which exist and changes which take place form two more or less coordinate categories of actual thing. If I say 'The tomato was red' I say that there was this tomato and it was red. If I say 'The tomato became red' I say that there *occurred a change* which was the becoming red of the tomato. I refer to this change much as in 'A tomato was red' I refer to a tomato.

There are certain purposes for which it is useful to analyse reports of change in Davidson's way. But there is no real analogy between objects and changes. Objects which exist are individuals; changes which take place are universals: they are possibilities of which there can be many fulfilments; there can be many takings place of them. A particular occurrence of a change is an individual and can be referred to. I can say

'Caesar's crossing of the Channel in 55 BC was a rough one.' But this is not a report of a change; 'Caesar crossed the Channel in 55 BC' would be that; and in this report I do not refer to the crossing but only to Caesar.

If I refer to an object I must predicate something of it; what do I predicate of the tomato when I say it became red? Alvin Goldman (1971, p. 769) says actions are predicates or properties of agents. Do I then predicate becoming red? Just as being red on Tuesday is not a different predicate from being red on Monday so becoming red is not a different predicate from being red. As there are no dated properties so there are no static or dynamic properties. If there were they could be acquired as well had; the tomato could not only be but become an example of becoming red; and we should have a regress.

In 'The tomato became red', then, 'became' does not combine with 'red' to determine what the speaker predicates. Rather it determines the way in which the speaker predicates the colour signified by 'red'. Saying that an object has a property and saying that it acquires or loses it are different ways of bringing the property into speech and expressing it.

How do they differ? To say that will be to say what change is.

I use the word 'explanandum' for something which is explained or which calls for explanation and 'explanans' for something which is put forward in explanation of something else. These technical terms signify roles which things can play in explanation and understanding. With their aid I can put my theory of change in two sentences. In 'The tomato became red' the colour red is predicated and expressed as a causal explanandum; in 'The tomato was red' it is expressed not as a causal explanandum but as a kind of non-causal explanans, as a reason for action or inaction.

The first of these claims has two parts: (1) if I think of a property rather as acquired than had I think of it as a causal explanandum; (2) if I think of a property as having or calling for causal explanation I think of it rather as acquired than as had. I shall take these in turn.

1 Suppose that five years ago I was heavier than you and now you are heavier than me. Russell's criterion shows that change has taken place, but cannot show whether it has taken

place in you, in me or in us both. Each of us has changed relatively to the other but if I am the weight I was and you are heavier than you were, only you have really changed. But what determines whether you are heavier than you were? Is it your weight relatively to everything else in the universe (or to the Standard Kilogram)? I suggest that you have really changed in so far as your changes relatively to other things are due to causal action on you. If that is right an object's acquiring a property, when that is a genuine change in the object, is always its being made to acquire that property.

Followers of Hume will protest that we have a clear idea of what it is for an object to become red but no idea of what it is for an object to be made red. I shall dispute the negative part of this objection in section 6.3; here I challenge objectors to say what non-Russellian idea they have of an object's becoming red as distinct from its being caused to become red. If ideas are conceived on the model of pictorial representations (which is the standard Empiricist way of conceiving them) we can have no idea of an object's acquiring a property as distinct from its having it. I say we have an idea of a change in so far as we understand how it could be effected.

There are various circumstances in which I may be said to think of an object as acquiring a property. I may *want* my skin to become brown. Then (as I shall argue in chapter 7) I must want to cause this change or at least be averse to preventing it; so I must think of it as causable or preventable. Or I may say to myself 'Here on sunny Corfu my skin is becoming brown'. Z. Vendler (1957, p. 145) has suggested that such remarks are covert predictions. If my skin fails to reach a passable shade of bronze my thought 'will turn out to be false'. That cannot be right. If it were, 'My skin was becoming brown, but it did not become brown because I was recalled to England' would be self-contradictory. 'My skin is becoming brown' is certainly different from 'Yiannis' skin is brown' but the difference is not that it is prophetic or that its truth hangs in the balance but that it is causal. It is true if something (the Sun) is causing my skin to acquire the specified property.

What if I think that the plums, by acquiring the size of normal ripe Victorias, are causing the branch to become curved? Surely I think of their change of size not as an explanandum

but as an explanans. Yes; but what is strictly speaking responsible for the deformation of the branch is not the change the
plums undergo but their undergoing of this change – the
importance of this distinction in causal thinking will be explained below – and in so far as I think of the plums as
acquiring one size rather than another I must think something
is making them acquire that particular size.

2   might be formulated: where the understanding is causal,
understanding a thing's properties is understanding its acquiring them rather than its having them. Holmes might say in
ordinary conversation 'Watson is brown because he served in
Afghanistan', but he must think of Watson as having become
brown, not as having been brown all along. Similarly, the
surprise of someone inexperienced in horticulture at the tomato's not being green or not being red is surprise at its having
ceased to be the one or its not having become the other.

What if you say 'That cup is fragile because it is made of
porcelain'? Fragility is a power, a liability to be changed in
certain ways by certain causal action, and powers are not
properties in the narrow sense in which I use the word. Furthermore I shall be arguing that the relation between having
certain powers and being composed of certain material is not,
in general, causal but logical. Part of what you mean when you
say 'That's made of porcelain' is that a blow will shatter it.
Sometimes, perhaps, an explanation of the form 'It has that
power because it contains this material' is causal; but then what
is really explained is the acquiring of the power or the coming
into being of something with it, for example, 'That drink is
intoxicating because I laced it with rum.'

The second claim of my theory, that thinking of a property
as being had is thinking of it as a reason, cannot be properly
defended until we have clarified the notion of a reason but I
can give an indication here of what I mean. If I pick the tomato
because of its redness I think of it rather as being red than as
having become red. Russell thinks it is red after not being red if
on Wednesday he picks it for the reason that it is red, having
on Sunday, for the reason that it was not red, refrained from
picking it.

What if Holmes tells me 'Because the tomato was red you
did not see the blood on it'? I agree that the redness is pre-

sented as a causal factor, not as a reason. Still, it is expressed as a kind of causal explanans – a condition without which the blood would have had a more distinctive effect on my eye – not as an explanandum; and I shall argue later that what appears in someone's thinking as this sort of cause also appears as a sort of reason.

That must do as a first outline of my theory; now for a pair of objections.

First, I seem to be saying that the difference between a tomato's being red and its becoming red lies in the way in which a single thing, its redness, comes into our thought and speech. Surely that is worse than Russell's reductionism. Russell does away with change but on my view neither being nor becoming is objectively real. For philosophical idealism does not that take the biscuit?

Not exactly. It would be idealism to deny that there is any difference, independent of our thought, between being and not being or between becoming and not becoming. I do not deny that. I do not even deny that there is a difference between being red, say, and becoming red, since if an object is becoming red it is not already red. My contention is that the difference between, on the one hand, being and not being and, on the other, becoming and not becoming is mind-dependent. When an object's redness enters your thought as a causal explanandum it is correct to say you think it has become or will become red; when it enters as a reason it is correct to say you think it is, was or will be red. This sort of mind-dependency is to be expected if objects and changes differ as I claimed on p. 22.

Secondly I hope to explain the difference between being and becoming by means of the notions of a reason and a cause. Will these extremely problematic notions stand the strain?

If reasons were simply causes of a special sort and understanding something causally were seeing that it is regular, my theory might come down to this: we think of the tomato as becoming red when we think of its redness as following regularly upon certain circumstances, and we think of it as being red when we think of its redness as having certain regular consequences. I should not expect such a theory to find many buyers. But I now want to attack this view of causation and replace it by a better one.

6.3   *Causal agents, causal action, causal conditions*

The idea that to understand an event is to fit it into a pattern, to see that it is not exceptional but conforms to some regularity or law, has held many philosophers captive. But if we can liberate ourselves for a moment from its spell, its inadequacy is fairly plain.

Understanding something is not, in fact, the same as seeing it as regular or being able to predict it. We often start by noting a regularity, a correlation, say, between divorce and cancer, and only later if at all come to understand it. Primitive people have been able to predict lunar eclipses without understanding them. And conversely when someone dies we can often understand the death though we were in no position to predict it. These and similar points have been put with force and eloquence by Rom Harré in his *Principles of Scientific Thinking* (1970, ch. 1).

But the inadequacy goes deeper. The regularity view of causation deprives material objects of all genuine causal powers and leaves them with nothing but geometrical properties and velocity. In the seventeenth century when causal thinking started to be construed like this, material objects were conceived as collections of corpuscular atoms which were, in fact, geometrical solids. For good reasons physicists dropped the concept of a corpuscular atom; but their conception of the basic framework of the world, of what an ancient atomist called the *primordia rerum*, remained mathematical. Their ambition is still to explain physical phenomena as far as possible in the way we explain the properties of numbers and geometrical figures, and their vision of the world is a counterpart to the atomistic philosophical theory I described in chapter 1. For many scientists and philosophers this way of regarding the world has a religious sanctity. The only alternative to it they can conceive is a strongly theistic vision (such as we actually find in Malebranche and, to a lesser extent, in Descartes himself) of velocities and configurations depending directly on the volitions of God. In their determination to expel divine purposes from the universe they sterilize away any kind of causation that goes beyond regular spatio-temporal conjunction.

This picture of the world stands to it rather as a map stands to a piece of countryside. For some purposes a map may be more useful than a picture by Poussin or Constable, but the painter can tell us things the cartographer cannot, and anyone who imagines that only what the cartographer can show is real has a seriously defective conception of countryside. The physical world contains objects with causal powers: objects which are capable of causing change in other things, and having change caused by other things in them, by definite causal action. Not to believe this is to have a seriously defective conception of the physical world, one which in the end will affect one's attitude both to inanimate nature and to other living organisms. That only geometrical properties are real is a false philosophical belief, and a false philosophical belief is a bad psychological condition fully as dangerous as a bad condition of blood or bone.

How are we to obtain a better understanding of causation? As elsewhere so here we may start with a linguistic observation.

We apply the noun 'cause' to at least three different sorts of thing. A material object which causes a change in another object is a cause in the sense of a causal agent. In this sense the Sun might be a cause of the evaporation of some water, and I am a cause of a change in the shape of a lump of Plasticine when I tread on it.

Second, the action by which an agent causes a change is said to be a cause of that change. So my pressing on the Plasticine is a cause of its change of shape, and the Sun's shining on the water or heating it is a cause of its evaporation.

Finally, a necessary condition of the effectiveness of some causal action can be called 'a cause'. If by dropping a lighted cigarette I cause a forest to go up in flames the dryness of the grass is a cause in this way of the destruction: had the grass not been dry my action would not have resulted in this change in the trees. The redness of the tomato because of which the blood on it goes undetected (p. 104 above) is a causal factor of this kind too, it is a sufficient condition of ineffectiveness.

The regularity theory feeds on a failure to draw these distinctions. Hume confused causal action with causal agents.

When an agent causes a change there must always be some action by which the agent causes it. The action connects the agent with the explanandum and is, in principle, open to observation. We have a clear idea of how the liquid makes the litmus paper red: it is by moistening it or soaking into it. Visiting Rome on the Ides of March we see how Brutus arrests the vital processes in Caesar's body, and if we have the right equipment we can record on video the action which connects him with Caesar's death. Hume looked for the sort of connection between the action by which an agent produces an effect and the effect which there is between an agent and an effect, and when he could not find it concluded that the notion of production is vacuous. But he was looking for an impossibility. There can be no action by which causal action causes change, nothing the action does, and hence no connection between the Sun's action and the evaporation of the puddle such as there is between the Sun and the evaporation.

Hume imagined that in ordinary thinking causes both produce: and are followed by effects. A wrong analysis. We think that causal agents produce effects but are not followed by them; the Sun is not followed, as it moves through the sky, by evaporations of puddles, nor is Macbeth followed through Scotland by deaths; whereas causal action may be followed by an effect but does not produce it. Mill (*System of Logic* III v 2–3) made the same mistake and compounded it by identifying the true cause of an explanandum with the complete set of conditions sufficient for its occurrence. That confuses causal action with causal conditions.

Causal agents are objects, a piece of causal action is some kind of event or occurrence and a causal condition is a state of affairs. It is impossible that things so different should be related in the same way to any explanandum. The relationship which most calls for analysis is that between causal action and a change for which it is responsible. 'Descartes', we say, 'caused the wax to become liquid by heating it': how must the heating be related to the change to liquidity if this explanation is to be valid?

Causal explanations in ordinary speech are various in form. To give a few examples:

1 The house caught fire (beginning of a process) because two wires came into contact (end of a process).
2 The wax changed from solid to liquid (complete process) because it rose in temperature by 20 degrees (complete process) or because it was heated for 60 seconds (going on of a process expressed as a piece of causing).
3 Odysseus caused the death of Antinous by releasing an arrow (cause and effect separated in space and time).
4 Othello caused the death of Desdemona by pressing on the pillow (effect later than the cause but not separated from it in space or, contrary to Shakespeare's account, in time).

Evidently we cannot expect the same relationship in all cases.

Often the explanans is less the rendering inevitable of the explanandum than the rendering of it likely or even possible. We also explain the non-occurrence of changes (though only when there is something to cause them) and here the explanans may render the change which is prevented impossible or only unlikely. For our present purposes it will be enough to consider three cases where a change is rendered inevitable.

6.4   Causal action and matter

We often think that an agent renders a change in an object inevitable by acting on the object for a time. Familiar modes of causal action are pushing, pulling and heating. 'Because', we say, 'an engine pulled those carriages for two hours the carriages moved from London to York, a distance of 200 miles' or 'Because I heated the butter for two minutes the butter changed from being solid and opaque to being liquid and transparent.' From now on I shall use the noun 'cause' only for pieces of causal action. In these explanations, which I call explanations of 'type-I', cause and effect are exactly contemporaneous. The carriages move the distance in the time for which the engine pulls them. Hume argued that if causes and effects are simultaneous history would be telescoped into a single moment (1888, p. 76), but he took all causes and effects to be momentary events; in my type-I explanations they have some temporal extent.

Besides being contemporaneous they coincide in space. But two changes can coincide in time and space without either being the cause of the other. When a slice of bread in the oven simultaneously turns brown and curls up, both changes are effects of heating, and if an object simultaneously changed colour and rotated, these changes might be effects of different causes. What further condition, then, must a piece of causal action satisfy besides spatio-temporal coincidence to be the type-I cause of a change? I suggest it must be the going on of that change. The hours of pulling are the going of the 200-mile translation of the carriages; the minutes of heating are the occurring in the butter of the change from solid to liquid. This suggestion is controversial; let me consider some doubts and queries.

Someone who wants to insist that we have no idea of causation beyond that of regular attendance may complain that to give pushing, pulling or heating as a cause is to beg the question. For heating is by definition causing something to become hotter. It looks as if pushing and pulling too are conceived as modes of causing. So to say that an agent causes a change by pushing, pulling or heating is vacuous or regressive.

It is hardly vacuous. That the gas causes the butter to melt by heating it is not an empty tautology; after all, it would not cause a piece of paper to melt by heating it. But it would be indeed regressive to say that an agent can cause a change only by causing another change. At that rate causing could never begin. Hence a basic type-I cause must be describable not just as a causing but as an undergoing of change. Pushing and pulling can be so described. An engine which pushes a carriage moves towards it in contact with it; an engine which pulls it moves away from it in contact with it. It causes the movement of the carriage by pushing, according to me, if its movement *is the going on* of the movement of the carriage. When one object heats another (as my hand heats this glass of brandy) the first becomes cooler or undergoes loss of heat or energy in the vicinity of the second, and this undergoing of change may be given as the causing or going on of the change in the thing heated.

In a type-I explanation, then, a going on of a change in the agent is given as the going on of the change to be explained. Are we here claiming an identity? That might seem impossible for the following reason. Identity is what is called a 'symmetrical' relation: if A is identical with B it follows that B is identical with A. But causality is asymmetrical: if A is the cause of B it follows that B is not the cause of A. Hence the relationship between cause and effect cannot be one of identity.

This argument is irrelevant. For the effect to be explained is a change which takes place, not a going on of a change. This will be confirmed in section 6.7 below. If I say 'The bow became curved because the archer's right hand moved back' the effect is the change which goes on in the bow and the cause is the hand-movement. The question is not whether I identify the hand-movement with the effect in the bow but whether I identify it with the going on of that effect.

Still, I think the answer is 'No'. Rather than assert that the hand-movement is identical with the going on of the change of shape I give it *as the going on* of that change. An utterance of the form 'A by ϕing caused B to become f' is in some respects analogous to the simpler 'B is f'. In 'B is f' the property signified by 'f' is referred to B as something B instantiates and we could say 'B is an instance of f'. But 'an instance of' here combines not with 'f' to determine what we predicate but with 'is': we do not predicate instantiation but 'is an instance of' is a variant for 'is'. When we say 'A by ϕing caused B to become f' we refer B's becoming f to A as something of which A's ϕing is the going on. We could say: 'A's ϕing was the going on in B of a change to f.' Here the words 'the going on' do not combine with 'in B of a change to f' to refer to something with which we say A's ϕing was identical. Rather they combine with 'was' to enable us to refer what is expressed by 'a change of f in B' to A. The structure of the sentence is not:

A's ϕing / was / the going on in B of a change to f.
It is:

A's ϕing / was the going on in B / of a change to f
or even:

A's ϕing / was the going on in B of a change to / f.

The property f is referred to A not as something A itself exemplifies but as something a change to which it causes in something else.

But even if a type-I explanation is not a straightforward identity claim, still cause and effect are spatio-temporally coincident. How, then, do we decide which is which? Why say that the horse moves the cart by pulling and not that the cart moves the horse by pushing?

The answer is obvious. The translation of the horse, the going on of which is given as the cause of the movement in the cart, is itself caused (we think) by action of its hoofs on the ground or of its brain on its legs. We should say that the cart was pushing the horse only if we could explain the translation of the cart without referring it to the movement of the horse, for instance if we could refer it to some third object as something of which a change in that third object was the going on.

Does a regress appear here? A change in A is the effect of a change in B because that change in B is the effect of a change in C. Must the change in C be the effect of a change in D and so ad infinitum? The regress may stop, I think, in two ways. The change in C might be not caused but natural like the approach of one massive body to another: that possibility will be explored in section 6.6. The other possibility, which many philosophers today would be unwilling to admit but which will be investigated in chapter 7, is that the going on of the change in C should be teleologically explainable: so, perhaps, the movement of the archer's hand. But it is not necessary to accept either of these possibilities to accept my analysis of type-I explanation which is simply that a period of action or change is given as the going on of the explanandum.

There is, however, a further difficulty. We can allow that the going on of one change in an object is identical with a going on of another change in the same object. The same object can be an instance of different properties – the toast in the oven is an instance both of brown colour and of curly shape – and if it is caused to acquire both by the same action the going on of the change to one is the going on of the change to the other. But I say that in a type-I explanation we claim that a going on of a change in one object is a going on of a change in another, and that might seem unintelligible.

To find it unintelligible, I suggest, is simply to be unable to conceive of material objects. The various kinds of matter in the world – air, water, gold, perspex etc. – are defined by causal powers. For an object to be composed of a particular material *m* is for it to be capable of having changes caused in it by certain action and of causing changes in other objects by certain action. So much might be agreed by someone who construed causing a change as being attended by it in a regular fashion. But on that view the notion of material *m* is not a notion of anything in objects. In themselves objects are geometrical solids which as a matter of fact change in a regular way; but nothing in them accounts for their changes. If anything in a candle is to account for its becoming shapeless and transparent when it gets hotter or when another object near to it loses heat, it must contain or be composed of something such that the change in the other object is the going on in it of the loss of shape and opacity. Wax is such a component.

My statement that materials are defined by causal powers may seem to be called in question by a thought-experiment devised by Putnam (1975, p. 223; see also Putnam 1988, pp. 34–6). We ascribe to water the power to refresh drinkers, the inability to intoxicate them, the liability to become solid when cooled to 32°F etc. But we can imagine a distant planet Twin Earth superficially like ours where the rivers are filled with stuff with all these powers, stuff which non-scientists could not distinguish from water here but which nevertheless has a different molecular structure. It consists not of oxygen and hydrogen but of the alien elements X and Y. Surely this substance would not be water. So to be water is not to have these powers; rather it is to have the same internal structure, whatever that may be, as the stuff called 'water' by us, or by those who first introduced the word.

I am not quite sure if this argument is intended to show that when we say 'That's water' *part of what we assert* is that the stuff has this structure. If not, I do not see why Putnam presents the argument as bearing on the meaning of stuff-words; if so, I find it unconvincing. We may distinguish three questions:

1   How do we conceive water? What structure, powers etc., do we think essential to it?
2   What conditions must a concept satisfy to be a shot at conceiving water, and not at conceiving something else?
3   What structure, powers etc., does water in fact have?

The answer to (2) may involve reference to some original samples. To be a concept of water a concept must be of the stuff Shakespeare called 'water' and Homer 'hudōr'. But the answer to (2) cannot be part of the answer to (1). What our concept of water is an effort at conceiving cannot be part of that concept. Just as it is not part of what I believe about the planet Mars that it is about the planet Mars that I believe this, so it is not part of of what I think it is to be water to be the stuff known to my ancestors (so too Putnam 1988, pp. 26ff.).

The answer to (3) is in general to be obtained by empirical enquiry, not by conceptual analysis; but the enquiry may affect the answer to (1). We cannot discover what water consists of by considering what we mean when we say 'That's water'; but discovering what it consists of may change what we mean. Our concepts of familiar materials like water (and also, though in a slightly different way, our concepts of familiar sorts of object) are neither immutable nor wholly definite. I hope to explain why that is so in chapter 9. When we find out that the stuff on Twin Earth is not H_2O but X_2Y the question whether it is water becomes one for us to decide. No doubt it is water only if it has the same essential nature as the stuff Shakespeare knew; but what is essential is what we decide is essential. Philosophers who hope that one day mathematics will do the work of physics may say that the essential nature of a material must consist in its microstructure, but even if their hope were reasonable this would not follow. Differences in structure must involve some difference in causal power; otherwise they will be undetectable. But if things composed H_2O and X_2Y have the same causal powers for all practical purposes we might say that there are two kinds of water. The rivers of Twin Earth contain stuff with the same essential nature as the Skamander and the Avon, and we loosen our concept to embrace it. If the difference in causal power, though not immediately obvious, could be practically significant, we should probably tighten our concept to exclude anything composed of X_2Y.

Not only do I wish to define materials in terms of causal powers; I wish to say they are causal powers. Philosophers since Descartes have found the notion of a causal power puzzling partly because they have tried to conceive causal powers on the model of properties. Locke thought that they are the geometrical and kinetic properties of corpuscular atoms; philosophers today reject corpuscular atoms but still mostly think that the only thing in an object which could make it not just regular but inevitable that certain action on it has a certain sequel would be some kind of microstructure. But these properties of this structure would have to be exemplified by what is, in fact, a geometrical abstraction, extension in three (or more) dimensions. This abstraction, like a powerful ghost, has made many appearances in the history of philosophy: as Platonic space, medieval prime matter, Cartesian extended substance, Lockean substratum and the transcendentally ideal substratum of Kant (*Critique of Pure Reason*, A 284–5/B 340–1). The only way to exorcise it from our thinking is to recognise that causal powers are not properties which materials exemplify.

When we ask 'What is it in an object by virtue of which it is affected by neighbouring changes?' we are apt to misunderstand the first 'in'. What we are seeking is present in the object not as a property it exemplifies but as something it consists of or contains. Gold, wood, wine and hydrogen are things in objects by virtue of containing which the objects inevitably change when their neighbours change. They are that in objects by being composed of which the objects belong to a physical system.

We are blinded to this by treating matter-concepts and concepts of sorts as similar in kind (so not only Locke, *Essay* III vi 2–3, but Putnam and Kripke). We then say that materials have causal powers whereas in fact objects have causal powers because of their materials. And we speak as if there were sorts of material *and* sorts of object when it would be more correct

to say that a matter-concept is a sort of concept of an object: a
concept of the sort of causal interagent it is.

6.5   Causal continuity

Locke uses the interaction of billiard balls to show that our
notion of power is 'obscure' (*Essay* II xxi 4) and Hume to
show that we have no genuine idea of causation at all (1902A,
pp. 28–30). When a ball *A* comes into contact with a second
ball *B A* presses on *B* and thereby causes *B* to change shape.
Having been deformed, *B* quickly regains its spherical shape
and in doing so acquires a velocity relative to the table. This
transaction is not detectable by the human eye (which doubtless contributed to Locke's and Hume's perplexity). But if
it did not occur the second ball would have to acquire considerable velocity in no time at all, a discontinuity which is
irreconcilable with an intelligible course of nature. (The point
is developed by Harré 1970, pp. 285–7.) As it is, between *A*'s
hitting *B* and *B*'s moving off there is a brief connecting process
of change of shape.

The type-I cause of *B*'s deformation is the going on of *A*'s
movement after the impact. It would be perfectly correct to
give this as a causal explanation of *B*'s starting to change shape.
But we can also give as the cause of *B*'s starting to change
shape *A*'s hitting *B*, that is, *A*'s reaching the point of impact
– with, of course, a certain momentum. I call this second
explanation one of 'type-II'.

In a type-II explanation the end of one process is given as
the cause of the beginning of another, and there is no temporal
gap between them. Hence they are simultaneous. Beginnings
and ends of processes are not temporally extended, so if there
is no interval between them they must be exactly simultaneous.
I suggest that a type-II explanation is valid if explanans and
explanandum are not merely simultaneous but identical, if they
are the same event under two descriptions.

In our example *A* does not stop at the point of impact. So its
reaching that point and its starting to move beyond are the
same event. But its motion beyond it is the type-I cause of *B*'s

starting to change shape. It follows that A's starting to move beyond the point of impact is identical with B's starting to change. So A's reaching the point of impact is the same event as this explanandum. We noted that identity is symmetrical and causality not. But there is no risk that B's starting to change will be given as the type-II cause of A's reaching the point of impact because I said that a type-II explanation is an explanation of the beginning of a later change by the end of an earlier, not vice versa.

If A's hitting B is identical with B's starting to change we can say that A by hitting B renders this event inevitable. But to see its inevitability is to accept the second change as a mere continuation of the first. When the end of one process is identical with the beginning of a second the second is continuous with the first. We do in fact regard the movements of A and B after the impact as a continuation of their movements (or A's movement) before it. If a stick's bursting in flame is the type-II effect of its reaching a certain temperature its turning to flame should equally be a continuation of its rise in temperature. Type-II explanations enable us to understand events by depriving them, so to speak, of their novelty: they appear no longer as new beginnings but rather at non-ceasings.

Type-II explanation, no less than type-I, involves applying concepts of material. The stick's reaching a certain temperature will be its starting to flame only if it is a stick of something like wood, not chocolate. A's reaching B is identical with B's starting to change shape because they are composed of some material like ivory. Were they just spherical expanses we could say the earlier and later movements were contiguous but not continuous.

6.6 Fundamental forces

The third case I wish to consider is that in which we attribute a change to a fundamental force of nature like gravitation or electromagnetism. Sampson pushes away a pillar which supports a beam and the beam comes down. The movement of the beam is not a continuation of the movement of the pillar or of

Sampson's hand. Sampson renders it inevitable, but only in that he stops the pillar from preventing it; he does not, strictly speaking, cause it.

We are inclined to say that the Earth is the causal agent responsible for the beam's movement and that it moves the beam by pulling it. But it does not pull the beam (or the Moon) in the way in which a horse pulls a cart: it does not move away in contact with it. No change has yet been discovered which it undergoes and its undergoing of which can be given as the causing of the movement in the beam.

Let us keep looking for such changes; but I do not think we need assume that they are there to be found, that there has to be some causal action by which the Earth moves the beam or a magnet a needle. Aristotle distinguished between an object's causal powers and its nature. Its powers are powers to affect and be affected by other things; its nature (strictly speaking, its material nature) is to undergo certain changes without being acted upon. Newton suggested it is natural for bodies to approach each other with a force proportional to their masses (and inversely proportional to the square of their distance apart). If that is indeed natural the mass of the beam, the amount of material in it, will be that in it in virtue of which it undergoes acceleration towards the Earth *without being acted upon*. Or, better, the amount in both is that in virtue of which action is needed to prevent their coming together.

To say that a movement is natural is to deny that it is due to causal action; it is not to say that it just happens or that it is inexplicable. If the beam falls 20 feet the 20-foot translation has a type-I explanation in its moving for a short stretch of time. The translation is natural in that this period of motion is natural. The period of motion is natural in that (unlike the motion of the pulled cart) it is part of what it is for the beam to exist. If it is natural for bodies to approach one another or to press on objects which prevent their mutual approach such moving or pressing is part of what it is for bodies to exist. As to think 'The apple becomes red because of action on it by the Sun' is to think of the apple (or its skin) as composed of a certain *sort* of material, so to think 'The fall of the apple to the ground is a natural movement' is to think of the apple as composed of a certain *amount* of material.

Aristotle believed in two fundamental forces. He thought that there is one particular point in the universe such that bodies composed of one sort of material ('earth') naturally move towards it, and bodies composed of another ('fire') naturally move away. This notion of a single central point independent of any object as the *terminus ad quem* and *a quo* of all natural movement is unsatisfactorily arbitrary. It is better to think of each material object as a terminus, and to allow, also, for the fact that objects are divisible and more massive in some parts than in others. But it does seem sensible to postulate two forces because, if there were just one, either things would become ever denser and more concentrated or they would be ever more dispersed. Harré would like a single force which acts in different ways at different distances, which is attractive, say, to objects until they become fairly close, but which then becomes repulsive and prevents the collapse of everything into a single point. Whereas Aristotle had to say that there are quantities of centrifugal stuff and quantities of centripetal, Harré would allow us to recognize only one kind of quantity: an elegant simplification, though not, of course, one achieved by science as yet.

6.7 Changes as explananda and explanantia

In section 6.2 I argued that the notion of a change is that of a causal explanandum. The discussion of sections 6.3–6.6 enables me to refine and supplement this account. It is considered as something which occurs or goes on that a change is a causal explanandum: the argument of section 6.2 applies to change only in that aspect. I now want to argue that considered as a going on of something a change is thought of (1) not as a causal explanandum but (2) as a causal explanans.

1   At first this negative contention may seem absurd. Surely to cause a change is to cause that change to occur. If the Sun, by shining, causes the strawberries to become sweet, is not the

occurrence in the strawberries of that change precisely what it brings about? Certainly we can say 'The Sun causes a change to sweet to occur in the strawberries,' but we have still to analyse that sentence. I suggest that the words 'to occur in the strawberries' should be taken with 'cause', not with 'a change to sweet'. The Sun causes-to-occur-in-the-strawberries something we call 'a change to sweet'; it does not cause (in what? the universe?) something we call 'the occurrence in the strawberries of the change to sweet'.

I favour this analysis for two reasons. First, whatever can be brought about can come about or go on. If, therefore, not only changes but also occurrences of changes could be brought about, occurrences of changes could come about. But that would be for occurrences to occur and goings on to go on: we should have a regress. Secondly we express the going on of change in English by continuous tense-forms. The strawberries *become* sweet *in* three days and *are becoming* sweet *for* three days; I move a distance in a time and am moving for a time. If there could be a cause not just of a change but of a going on of a change there could be a cause not just of my moving a distance but of my being moving, not just of a strawberry's becoming sweet but of its *being becoming* sweet. But that is something English does not permit us to say.

The ablest of Hume's modern followers is here false to his leader. Mackie says that if a top spins for a time the earlier seconds of its spinning can properly be given as the cause of later; he even says that earlier seconds of an object's existence can be counted as the cause of later (1974, pp. 155–6). I have just argued that it makes no sense to ask for the cause of a top's spinning (that is, of its *being* spinning) for a time. In general a change in an object's uniform motion is something which calls for causal explanation; but the absence of a cause of a thing's stopping is not a cause of its not stopping. And that an earlier period of existence cannot be the cause of a later is the valuable insight which underlies Hume's critique of causal thinking.

It is true that we do not expect things to undergo annihilation. Materials like bronze, wood and milk are produced out of other materials and when they cease to exist other materials come into being out of them. That being so we feel that if anything (and still more if everything) just went pop that would be a flagrant violation of natural laws. But natural laws are laws to which natural things conform while they exist and in their mutual transformations. If everything went pop there would no longer be anything for natural laws to apply to, and that would not be a breach of any natural law. It could not be a natural law that there will always be things for natural laws to apply to. Similarly with particular objects. Suppose that when Dido's pyre is lit her body, instead of turning to smoke and ashes, turns into a large and beautiful bird: that would be a violation of natural law. But if it ceases to exist and nothing arises out of it that is neither natural nor unnatural. The coming into being of something calls for explanation but the not coming into being of something does not. If nothing happens there is nothing to explain, and the absence of anything to explain does not require explanation.

Anyone who doubts this must think it is natural for new things to arise when old cease to be, and therefore for there always to be things for natural laws to apply to. How does this differ from the view, abhorrent to philosophers since Kant, that it is natural for God to exist? Spinoza held it is natural for extended substance to exist. In claiming that an earlier period of existence can be causally responsible for a later Mackie is forsaking Hume for Spinoza.

2   But even if thinking of a change as a going on of a process is never thinking of it as a causal explanandum, need it be thinking of it as a causal explanans? Could I not think of a change as so many hours of moving or getting larger without thinking causally at all?

Certainly I can *say* 'The melon was getting bigger for weeks' without expressing the change either as a cause or as an effect. But it does not follow that I can *think* of it without thinking of it as one or the other. If I think you walked for two hours in order to reach the top of the mountain I think of your movement as two hours long. Here the movement appears primarily as something I explain by means of your purpose; but it also appears as the causal action by which you hoped to effect that purpose. If I do not think either that for several weeks the Sun and the rain were making the melon bigger, or that for several weeks by getting bigger the melon was causing changes in the rest of the plant and the ground beneath it, how do these weeks come into my thought? Their presence will be completely idle like a sentence on a piece of paper no one is reading; they will have no relation to any practical interest of mine. I think we have no idle thoughts. Either I want the melon to get bigger. Then the change appears as measurable not in time-units but in volume-units; it appears as a causal explanandum and the weeks are weeks of action causing it. Or else I am concerned about other objects and changes; and then the melon's getting larger appears as a period of causal action.

This argument depends on the premise that thinking is never completely idle or disinterested. I shall try to show that in the next chapter; meanwhile here is a second defence of (2).

Considered as a going on of something, a change is measurable in time-units: it is so many hours or minutes of change. So considered, it is a period in the existence of the changing thing. Objects exist for hours or minutes, and an hour for which an object is changing is an hour in its existence. So a change considered as a going on of something is considered as a period in the existence of the changing thing. I suggest that we conceive the existence of an object, at least in so far as it is measurable in time-units, as consisting in causal action. If that suggestion is right, (2) is confirmed.

Is the suggestion right? The words 'causal action' must be taken to cover not only the causing of conspicuous changes but the preventing of natural changes and such action as that of the beam on the pillar which prevents it from falling. That being understood, it is plausible to say that any period for which an object exists is in fact a period of causal action. But the question is whether this is a conceptual truth. Is it not conceivable that an hour in an object's existence should be an hour simply of acquiring properties? Or even simply of having them? That, in effect, is what Descartes claimed when he said that the nature or essence of material things consists simply in extending in three dimensions (*Principles of Philosophy* II 4): their exitence could consist in having the size, shape and spatial relations they have.

How do we determine what the existence of things consists

in? Existence is not, strictly speaking, something that enters our thought. To say 'We are aware of the existence of objects' is to say how *objects* enter our thought. The issue between Descartes and me, therefore, concerns the way in which objects appear in our thinking. Can they appear simply as instances of properties? If they did, how could we be aware of them as *really* existing, as objectively real? How could we relate them spatially and temporally to other objects? As it is, we are aware of objects we perceive as interacting causally with our sense organs and of objects the existence of which we infer as interacting with other objects. (This seems to be the point Kant wishes to make in his Transcendental Analytic.) Any object is apt to appear in our thinking as a causal agent, and when we act to benefit or harm other people they appear as purposive agents. In so far as something appears as a causal agent we are aware of its existence as a causal agent and conceive its span of existence as a span of causal action in the broad sense. Many philosophers think that a causal agent is the only sort of agent of which we have any notion. Were that correct it would be true without qualification that we conceive the existence of objects as causal action. If I am right and sentient beings enter our thought as purposive agents we may be able to conceive their existence as something other than causing; perhaps (as Descartes hoped) as some kind of mental activity. But in so far as existence is not conceived as causing, neither, I think, is it conceived as temporal or as the going on of change. The only years or seconds of existence we can conceive of are years or seconds of causing.

In chapter 5 I said time is the going on of change; now I say it is the causing of it: not, as Shakespeare makes out, a causal agent, but a kind of formal cause of causal action.

7

Teleology and Mental States

7.1 Theories of mental states

Perception, thought and volition seem to be elements in human life almost as flying and laying eggs are elements in the life of birds. Unlike flying and egg-laying, however, they are studied by philosophers. That is not because there are no scientists to study them; on the contrary, zoologists, neurologists, empirical psychologists and even anthropologists and sociologists buzz round them like wasps round a jam jar. Why philosophers shove their way in here, whereas they are content to leave other features of human life like digestion and the growth of body hair to scientists, is a question to which a satisfactory philosophical account of mental states and activities should suggest an answer.

Descartes claimed that the mental or psychological side of our existence is directly open to our view: we can, so to speak, look into ourselves and contemplate our mental states and activities rather as a bee-lover can look into a beehive and see the activities and domestic arrangements of the bees. He conceived these activities and states (unconsciously, no doubt) on the model of physical states and processes. Believing that the Moon is spherical or wanting a sandwich, he thought, is having a property in the same sort of way as being spherical or a mile from the Eiffel Tower; and deliberating, wondering etc., are processes analogous to digesting or melting. The difference is that mental processes and states are not physical; which means, among other things, that they are not spatial in the same way as shape and movement. Descartes, then, bequeathed a double legacy to his successors: introspection as a mode of access to our mental life and physical states and processes as models for conceiving it.

Modern analytical philosophers are divided over both bequests. D. M. Armstrong (1984) believes we know about our mental states by means of something like a sense; Norman Malcolm (1984) denies this. I take up this issue in chapter 10. On the nature of mental states we find at least three positions (for a more finely grained classification see Fodor 1985).

A few people still hold that they are non-physical properties which we exemplify in the same way as physical. Geoffrey Madell (1988) offers a defence of this position but the majority of analytical philosophers will have no truck with the non-physical. They hold that all our intentional movements, whether in carousing, building cathedrals or helping the unfortunate, have a complete causal explanation in terms of events in our brains and stimulation of our sensory system. The attribution of beliefs and desires belongs to what they call 'folk psychology'. Just as there is folk medicine which exists among primitive people and sometimes gets results, so we in ordinary conversation offer explanations of each other's behaviour in terms of beliefs and desires and these explanations are often satisfactory for the purposes for which they are advanced. But has folk psychology any more basis than folk medicine?

Paul Churchland (1984) and D. C. Dennett (1989) say not. There is no correspondence between the cerebral events which are the genuine causes of our behaviour and the beliefs and desires we attribute to one another. The play of psychological phenomena of which we are conscious has no isomorphism with what goes on in the depths of the brain.

Jerry Fodor (1981) and Colin McGinn (1989) shrink from this conclusion. They want to have their brain-processes and also think them; or at least assign to them some definite cognitive, propositional or representative content. What is it, then, for some event or state of affairs in my skull to be the belief that this glass contains wine? Various answers are canvassed. The cerebral item is due to stimulation of my optic nerve by something glass-like and causes my limbs to move in a manner appropriate to the proximity of wine; or it is causally related to other items which constitute logically related beliefs: it causes an item which constitutes a belief that the glass contains liquid, and prevents an item which constitutes a belief that no glass is to hand; or perhaps it has a special biological function, that of indicating the presence of wine and thereby enabling me to survive and transmit my genes.

For those who take the first position my being in a certain mental state is as hard a matter of fact as my being a certain weight. For Dennett and Churchland it is not a matter of fact at all. They are therefore better placed to say why mental states are, and digestion and body hair are not, topics for philosophical discussion. In the way in which a scientist from Mars could discover that we digest various substances and have hair in various places, such a visitor could not discover that we have certain beliefs and desires. That can be revealed only by philosophical analysis. Primitive people understand each other's behaviour but they do not separate their psychological from their physical attributes. The idea that there is a side to our existence which consists in perceiving, feeling and understanding results from philosophical interpretation, evaluation and selection. The mind could not be a scientific discovery because it is a philosophical invention. Here too the third position is intermediate between the first and second: it makes the existence of mental states a fact, but a soft one.

There is keen debate today between philosophers who uphold the second and third positions but what unites them is more important than what divides them. This bond is physicalism. It comprises two theses. There is the negative ontological thesis that there are no non-physical objects or properties, and there is a positive thesis about explanation, namely that (mathematics apart) everything, including our voluntary actions and our thoughts, has a physical explanation. By a 'physical explanation' is understood a causal explanation in terms of entities recognized by physical science and in accordance with physical laws.

Whether physicalism is true is one of the big questions to which philosophy keeps recurring; but like other big questions it presents itself differently to different ages. To Descartes and many of his successors the ontological issue was crucial. He himself wanted entities – minds with mental states – which are not known to science, but he had no objection to thinking about these causally; on the contrary he supposed that our thoughts determine our bodily movements in a causal way. As K. W. Wilkes (1978) makes clear, the emphasis is now on the thesis about explanation. If physicalism is to define itself in opposition to dualism the idea it opposes is not that the universe contains two different sorts of entity but that there are two irreducibly different kinds of explanation.

It seems to me that the notions of an object and a property belong to the sphere of physical explanation, so I sympathize with physicalists who say there are no non-physical objects or properties. I am also attracted to the second position on mental states in so far as it differs from the third: I agree that mental states are an invention of Plato's. But I shall argue that to give a satisfactory analysis of mental states we must recognize a kind of understanding that is as valid as causal understanding but irreducible to it.

7.2   Action theories of belief and desire

Any attempt to give us insight into mental states by using as a model a picture or a written sentence must fail for the reasons indicated in chapter 3. A satisfactory theory of mental states must make them explanatory in one way or another. A theory which I believe to be on the right lines and which, following Mellor (1977/8) I shall call the 'action theory' goes back at least to F. P. Ramsey (1990, papers 3 and 4) and R. B. Braithwaite (1932/3). Its originators expected it to be developed in a physicalist way but it does not have to be. They also believed that thinking involves entertaining propositions and having feelings (described in Russell 1921) of desire and belief, but the theory can be freed of these appendages. A first outline is this:

1   A believes that p = there is some behaviour ϕing such that for the reason that p, A ϕs (for short, $Rp\phi A$).

2   A desires that B should become f = there is some ϕing such that in order that B may become f, A ϕs ($TfB\phi A$).

That is only the roughest of sketches and two or three qualifications should be added at once. First, I use 'believe' as a generic term to cover what is common to knowing, perceiving and opining or imagining that something is the case. So in this sense of 'believe' I believe I am in London when I know perfectly well I am, and believe there is a glass of wine in my hand when I can see and taste it. Next, belief and desire may be manifested not only in doing things but in not doing them. I believe that the ice is thin if I refrain from skating for that reason; I want the baby to fall asleep if for that purpose I refrain from practising the trumpet. In the definitions ϕing covers inaction as well as action. Thirdly I can believe that there is a reason for ϕing yet not ϕ. The theory requires that in such cases I should have some reason for not ϕing, that but for this counter-reason I *would* ϕ, and that I refrain from ϕing in spite of the reason for ϕing. Finally besides desiring changes we can be averse to them. According to the theory:

3   A is averse to B's becoming f = for some ϕing, in order that B may not become f, A ϕs ($TNfB\phi A$).

On this view the concepts of belief and desire are not concepts of properties whether relational or non-relational, physical or non-physical. They are explanatory concepts, concepts of roles which things play in explaining or understanding behaviour. A thing may play the role of *that from desire for which* or *that from aversion to which*. The notions of desire and aversion are notions of these roles (and according to chapter 6 the notion of a change is a notion of how something appears when it plays these roles.) Alternatively a thing may be thought of as *that because of which as a reason*. It is then thought of as an object of belief (and according to chapter 6 properties enter our thought rather as things had or lacked than as things acquired or lost).

Explanations of the forms $Rp\phi A$ and $TfB\phi A$ are current, I think, even among primitive people, and to the extent that they are, but only to that extent, primitive people may be said to have concepts of belief and desire. Such explanations can be valid, of course, even when they are not given. Most people imagine they are valid for animals like dogs and horses. They think that animals perceive things to be the case and move to seize prey or to avoid predators, and hence they attribute psychological states to these animals. Inasmuch, however, as we think animals do not explain or understand behaviour in these ways we cannot credit them with concepts of mental states.

These ways of understanding behaviour, at least at first sight, seem quite different from the modes of causal understanding I described in chapter 6. I label them 'teleological'. The notion of teleological understanding and explanation in this sense is, I believe, the key to all our psychological concepts, and the distinction between teleological and causal understanding is the true basis of the distinction between the psychological and the physical or between mind and matter.

Philosophers today mostly use 'teleological' in a slightly different way. By a 'teleological' explanation they mean one in terms of function. The function of an artifact is what it is designed to do and the function of a biological process or an organ of a living thing is what it was selected for in the process of evolution (so L. Wright 1973). According to this usage, to say that the notions of belief and desire are teleological is to say that they must be explained in terms of biological function and natural selection. Such a view is, in fact, becoming fashionable. A number of philosophers say that a brain-state can be a mental state with content, it can relate to something external to the thinker, because its function must be specified by reference to something external. This view is completely different from the one I am proposing. It represents a mental state as a kind of teleological explanandum whereas I am suggesting that the notions of belief and desire are notions of ways in which things can be teleological explanantia.

Explanations in terms of beliefs and desires are distinguished from causal explanations by Plato (*Phaedo* 96–100) and Aristotle (*Nicomachean Ethics* III and elsewhere). But the distinction has been resisted. Spinoza reduces explanations by desire or purpose to causal explanations: to say that I built a house *in order to* have shelter is to say I was caused to build it by a desire for shelter (*Ethics* IV, Preface). Davidson (1980, essay 1) extends this analysis to reasons. My desire that my skin should become brown and my belief that I can most readily effect this change by going to the beach together make up both my reason for going and the cause of the movements of my limbs. Action theorists cannot say this because they define mental states with the aid of the teleological conjunctions. But they can offer accounts of what it is to act for a reason or purpose which have the consequence that understanding action in these ways involves understanding it as causally determined. Those using the notion of biological function want a similar analysis of that: thinking that something was made or selected *for the sake of* something ought not to require any non-causal type of understanding. The sort of analysis favoured by physicalist action-theorists is superior to Spinoza's, but will either of them do?

7.3   Theories of teleological explanation

A Spinozist must say something like this:

$Rp\phi A$ = A's ϕing is caused by the belief that p.

$TfB\phi A$ = A's ϕing is caused by a desire for fB.

I agree that if $Rp\phi A$ we can say 'Because he believed that p, A ϕed' and if $TfB\phi A$ we can say 'Because he desired fB, A ϕed'. But in both cases the verb of thinking can be put in parentheses. We can say: 'Because, as he believed, p, A ϕed'; 'In order that, as was his desire, B might become f, A ϕed.' When the verb in a 'because' clause expresses a genuine cause, this grammatical transformation is impermissible. In 'Because Othello pressed on the pillow, Desdemona died,' 'pressed' signifies a mode of causal action; and it is not English to say 'Because, as Othello pressed on the pillow, Desdemona died.' This argument proves that mental states are not conceived as causes in ordinary thinking. A philosopher can still, of course, argue that we ought to think of them as causes, perhaps by arguing that there are no non-physical states or events and also that there is no non-causal way of understanding things.

The idea that we conceive mental states as causes has been reinforced or protected by the regularity theory of causal understanding. If I think that $Rp\phi A$ I probably think that anyone who is in A's position and believes that p or something analogous will ϕ. If causation, then, were nothing but regular attendance A's ϕing *would* be caused by the belief that p. This shows how a philosophical mistake about something that looks purely academic and unrelated to human interests, in the case the way causes generally are related to effects, can obscure our understanding of human nature.

I take Jonathan Bennett (1976, ch. 2) as representative of physicalist action-theorists. Shorn of its refinements his theory is as follows. A desires fB (Amanda wants her baby to become fat) if she is so constructed or fixed up internally that in different circumstances she does what in those circumstances conduces to fB: any circumstance (within certain limits, no doubt) which makes it necessary to do something (also within a certain range) if B is to become f causes her to do that thing, and causes her in a special way, by stimulating her nervous system. If (1) A desires fB, (i.e. if fB is her goal), (2) a circumstance C makes it necessary for her to ϕ if the goal is to be attained, and (3) C in fact causes her to ϕ, then she *believes* that C. If crying in the next room makes it necessary for her to fetch a bottle and does in fact, by stimulating her auditory nerves, cause her to fetch a bottle, she thinks there is crying in the next room. And she also thinks this if something similar to crying, say the cat's yowling on the roof, causes the same behaviour in the same way.

This is a highly ingenious theory. It will allow things like chess-playing computers and homing missiles to have mental states of a sort, but in the eyes of the physicalist that is rather a merit than a defect. I think the theory breaks down, however, when applied to beliefs about the mental states of others.

A human being is conceived as an object which has a variety of goals (now drinking wine, now going to the opera, now winning this other person's esteem). But the concept of an object with many goals is purely formal: it applies to other animals besides men and would not, by itself, enable us to pick out any physical object as a human being. It could be that quantities of material, sets of atoms, which at the moment we do not think of as constituting individuals at all, might still satisfy the formal concept of an object with goals, though in that case the goals would not be ones which had any significance for us as we are. A disconcerting thought: there might be a highly intelligent goal-seeker composed at this moment of part of my right eye, part of the carpeted floor in this room, parts of a rat and two earwigs. (Scindapses are like that; blarving and spintling are among their favorite goals.) But so far as human beings are concerned it is natural to suppose that infants start by picking out the people around them not as goal-seekers but as objects which are useful, beneficial and harmful to them in various ways.

How, then, do we come to attribute goals to other people, and why do we attribute to them the particular goals we do? The second question sounds easy: we attribute to them the goals we have ourselves; we think they act to obtain things that benefit us and to avoid things that harm us. But how do we know what our goals are? An organism can have a goal without knowing it has it; so, perhaps, lizards. To know that getting chocolate is a goal of mine I need some concept of myself. Nettles and chocolate may force themselves, so to speak, on a child's attention, in that touching the first and eating the second are experiences with a particular kind of self-intimating luminosity. But on Bennett's analysis to think of them as goals to itself the child must think of them as related in a special way to movements of the particular object which is itself: how does it come to notice and have an idea of that?

As to how we come to do any attributing of goals to others at all, Bennett might say (cf. p. 111) that this increases our ability to predict how they will behave, and thereby our ability to achieve our own goals. But this answer seems to do away with altruism. When I act altruistically I make your goal my own, not in the sense that I try to achieve that goal for myself, but in the sense that I act to enable you to achieve it. Now there is no difficulty, on Bennett's theory, in my acting in order that you may obtain something you want. But is this just a means to some ulterior objective of mine like obtaining food or escaping bodily harm? Then the altruism is merely superficial. Or is your achieving your goals a goal in itself to me, and one I may pursue in preference to more egocentric goals like getting food for myself? That seems deeply puzzling so long as I am thinking of the changes you desire simply as changes your movements tend to effect. On Bennett's analysis, in so far as I act in order that you may achieve certain goals we appear to form a single system seeking those goals; we constitute one person, not two. What keeps us separate in reality is that I *think you want* certain things. Bennett's account fails to explain this awareness of you as a person.

Supplementing it with the notion of a biological function will not help. We should have to say that Philip thinks the other soldier desires water through thinking the other soldier has a certain state because it puts him in touch with water or enables him to achieve some further goal through being in touch with water; but why should Philip think that? And since amateurs of biological function believe that our ultimate goals are those of our genes and that our genes are incurably selfish, they are no more able than Bennett to account for altruism. In chapter 8 I shall try to explain how we can have thoughts about thoughts by exploiting precisely the ideas of disinterested friendship and enmity.

Bennett's theory and the Spinozistic theory reduce teleological understanding to causal. Such a reduction is a disastrous impoverishment of our thought. Teleological and causal explanation are two different kinds of explanation, applying to different things and providing different modes of understanding.

Causal explanation, I have argued, applies to changes which take place. Considered not as something which occurs but as an occurring, a change is thought of not as a causal explanandum but as a causal explanans. The types of causal explanation I described all exhibit the explanandum as necessary or inevitable. The understanding they provide consists in seeing the inevitability of what is understood.

Teleological explanation has a converse application. There is no teleological explanation of changes which take place or are brought about. Considered as something which takes place, a change can figure in our thought as a teleological explanans: it can play the role of that to effect which or that to prevent which. But it is effectings and preventings and changes considered as occurrings that we explain teleologically. If I walk a mile in 20 minutes what is for a reason or purpose is not the mile I walk but my 20 minutes of walking.

Teleological explanation applies not only to causal action but to inaction, to refrainings from causing or preventing; and it exhibits its explanandum not as inevitable but rather as an exercise of free will or spontaneity. The understanding it offers consists in seeing the voluntary character of the behaviour understood. That is a much richer notion than the notion of causal necessity. It is part of seeing someone's behaviour as voluntary or intentional to see it as skilful or unskilful, original or unoriginal, intelligent or foolish, enjoyable or tedious, virtuous or vicious. All these mental and moral concepts belong to teleological understanding.

When I say that teleological explanation applies to causal action I do not mean that all causal action can in fact be explained teleologically. I mean only that it is proper to look for a teleological explanation of any piece of causal action. We can easily draw a blank. Most of the causal agents which affect us and our environment act for no reason or purpose. Their action is teleologically inexplicable and we consider it mindless or blind. Agents which never act for reasons or purposes we call 'inanimate'. But these notions of the mindless and the inanimate are just as teleological as those of the purposive and the conscious. And they apply primarily to the going on or the not going on of change: in so far as a change is thought of as something which takes place it is neither purposive nor purposeless.

But even if teleological understanding is radically different from causal, can we really analyse our concepts of mental states in terms of it alone without any invocation of non-physical properties? I shall now consider some objections to my action theory.

7.4 The action theory defended

An obvious objection is that we can have beliefs and desires which are not manifested in behaviour. I do not mean merely dormant beliefs like the belief that the Battle of Hastings was fought in 1066 which many people keep stored up throughout their lives without giving the matter any thought; I am talking of actual thinkings of thoughts. Cannot a belief, as Russell puts it (1921, p. 246) 'exist actively' in mere 'thinking'?

We have many different sorts of belief and desire. Here is a selection:

1 I believe that there are crocodiles in this pool. I should like a glass of wine right now.
2 I believe that you wrote to me last week. I am glad you did.
3 I believe Charles I was executed. I wish he had not been.
4 I believe that Elizabeth Bennet loves Mr Darcy. I hope she gets him.
5 I believe that for every transfinite cardinal number there is a greater. I wish there were no number greater than $Aleph_0$.

When do these mental states 'exist actively'? When do I actually think, say, that Charles I was beheaded? We date things by saying with what particular rotation of the Earth they are simultaneous. The only things that can be directly simultaneous with a given physical event are other physical events. A belief can be simultaneous with a physical event only through some more than merely temporal connection either with that event itself or with some other. This is not just a point about how we find out whether a claim of simultaneity is true. Unless we think that there is absolute time and that everything stands in direct temporal relationships to parts of that, we need to say what it means to claim that a thought is simultaneous with Big Ben's striking noon on the third day of the year 1984. Some philosophers could say that thoughts get a place in the temporal order through being identical with physical events in the brain; my suggestion is that it is through the behaviour in which they are expressed. In general A believes that p when $Rp\phi A$.

In cases like (1) my not taking appropriate action is itself a reason for thinking I do not have the belief or desire. If I am swimming blithely in the pool you must suppose I do not believe it contains crocodiles unless you have some special reason to the contrary. (And it is not a decisive reason that there is one in my field of vision.)

In chapter 6, trying to explain the difference between thinking of objects as having properties and thinking of them as changing, I said that a property is thought of as had when it enters our thought either as a reason or as a causal condition. I did not mean that appearing as a causal condition is incompatible with appearing as a reason and therefore constitutes an exception to my present thesis. If I think 'It is because the grass is dry that the fire is spreading' the dryness of the grass certainly appears as a causal condition, but fires are not a matter of practical indifference. We notice whether fires are spreading because we want them to spread or, more commonly, are averse to their spreading. If I fear that this fire will damage useful things or harm people, the dryness of the grass appears as something which makes it necessary for me to increase my efforts to stop it spreading. If I am a shepherd burning the heather to improve the grazing, the dryness appears as something which makes it unnecessary for me to increase my efforts to promote the spreading.

It sometimes happens that an agent believes something of practical importance but does not act on the belief. Boating on the river I believe it to be crocodile-infested but I still dive in because my infant daughter has just fallen overboard. Is there anything I then do for the reason that there are crocodiles? I keep a special lookout. But my belief here consists less in doing something *because* there are crocodiles than in doing something (diving in) *although* there are. What is it to act in spite of a circumstance? No doubt if I ϕ although p then had some condition not been fulfilled (had my daughter not fallen in) I should have refrained from ϕing; but we do not have to depend wholly on this counterfactual analysis. The soldier who advances although there are enemies ahead (unlike his bloodthirsty comrade who advances *because* there are) advances with some reluctance. The reluctance may involve doing certain things (tensing muscles, muttering wishes, running to get it over) but it is enough if the thing done in spite of the fact that p is done with less alacrity, calmness, insouciance etc., than it would have been had the agent been unaware that p. When I say mental states must be expressed in behaviour I count as behaviour not just pushing and pulling but imagining and trying not to imagine; and when I ϕ for the reason that p and in spite of the fact that q my belief that q will normally be manifested as a modification of my ϕing, not in my doing something else, ψ ing, as well.

Mental states like (2) are not, I think, significantly different from those like (1). Your having written to me last week would be a reason to me now for replying, for counting on you etc. What happened near us in the recent past is often of live practical importance. We attribute mental states like (2) as well as like (1) to dogs and elephants. But states like (3)–(5) are different. We hesitate to attribute them to animals and one reason for our reluctance may be that they depend on being formulated in language. If that is right – if to think not that Louis XVI but that Charles I was beheaded I must put this to myself in words – there is already some behaviour we can offer as the expression of my mental state. I have the belief, we may say, when I mutter the name under my breath.

In fact, however, such muttering is at best a necessary, not a sufficient, condition of having the corresponding thought. Even when I say, 'There are more real numbers than rational fractions,' I need not believe it. I believe it, perhaps, if I am prepared to use it as an example here, since I should look ignorant if I gave as an example a mathematical belief which was false. History, mathematics and philosophy are enterprises pursued by loosely organized communities in accordance with rules and customs. They are like games. We have theoretical thoughts while engaged in them and I believe that p when I am prepared to declare that p or at least to include it in a draft of a paper.

Desires concerning transfinite numbers, if they really occur, may be compared with the sort of desires that are part of playing bridge or cricket ('If only the King were in the other hand!'). Literary criticism can be something of a game too; but our emotional involvement with persons who are either completely fictitious (Elizabeth Bennet) or inaccessibly remote (Charles I) deserves special treatment. I think that it is expressed not only in trying to find out more about the person (in fiction, by reading on) but also in having hypothetical desires about how we should behave if accessible persons were in the same situations.

Russell questioned whether every mental state must be expressed in behaviour; but the version of the action theory which I favour claims more than that. In a way it reduces mental states to behaviour: it says there is no more to believing that p than being active or inactive for that reason. Does this not, it may be protested, do away with mental states altogether? What difference is there, in reality, between doing something for a reason and just doing it? If I think that Othello is pressing on the pillow for the reason that Desdemona loves Cassio, her love for Cassio plays a certain part in my thinking. But we all know that she did not really love Cassio. What if nobody thought about Othello? Presumably he would just press. But in fact (the protest continues) far from being reducible to intelligent or foolish behaviour mental states are presupposed by it. Othello can act for the reason that Desdemona loves Cassio only because he believes this.

This really amounts to refusing to take the action theory seriously. I agree that if $Rp\phi A$ A must believe that p; but according to me that is not because believing that p is a cause of ϕing for that reason; it is because ϕing for that reason is what it is to believe something. 'If A acts for the reason that p A must believe that p' is like 'If A is an unmarried female A must be a spinster.'

If mental states are properties or processes distinct from behaviour either they are not related to behaviour at all, but just run parallel to it; and then it is amazing that there are the correspondences we find; or else they must be related to it causally. (A belief or desire can, of course, be a reason; believing that the Pope is trying to poison you or wanting to have sex with a dolphin might be a reason for going to a shrink – but that is beside the point here.) On any robust view of causation, relating mental states causally to behaviour involves profound difficulties. And the action theory does not, in fact, make it depend on someone's thinking about him whether or not Othello believes something. It can be for the reason that p that he ϕs, whether or not anyone else understands his behaviour in this way: witness Freud's Table Cloth Lady.

An exasperated physicalist might say: 'Either the teleological relations are reducible to causal or they are totally unintellible, and the syllables "for the reason that" and "in order that" are just noises.' I reply: 'If that were so, mental states would be totally unintelligible and we delude ourselves in imagining we attach some meaning to the sounds "think" and "want". But we don't and they aren't. So causal understanding is not the only kind of understanding we have.' Perhaps that looks like a deadlock. If so I hope to break it below when I argue that we need non-causal understanding, not, indeed, to understand causally, but to understand causal understanding.

Meanwhile the conclusions of this chapter may be stated as follows. The verbs 'to think' and 'to want' have a primary use in describing forms of thought and expression. If I believe that $Rp\phi$ or $TfB\phi A$ you can say that I believe A *thinks* that p or *wants* fB; and if I declare these things you can say I express the circumstance that p or the change fB as an object of *belief* or *desire*. But although verbs of thinking and wanting therefore belong primarily to a second-order vocabulary for describing thought and speech they can be used in first-order speech to achieve explanatory modes of expression. I give my utterance an explanatory form by saying 'A thinks that p' 'A wants fB.'

8
Moral Concepts

8.1 Theories of good and evil

Actions, states of mind and human beings are thought to be
good or bad. What do we think about them when we think
this? How do good actions, for example, differ from bad or
evil ones? And how can we tell to which of the two classes an
action we are contemplating belongs? Philosophy as a discipline began when Socrates and his disciples saw that these
questions cannot be answered by any ordinary type of exper-
tise comparable with medicine, architecture or navigational
skill. Navigational skill may tell us how best to accomplish a
journey, but not whether or not it will be best to undertake it.

The words 'good' and 'bad' are adjectives which look at first
as if they have meaning in the same way as 'green' and 'circular' or at least in the same way as 'large' and 'fast'. They look as
if they apply to objects or changes either because of properties
those things exemplify by themselves or because of how they
are related to other things. Socrates and his followers, however,
were convinced that there is no one property which all good
actions or all good people or all good states of mind possess;
and though they thought that 'good' and 'bad' are relative
terms in a way they did not think them relative in the same
way as 'large' and 'fast'. Xenophon, for example, says that
what is good must be good *for* someone or something (*Memorabilia* III viii 3); whereas what is large is not large *for* anything
(though it may be *too* large for something and on that
account unsuitable or harmful for it).

The earliest philosophical analysis, then, detected that the meaning of moral terms is problematic; and Aristotle articulated a theory variants upon which are accepted by medieval Christian thinkers like Aquinas and by Spinoza. He suggested that the basic notion of goodness is that of an end, objective or object of desire. The good is that to obtain which a purposive agent acts; or else that to effect which we act or lest we lose or prevent which we refrain from acting. To think of an object or change or property as good is to think of it as a teleological explanans of this kind. And to think of it as bad is to think of it as an explanans of the contrary kind, something to avoid or prevent which we act or something lest we cause or preserve which we refrain from acting.

That we try to obtain things we think good and are averse to things we think bad is pretty clear. But do we aim at things because they are good or are they good because we aim at them? Do we see they are good and for that reason try to obtain them, or is their being aimed at what makes them good?

One way of being good is by being conducive to some further good thing. We aim at things which are good in this way, good as means, because they are good as means, not vice versa. But the position over things like pleasure, knowledge and friendship, which are good in themselves and aimed at for their own sake, is more doubtful.

If we say 'We aim at these because they are good', what makes them good? What does their goodness consist in? Moore, the leading modern thinker to embrace this horn of the dilemma, jettisoned the original Greek insight and made goodness a property. He says that the only things which are good as ends in themselves are certain pleasurable states of mind; and he claims that the goodness of these states of mind is a kind of property they exemplify rather like the unity or the balance or the exuberance which might be exhibited painting (1903, chs 1, 6). The strangely aesthetic character of Moore's theory probably derives from Shaftesbury (*The Moralists* III ii). Whereas most of Shaftesbury's followers, however, identify the goodness of an action or a state of mind with its power to cause feelings of pleasure in intelligent, sensitive, unprejudiced people who contemplate it, Moore wanted the goodness of a state of mind to be an intrinsic, non-relational property which it has

independently of how anyone reacts to it. This idea inspired
Bloomsbury but now seems unrealistic. The states of mind
which Moore identified as intrinsically good are admiring contemplation of beautiful objects and admiring contemplation of
beautiful people who are admiringly contemplating beautiful
objects (ss 113, 122). There seems to be no one property shared
by these states of mind; and if there were it would be hard to
make sense of the suggestion that it is identical with goodness.
The connection with desire has been completely severed: why
should we aim at states of mind which have 'goodness' of this
kind?

If, on the other hand, things are good because we aim at
them, why do we aim at them?

It is easy to speculate as follows. There are certain things we
seek and others we shun for their own sake. Various pleasant
sensations fall into the first category and feelings of pain and
nausea into the second. We aim at other things or avoid other
things because of their conduciveness to these ultimate objects
of desire and aversion. We can give a rational justification of
actions which are means to our ultimate goals. To give a reason
for doing something or wanting something is precisely to show
how it leads to some further benefit. But that being so, there
can be no justifying our ultimate goals themselves. My aiming
at something for its own sake may not be completely inexplicable, but the explanation cannot be a rational justification.
It must be a causal explanation: I aim at this and avoid that
because of how I am made. Hume sketches this view in a
famous passage at the end of his *Enquiry Concerning Morals*.

> The ultimate ends of human actions can never, in any case, he
> accounted for by *reason* ... Ask a man *why he uses exercises*;
> he will answer, *because he desires to keep his health*. If you then
> enquire *why he desires health* he will readily reply, *because
> sickness is painful*. If you push your enquiries further and desire
> a reason *why he hates pain*, it is impossible he can ever give any.
> This is an ultimate end, and is never referred to any other
> object. (1902B, p. 293)

There are really two ideas here. One is a sceptical theory of
rationality. Our ultimate aims are fixed by our physical make-

up and do not admit of rational justification; rational justification consists in showing conduciveness to an ultimate end. The second is a hedonistic or sensual theory of motivation: the only things at which we aim or to which we are averse for their own sake are certain sensations.

These ideas go naturally together. For what things give us pleasant sensations and what cause pain or nausea really do seem to be matters determined by our physical make-up; whereas it is hard to see how our physical make-up could be responsible for our aiming at knowledge for its own sake or at benefiting our friends. The trouble is not just that these goals are too edifying and spiritual in character to be due to physical structure. They can be achieved in an excessively wide range of ways. Almost anything might, in the right circumstances, count as helping a friend or enlarging one's knowledge. So anyone who subscribes to a Humean theory of rationality will be inclined to say that the sole things at which we aim for their own sake are certain feelings, and we pursue friendship, knowledge etc., for the sake of these. Nevertheless the two theories can be considered separately.

We may be tempted to think that 'People aim at sensations of pleasure and are averse to pain' is a kind of empirical law of human psychology. But that must be wrong. To establish it as an empirical law we should have to be able to tell whether a sensation was pleasant or painful independently of whether it was sought or shunned. No means of determining this are ever proposed, and in fact 'We pursue pleasant and avoid unpleasant sensations' is a logical, not an empirical truth. 'Pleasant' and 'unpleasant' or 'painful' are explanatory terms in the same way as 'good' and 'bad'. We class a sensation as painful if it is experienced straight off as an object of aversion, if it is part of experiencing it to want to avoid whatever is causing it. We class a sensation as pleasant if it is part of experiencing it to want it to continue or to be averse to losing it – and perhaps also if it helps to make an activity enjoyable, in which case, as we shall see, the activity is desired for its own sake.

We certainly avoid the sensations of being cut or burnt, pursue certain erotic sensations and so forth. But can it seriously be held that all human actions are done in order to

obtain or avoid feelings like these? It is too obvious that people
forego pleasant sensations and endure unpleasant ones in order
to discharge obligations, help friends, injure enemies and pro-
secute artistic or scientific interests. Hume (1888, pp. 319, 576)
tried to explain some altruistic behaviour by saying that the
thought of other people having pleasant or painful sensations
causes similar sensations in us. He compared this to the sym-
pathetic resonance of strings. If anything deserves to be called
'folk psychology' it is this. A more popular strategy is to
postulate certain refined feelings of pleasure and distaste which
are not localized in any part of the body and which are caused
by imagining various actions and states of mind. It can then
be said that we keep our promises, refrain from crime etc., in
order that when we review our conduct we may experience
these finer pleasures and escape this more delicate disgust.

This leads to the position that whether an action is good or
evil ultimately depends on how the thought of it affects our
sensibilities. 'Quite right,' some will say, 'that is how the
autonomy of conscience works.' 'Beware,' say others, 'that
way lie hypocrisy and self-deception.' But the serious doubt is
different in character. These pleasant and unpleasant feelings
are supposed to be like bodily sensations in that in themselves
they do not involve any thought or cognitive judgement, but
unlike in that they are not associated with any part of the
body. Are such feelings possible? 'They must be,' say their
defenders, 'not to have them is to be lacking in moral sense.'
Then I fear that I, for one, must admit to that deficiency.

The theory of rationality is that an action can be reasonable
only in so far as it is a means to some further good (or to
avoiding some evil). Of course there are actions like that. I
walk for an hour to see a view at the end of it; Odysseus
shoots an arrow from the doorway to kill an enemy at the end
of the hall. But sometimes we act not to effect some further
change or obtain some benefit when the action ceases but to
comply with a rule or to behave in a certain way. We do things
to be friendly, refrain from doing things in order not to break
the law. The relationship here is not one of means to end.
Doing something generous is not a means to behaving gener-
ously but rather a specimen of it. Adherents to the Humean
theory of rationality have to choose between forcing an means–

end interpretation on behaviour to which it does not apply and taking the cynical line that we do virtuous or friendly acts as a means to feeling smug.

The source of the trouble is too narrow a notion of a reason. Showing that an action is conducive to some ulterior goal is only one way of justifying it; others are showing that it is obligatory, friendly or enjoyable. A circumstance which makes an action one of these things is a reason for doing it not just as a means to something else but for its own sake. Seeing the friendliness of an act, for example, is a way of seeing its reasonableness alternative to seeing how it conduces to further benefits: doing something for a reason that makes it friendly is an end in itself.

To achieve an adequate theory of rationality we need to see that there are many different ways in which something can be a reason. Figure 2 may serve as a guiding thread in the discussion which follows.

Figure 2

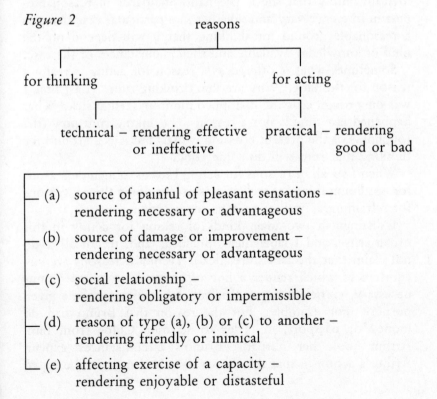

8.2 A taxonomy of reasons

By 'a reason' I mean any circumstance or state of affairs, real
or fancied, which may be introduced into an explanation by
some conjunction like 'for the reason that'. If Othello kills
Desdemona for the reason that she loves Cassio the fancied
circumstance that she loves Cassio is his reason, or one of
his reasons, for killing her.

I begin by distinguishing reasons for thinking and reasons
for acting. A reason for thinking something is a *ground* for
thinking it. The notion of a ground, or at least of a good,
reasonable ground, for thinking that p is not quite the notion
of something which logically implies p. On the one hand, that
the Moon is uninhabited implies that no one lives on it, but it
would be silly to give it as a ground for thinking that no one
lives on it. On the other hand that Niobe feels sick might be
a ground for thinking that she is pregnant, but it does not
logically imply that she is pregnant. Standards of reasonableness in inference vary and whether in a particular case that p is
a reasonable ground for thinking that q will depend on the
kind of knowledge available and the circumstances of the case.

Sometimes what is offered as a reason for acting is really a
reason for thinking. 'Why are you drinking rum?' 'Last time I
was on a rough crossing it stopped me from feeling sick.' What
happened last time is not a reason for drinking rum now (the
roughness of the present crossing is that) but it is a ground for
thinking that rum will do some good.

When I speak of reasons for acting I mean to include reasons
for not doing things as well as reasons for doing things, reasons
for refraining as well as reasons for exertion.

I distinguish two main kinds of reason for acting in this
broad sense, and I label them 'practical' and 'technical' (I do
not claim that the labels are ideal). Technical reasons are circumstances which render a line of conduct necessary or unnecessary, sufficient or insufficient, for achieving some given
purpose. For example: 'For the reason that Bruno had no
money or passport, in order to separate Chloe from him,
Arthur took her abroad.' Bruno's circumstances explain
Arthur's action in that they show its sufficiency for the stated

purpose. 'For the reason that Duncan was a light sleeper, in order to approach him undetected, Macbeth held his breath': the King's being a light sleeper made it necessary for a would-be assassin to hold his breath. Technical reasons explain action or inaction by showing its effectiveness. They also explain not acting or not refraining by showing it to be unnecessary or insufficient. 'For the reason that Bertram had a passport and plenty of money Arthur did not, in order to separate Chloe from him, take her abroad'; 'For the reason that the elder Hamlet was dead drunk Claudius did not, in order to approach him undetected, hold his breath.' Explanations by technical reasons may have not only the form $RpTfBN\phi A$ but also $RpNTfB\phi A$.

A practical reason (I use this phrase in a slightly different way from Thomas Nagel 1970) is a circumstance which renders a line of conduct not merely effective or ineffective of some given purpose but good or bad. It is reasons of this kind which followers of Hume find problematic – they raise no difficulties about technical reasons or reasons for thinking. I shall now distinguish five varieties of practical reason concerned, respectively, with (1) bodily sensations, (2) utility, (3) duty, (4) friendship or enmity and (5) enjoyment or boredom.

1   We are averse to the sensations of being cut and burnt independently of their being signs of injury to our limbs; we desire erotic sensations independently of their indicating that we are peopling the world with little Calibans. Some people are more or less insensitive to pain; so it looks as if it is thanks to our physical make-up that we find pleasant and unpleasant the sensations we do. But given our make-up, the presence of a source of such feelings is a practical reason for action or inaction. Wasps cause pain by stinging, so the presence of one makes it good so to comport yourself as not to be stung. The presence of a shady tree in a hot place makes it good to sit under it and bad to leave its shade.

Could such a circumstance be classed not as a reason for acting but rather as a reason for thinking? Certainly I may say, 'For the reason that the poker was red hot George thought it would be extremely unpleasant to put his hand on it.' But I am not here giving the presence of a hot poker as George's ground for thinking that a certain hand movement would have the property of unpleasantness. Pleasantness and unpleasantness are not exemplifiable properties; the notions of them are explanatory. The utterance 'George thought grasping it would be painful' is not of the form 'A believed that B was f'; rather it is of the form 'A was averse to ϕing'. 'Think pleasant', 'think painful', and we shall find the same goes for other moral terms, signify modes of desire and aversion. To think that grasping the poker would be extremely painful is to *fear* to grasp it; to think that embracing Nicky would be extremely pleasant is to feel an erotic desire to embrace Nicky.

But even if the presence of a source of pain or pleasure is a reason for acting, is it not rather a technical than a practical one? The presence of a scorpion in my slipper is a reason for not inserting my foot in that it makes refraining necessary in order not to be stung. The presence of the Sun in the sky is a reason for going out in that it renders going out sufficient for being warmed.

It is true that going out of doors is not an end in itself; I want to go out only because the warmth of the sun is pleasant. Equally I am averse to putting my foot into the slipper out of fear of being stung. But precisely because I am so made that scorpion stings hurt and sunshine feels nice it is, so to speak, practically necessary for me to refrain from inserting my foot and practically advantageous to go outside. The necessity in the one case, the advantage in the other, are not conditional upon any choice of mine. That makes the reasons different from ordinary technical reasons. It is Macbeth's choice to murder Duncan and the need to cross the courtyard, to hold his breath etc., are contingent on that. We can say, 'No doubt he had to hold his breath if he was to encompass Duncan's death; but what was his reason for wanting Duncan dead?' We cannot say, 'No doubt he had to refrain from putting his foot into the slipper if he was not to be stung; but what reason had he for being averse to scorpion stings?' Because aversion to certain sensations is not rationally explainable the presence of something which can cause such sensations provides a complete rational explanation for certain behaviour.

2 By 'damage' to an object we mean a change to it which makes it less useful. Anything which makes ϕing necessary to prevent damage to an object I use or might use makes it good to ϕ. That is most obvious when the object which might be damaged is a part of my body like an eye or a leg; but the same is true when the object is an artifact like a car or even a living organism like a tree, a horse or a physician. Anything which makes doing something sufficient for causing damage makes it bad to do that thing and good to refrain. The goodness and badness here are similar to the goodness and badness of doing ·what is necessary to avoid pain or what is sufficient for experiencing it. Both may be called 'practical necessity and impossibility'. The difference is that if I think doing something is sufficient for experiencing pain I fear to do it, whereas if I think only that it is sufficient for causing damage, though I am averse to doing it my aversion is not a visceral kind of fear. There are also practical reasons connected with improvement. Whatever makes the act of ϕing sufficient for causing an object to become more useful makes it advantageous to ϕ. On the other hand if something makes ϕing sufficient for preventing my lambs from getting bigger or my employees from becoming more skilful, it makes it advantageous for me to refrain from ϕing.

Is improving things or preventing them from being damaged an end in itself? We sometimes act as if it were, but I think we can be irrationally scrupulous about damage and attach excessive importance to having our possessions and even our limbs in the best possible trim. On the other hand 'Why do you not want your limbs to become useless?' is as inept or offensive a question as 'Why do you not want to experience pain?' The notions of damage and utility embody notions of evil and good. For what is useful is useful for a particular sort of work and to a particular sort of agent. A knife is useful for cutting or dividing, but only to something with aims that can be served by cutting, and hands of a suitable size. A knife would not be useful to a hooked salmon, still less to a mosquito. An orangutan has hands; but if (contrary to the opinion of Lord Monboddo) enjoying music is not a goal of orang-utans, a violin bow is not useful to them for obtaining music from violins. But given that knives and violin bows are useful to me in the way they are, a circumstance which makes moving one necessary to prevent damage to it is a practical and not just a technical reason for moving it.

3   Everyone recognizes some positive and negative obligations or duties: to cherish parents or children, to attend to patients or pupils, to refrain from taking things that belong to others and so forth. Such obligations, I suggest, are essentially social. They are attached to relationships which, even if they have a basis independent of society are recognized by society: relations of being a parent or an employer or a fellow-citizen. And a relationship to which society attaches an obligation makes discharging that obligation an end in itself. If in my society a father has a duty to ensure that his daughters find husbands then that Miranda is my daughter is a practical reason which makes marrying her off an end in itself. This suggestion contains two points that need development.

First, are obligations confined to societies? Do we not have duties to our parents and children simply by virtue of our biological, our causal, relations to them? Do not all human beings have a natural right, independent of any society, to live and seek food, and does it not follow that we have a negative duty not to prevent them?

It is notorious that different societies see the parent–child relationship as carrying different duties and rights; and Hume argues strongly (*Treatise* III i 1) that there are no duties which can be deduced simply from the causal relationships involved. As for natural rights, confidence in them has been fostered by error or confusion. Their champions in the seventeenth and eighteenth centuries made the very questionable assumption that it is possible for intelligent, self-conscious agents to exist in a so-called 'state of nature' independently of any society. That made it seem there must be a pre-social morality. They were also brought up in the Judaeo-Christian tradition according to which all human beings do in fact form a kind of theocratic society. And they did not distinguish sharply between discharging obligations and behaving altruistically. We can behave altruistically towards people not of our society and

even, perhaps, towards animals not of our species; whether our
obligations extend beyond our society I doubt. But if they do I
do not think my main line of argument is affected.

More important is whether discharging obligations is really
an end in itself. For the reason that Phaedra was his stepmother
Hippolytus was averse to sleeping with her. Did this relationship make it good to refrain merely in the way in which
the presence of crocodiles in the estuary might make it good
to refrain from bathing? It is good to refrain from bathing
(primarily, at least) because refraining is necessary in order
to avoid the evil of being eaten. The crocodiles do not make
bathing an object of fear independently of that further evil.
It is not, I suggest, in order to avoid some further evil that
Hippolytus is unwilling to embrace Phaedra. The evil he wants
to avoid is precisely the evil of embracing one's stepmother.
His awareness of her relationship to him takes the form of a
kind of horror at the act of embracing her itself. Equally, when
Prospero is aware of Miranda as his daughter, fixing her up
with a suitable husband becomes to him an end in itself.

Some people may find this hard to believe. 'It would be
utterly in vain' says Locke (*Essay* II xxviii 6) 'to suppose a rule
set to the actions of man without annexing to it some enforce-
ment of good and evil to determine his will.' Surely people
do what is obligatory in their society and refrain from what
is impermissible because this is necessary in order to avoid
punishment or censure and to obtain the benefits of human
society – security, material comforts and leisure for friendship,
art and academic research?

In chapter 3 I compared a society with a language and a
game: I said that each has its own purpose and rules. The
purpose of a society, or at least a society like a family, a tribe
or a state, is a kind of life. The life does not consist in acts of
pure, unmixed duty-discharging; it consists in a wide range
of activities, some of which may be solitary. But we share in
social life by conducting these activities in accordance with
rules of duty. Social life in this sense is not something we can
choose whether or not to engage in. It extends to animals:
chimpanzees, wolves and vampire bats are among species that
have something of the sort. It is almost certainly a precondition

of the emergence of the intelligence, the ability to deliberate and make long-term choices, which Hobbes and Locke attribute to their presocial individuals. For human beings society *is* the state of nature.

Social life is what carries us from the goals of mere sentience to the goals of intelligence. Unless we can see it as an end in itself we shall find totally bewildering or even incredible the existence of conscious altruism. But having it as an end in itself is not having it as something to which doing what is obligatory is a means; it consists precisely in a disposition to regard social relationships as practical reasons for doing some acts and refraining from others independently of any further benefits.

A disposition of this kind cannot be due simply to our physical make-up because different societies have different rules; they conceive the same biological or economic relationships in different ways. Our social dispositions are plainly due to our upbringing. We are taught the rules of the society in which we find ourselves and most of us are won over to accepting them. What wins us over is not, in the first instance, fear of punishment or desire for policemen and anaesthetics, but the apparent goodness of the life around us; though I shall suggest in chapter 10 that kindness and friendship also play a part.

4   A reason for action to me is, so to speak, a second-level reason to my friends. The presence of a scorpion in my slipper makes it good for my friends to act in order that I may not be stung: either by dealing with the scorpion themselves or by alerting me to it. In the latter case they act in order that I may act for that reason: $RpTRp\psi B\phi A$. If Jocasta's being Oedipus' mother makes it obligatory for him to refrain from marrying her it makes it good for his friends to act to prevent him: if not by force, at least by disclosing the relationship.

What is good in this way may sometimes be described as necessary but it is different from the necessity of doing what will prevent pain or damage and also from the necessity of doing what is obligatory. It is necessary for a friend. Second-level reasons render lines of conduct friendly or unfriendly. But there is a complication: we are capable of enmity as well as friendship. To Oedipus' enemies the presence of Gorgons on the beach is a reason for urging him to go shrimping; his relationship to Jocasta makes it good to tamper with the Theban register of births. I shall say more about inimical or malignant behaviour in a moment.

To deal first with friendly behaviour, it would be childishly cynical to say we benefit others only in the hope of receiving benefits in return. Vampire bats regurgitate blood they want themselves in order to save the lives of friends (not just relatives) in need (G. S. Wilkinson, 1990); to attribute such calculations to them would be fanciful indeed. Hardly superior is the suggestion that friendly action makes us feel good, and altruists act in order to obtain feelings of virtuous complacency. Feelings play a part in friendly action but they are feelings neither of smugness nor, in many cases, of being personally attracted. They are feelings of fear or hope, grief or joy, directed at what is good or bad for those we wish to benefit.

Nagel (1970, chs 11–12) has two suggestions about friendly (or, as he calls it, altruistic) behaviour. One is that if I think it is rational for me to act to avoid feeling pain myself I must think that pain is intrinsically evil whoever it is experienced by; and I shall therefore want to prevent others from feeling it. The second is that I have to want to prevent others from experiencing pain in order to think of them as sentient beings at all. The first suggestion seems to involve the idea that I can understand my own behaviour teleologically and form a conscious moral judgement on it independently of caring for others. In chapter 10 I argue that that is impossible. Nagel himself has expressed some doubts about the second suggestion (1986, p. 156) but I think it is fundamentally sound. We should not infer, however, that we do friendly acts merely as a means to being conscious of others as persons. The two are inseparable: acting out of concern for you and acting to be aware of you as a person are the same thing.

Friendly behaviour is an end in itself in the same way as social life. To put it formally, A is a friend to B in so far as A has the following disposition: when a circumstance that p is a reason to B for ϕing, A's awareness that p takes the form of a desire to act $TRp\phi B$, and to act in this way without regard to any further benefit. We might fear that either A must desire the friendly act not as an end in itself but as a means to B's ϕing, or else that A is not really concerned about B at all but merely has a narcissistic desire to play the role of friend to perfection. But that is a false dilemma.

Suppose you see that there is some hazard, say a dangerous pit, near where my child is playing. That is a reason to me for precautionary action. That I should act because of it is not a change you can bring about in me in the way in which, by exposing yourself to the sun, you can bring about a change in your skin. When you say 'There is a dangerous pit over there' (in order that, for the reason that there is a pit, I may recall the child) your speaking is different from my precautionary action, but these are not separate objects of desire to you. You can be aware of my action as something good only through making my reason your own and identifying yourself as a purposive agent with me. Action which benefits our friends is an end in itself because in it we are at one with them.

This distinguishes friendly from inimical action. If Iago hates Othello he will act to harm him without expecting any ulterior benefit to himself, but such behaviour is not intelligible straightforwardly as an end in itself. People will understand your telling me of the danger to my child without any special explanation. Suppose, however, that, seeing the danger, you pretend to collapse in a fit or start making passionate love to my astonished elderly cousin: people will be unwilling to understand your behaviour as action to distract me unless they can see some special purpose you have in harming the child or know of some past injury I have done you. Why the difference? Because to the extent to which you make my evil your good you are at variance with yourself.

5   If I exercise some capacity for a practical reason I may be expected to enjoy exercising it unless there is something to impede the exercise or make me reluctant to continue it. Obstructions can be various. Reading a book is an exercise of the sense of sight, of knowledge how to read and of knowledge of the things that form the subject-matter. My reading may be impeded by a headache, by men drilling in the road outside, by grief at the recent death of a friend, by consciousness of a powerful reason for doing something else. These are factors

external to the book but there can be things about the book itself which prevent me from enjoying reading it. The style may be monotonous or even illiterate; the contents may be unintelligible to me. Things like this are practical reasons for not reading the book: they make further reading bad in that it is boring or tedious. And other features can have a contrary tendency: they make reading good in that it is exciting, moving, amusing, instructive or enjoyable in some other way; they enable me to forget my grief or ignore the noise outside.

Similarly with other activities. In exercising any capacity of my own free will I am aware of things which affect the enjoyability of the exercise. Good weather makes outdoor pursuits more enjoyable and bad weather makes them less (perhaps that is part of what we mean by 'good' and 'bad' weather). Awareness of these factors takes the form of wanting or being averse to continuing the activity and the desire or aversion is independent of any ulterior benefit or cost. A reason for enjoying reading or walking is a kind of reason for reading or walking as an end in itself.

A reason for acting of this kind is an *additional* reason: since we will hardly enjoy doing what we do against our will it normally presupposes some practical reason of a different kind (exceptions might be walking simply because it is a nice day, talking just because your interlocutor is good company). Hence enjoyment could not be anyone's sole aim in life: we need other aims to enjoy pursuing. But reasons of this kind can make actions ends in themselves which are originally undertaken for ulterior purposes like avoiding damage or obtaining pleasant sensations. Gardening and cooking can be fun. And things that make actions which belong to friendship or social life enjoyable make them ends in themselves twice over.

This survey of practical reasons was undertaken partly in response to the Humean claim that we have no reason for aiming at things which we aim at for their sake. That claim fits pleasant sensations. Which sensations we aim at for their own sake and which we avoid seems to be determined by our physical make-up. But it does not fit social life, friendship or enjoyment. It may be said, indeed, that these things are ends in themselves and that we have no reason for aiming at them. But they are not, like pleasant sensations (or diamonds) things distinct from our actions which we obtain by acting. To say that they are ends in themselves is to say that social relationships, the first-level reasons of others and reasons for enjoying render certain actings or refrainings good in themselves. We have no reasons for aiming at them not because we are physically so constructed as to aim at them but because they are types of rational justification. One rational justification for doing something for its own sake is that it is enjoyable; another is that it is socially obligatory, a part of social life; a third, that it is friendly. These justifications do not show that the action is better than any other open to the agent but they are complete in that they do not depend on anything further. Burying Polyneices because he is your brother, telling me that there is an adder where my infant is crawling for the reason that there is and reading Shakespeare's sonnets because of the language and the imaginative power are paradigms of rationality.

Even about pleasant and painful sensations Hume's claim is not the whole truth. If I reflect on my behaviour I may decide that the presence of the sun in the sky is a *good* reason for going out, and the presence of crocodiles in the river a good reason for not bathing. To decide this is to opt for being the sort of person who acts in this way, and that is to make such action an end in itself. There is a difference between being averse to certain sensations and desiring that awareness of a source of those sensations should be expressed in preventive action. Perhaps any sentient organism is averse to some sensations; it is only if I am aware of myself as something which acts for reasons and purposes that I can want certain circumstances to be reasons to me for certain behaviour. But once I have this sophistication a circumstance which makes an action good as a means can make it good as an end too. A reason connected with pleasant or unpleasant sensations or with utility, besides functioning in the ordinary way, can function at a special, conscious level making the action for which it calls an end in itself to the agent as a self-conscious being. The same, of course, holds for reasons connected with social life, friendship and enjoyment. For the reason that his wife is weeping and falling on the bed Romeo goes to see her not only because he thinks this friendly or obligatory on a husband but because he thinks friendly and dutiful behaviour good.

8.3   Moral terms

By 'moral terms' I mean such linguistic items as the English words 'ought' and 'good' and the Latin gerundive construction (as in *delenda est Carthago*). In this century analytical philosophers have hoped to discover what good and evil are by considering what these terms mean, and to grasp the character of the difference between them by asking whether saying 'Discrimination on grounds of colour is evil' or 'You ought to keep your promise to repair my burst pipe' is saying something strictly speaking true or false.

As to this last question, it is sometimes imagined that these utterances can be true or false only if there are properties of goodness and badness, rightness and wrongness, which actions can exemplify. I dare say we could define a moral fact as an action's exemplifying such a property. In that case I do not think there are any moral facts. But it does not follow that the utterances of moralists cannot be true or false. On my view they are explanatory. When I discussed truth and falsity in chapter 4 I did not mention explanatory remarks but the account I offered can be applied to them.

Suppose I say, 'Because the wires came into contact, they became red.' I do not state a causal fact, if by a 'causal fact' we mean the exemplifying by two events of a special relation of causality. But I express the colour red as one some objects are caused to acquire, as an effect in them of a change in spatial relation. If the property was in fact caused in them by that change my mode of expression corresponds to reality and I speak truly. It is similar if I say, 'My hair's being red is not a reason for refusing me your daughter's hand in marriage' or 'It would be good to cause George's face to become red.' In the first of these remarks I express the colour (in a negative way) as a reason for not consenting to something, and I speak truly if the property does not in fact make consenting impossible or disadvantageous. In the second I express the property as one there is reason for causing in a certain object, and I speak truly if such a reason in fact exists.

Philosophers who accept the Frege-Austin theory of meaning give wildly implausible accounts (see pp. 47 above) of how moral terms have meaning. How can we do better?

The English word 'ought' is used in two ways. If I have a duty to do something I may say, 'I ought to do it.' But I may also say 'I ought to go to London' if that is, in the circumstances, the right thing or the best thing to do. I have claimed that the notion of duty is a social one applying only within societies. If we use 'ought' in the first sense what I ought to do is what I am under an obligation to do by virtue of my relation to other members of some society. That may not be the best course in the circumstances. I may have overriding reasons for doing something incompatible. Hence what I ought to do in the second sense is not what I ought to do in the first, and to avoid confusion I perhaps ought to use some word other than 'ought'.

To think that it is good to do something is always to think it is good in some specific way: advantageous, necessary, obligatory, friendly, pleasant. I can say, 'It would be good for me to go to Paris', without saying it would be good in one of these ways, but I cannot think it would be good unless there is at least one of them in which I think it would be good. Hence I must think that there is something *making* it advantageous, necessary or whatever it is. Hence in saying it is good (and equally in asking if it is or expressing the wish that it were) I express the change as one for which there is a reason. To ask 'Would it be good to lose 4 kilos?' is as much as to ask 'Does anything render it advantageous or necessary to lose 4 kilos?' More precisely, I express a property as one a change to (or from) which is something there is a reason for effecting (or preventing).

What mode of expression is that? The property or change is expressed as a teleological explanans. It is not given as the explanation of any specified behaviour. But in 'It would be good if A became f' fness is expressed as something we could understand an unspecified agent acting to bring about. When I ask, 'Must I lose 4 kilos?' I express the weight 4 kilos in an interrogative way as something abstinence by me could be understood as abstinence in order to lose. We can say things, of course, like 'You ought to visit your aunt' or 'It would be good if Medusa washed her hair' without really having the corresponding thoughts. Exactly what it is to have such thoughts I shall consider in chapter 9. Here I wish to emphasize only that thinking of a property as good or bad is thinking or it as a teleological explanans of unspecified behaviour – whereas thinking of it as causally necessary, possible or impossible is thinking of it as a causal explanandum.

Speaking of one course as better or worse than another is comparing them as explanantia. Sartre in a famous passage (1989, p. 35) describes the dilemma of one of his pupils in the 1939–45 war: would it be better to stay at home with his widowed mother or go off and join those of his compatriots who were resisting the German occupation? That is the question whether joining the Resistance or staying at home is something it would be easier to interpret the student's future/behaviour as behaviour to effect. Such a question is not purely theoretical, especially as there is as yet no behaviour to interpret. Sartre says the student is trying to decide what sort of person he is to be and I have already indicated that I agree. Suppose the student decides it is better to join the Resistance: that is wanting to be the sort of person who would join the Resistance *because* a foreign enemy is occupying his country and *although* his mother needs him; and wanting this more than to be the sort of person who would stay at home *because* his mother needs him *although* a foreign enemy is occupying his country. When he vanishes into the woods it is not only in order to impede or expel the Germans but also in order to be an agent who acts in this way.

In practice it is often very hard to decide whether one course is better than another. It can be still harder to decide which of the courses open to one is best. Economists who look for some set procedure which, when properly applied, is bound to yield the right answer are probably looking for El Dorado. Here, however, we are concerned not with how we decide what is best but what it is to think something best. I shall confine myself to three remarks.

First, I take it that thinking a course best is thinking it better than any alternative, including waiting and seeking more information.

Secondly, deciding when to act and when to wait and seek more information requires a special kind of practical judgement distinct from the ability to balance pros and cons. To act when it is not necessary to act and when you lack grounds for certainty that there are no reasons against acting is, in serious matters, imprudent or rash. It would be imprudent to marry someone you do not know or to plunge without precautions into a pool deep in a hitherto unexplored tropical forest. This is a dimension of practical thinking which has not received much attention from philosophers. One might treat it as a variety of considering what is necessary in order to avoid harm. Since spouses are able to cause each other great misery, that this man may become your husband makes it necessary to find out about him, rather as the fact that enemies were in an area last week makes it necessary for soldiers to look out for ambushes. But whereas marrying a man although he is a scoundrel because he is attractive shows imperfect mastery of one's feelings, marrying a man without troubling to find out anything about him at all is childish or silly.

Finally I shall argue in chapter 9 that thinking a course best for someone else can never be a purely detached judgement but always involves some interpersonal engagement.

9
Conceiving and Understanding

9.1 A holistic theory of thinking

In chapter 7 I sided with those modern philosophers who deny that having a thought or desire is a real event on its own: thinking that your face is red or wanting a pear is not like becoming spherical or turning through 90 degrees. Reports of the forms 'A thought that p' and 'A wanted fB' call attention to elements in, or features of, A's mental life which illuminate aspects of A's behaviour but which are not in themselves marked off from one another. In that respect they are like warm or healthy areas in geography or ages of advance or consolidation in history.

The view I favour may be called 'holistic'. To view something holistically is to view it not as an aggregate of atoms but as a whole. I see a person's mental life as a whole, interrupted by periods of sleep or unconsciousness but otherwise continuous. While awake we are more or less aware of more or less of the world even if our conscious attention is concentrated on something remote like Bronze Age China or outside the world altogether like the square root of two. It is for those who want to explain our actions and utterances to differentiate particular beliefs and desires.

Many analytical philosophers would agree that mental states should be viewed holistically, but their emphasis would be slightly different. So far as I know I am alone in treating mental states as explanantia in irreducibly teleological explanations:

the general view is that we need not think of them as explanatory at all, and if we do we should think they explain causally.
And the ground for saying we should view them holistically
is that we cannot attribute them to a thinker one by one, in
isolation from one another, but only collectively or in groups
(so Davidson 1987, p. 167). I do not wish to dispute this idea
(for the origin of which see W. V. O. Quine 1961, ch. 2 and
Wittgenstein 1979) but it is not what I shall be developing in
this chapter.

Nearly all philosophers who try to describe our mental life
think we have complex thoughts which are somehow constructed out of or analysable into simpler ones, and that we
apply complex concepts which are definable in terms of simpler
ones. One can think this without wanting to give the austerely
atomistic account I sketched in chapter 1. Here is a synopsis of
the description I shall be offering.

The simple concepts we use are concepts of what I call
'properties', that is, spatial relations and attributes like shape,
volume, temperature and colour. We apply these concepts in
thinking of objects as having, acquiring or losing the corresponding properties. We do this primarily in responding to our
surroundings as sentient, purposive agents. We think of an
object as *having* a property in acting for the reason that it has
it; we think of an object as *acquiring* a property in acting in
order that it may acquire it or in order that it may not – that is,
the change to the property appears to us good or bad.

In acting like this we are already applying concepts of objects. These are not concepts we apply in addition to concepts
of properties. A report like 'Amos applied the concept of a
scorpion' or 'Ada thought the object was a scorpion' is a
description of the thinker's applying of unspecified concepts of
properties. Ada might, for example, apply the concept of the
relationship *being in contact with*: she is averse to the object's
acquiring that relation to her toe.

Thinking is never idle or purely academic: it is always purposive. But it is not always intelligent. We think intelligently in so
far as our applying of concepts of properties is understanding
or trying to understand. Things then come into our thought
not just as reasons or purposes to ourselves but as explananda
or explanantia.

There are two kinds of understanding, causal and teleological. We apply concepts of materials, that is, we think of objects as composed of wood, water, hydrogen etc., in thinking causally. We apply psychological concepts, we think of agents as having beliefs and desires and also such qualities as skill, incompetence, virtue and vice, in thinking teleologically. I have argued for these claims, at least up to a point, in chapters 6 and 7 and shall only adumbrate further arguments here. But this does not exhaust the richness of causal and teleological understanding.

In chapter 10 I shall argue that it is in understanding the changes we bring about that we are aware of ourselves as causal agents; and it is in understanding our bringing about of these changes, in understanding our own behaviour teleologically, that we are conscious of ourselves as purposive agents or persons.

9.2   Sortal concepts

I call concepts of sorts of object 'sortal concepts'. (The term was originally used in connection with sorts of material as well as sorts of object (so Locke, *Essay* III iii 15) but matter-words have a different grammar from object-words and their concepts should be classified separately.) They are of various kinds. We have concepts of sorts of artifacts like knives, cars and houses, and concepts of species of plant or animal like oaks, alligators and human beings. And besides concepts simply of species we have concepts embracing a species and also something else: sex, age, a causal or social relationship, a physical condition, a mental or moral quality. Examples of these are the concepts of: a ewe, a lamb, a sibling, an employer, an epileptic, a botanist, a bully. I shall start with concepts like that of a knife or an alligator and pass to the more complex later.

A traditional view is that words like 'knife' and 'alligator' are primarily used predicatively, in utterances like 'That is an alligator,' and signify properties; the concepts are concepts of sets of properties. I argued in chapter 3 that the words are primarily used referentially, not predicatively, and it is awkward to hold that the concepts are concepts of sets of properties. What properties are comprised in the concept of a knife? Knives come in many different shapes and sizes, and there are no clear constraints on what as yet unguessed products of human ingenuity will be classed in the future as knives. There may be a constraint on what could be an alligator: it should be able to interbreed with the alligators we have now. But we saw in chapter 6 that there does not seem to be any set of intrinsic properties we *conceive* as essential to being water or gold, and neither, I think, are there any such properties we conceive to be essential to oaks or armadillos.

Nevertheless it is perfectly correct to say things like 'Alice applied the concept of a snake. She thought that there was a snake under her bed. She thought that Boris's tie was a snake.' I do not think we need bother about the difference between the forms '*A* thought an *s* was present' and '*A* thought that *B* was an *s*': what makes such utterances true?

I am here using 'concept' as a non-technical term in common use. I am not giving it as special sense (as I have given to 'object', 'property' and 'change') still less am I using it as a word for a sort of object – a special, non-physical object – so that I can be asked 'What is a concept?' in the way in which, when I say, 'My aunt is using her compact,' you may ask, 'What is a compact?' I *apply* the concept of a snake if I think that something is a snake, or wonder if it is, or wish there were snakes in Ireland, or use a word which means a snake knowing what it means; and I possess a concept if I am able to apply it.

For most people it is part of possessing an ordinary concept like that of a dog or chair to be able to recognize a dog or chair for what it is when they see it. (A person without sight, of course, would have to rely on other senses like hearing, smell and touch.) To be able to recognize something as a dog or chair by sight is to be able to recognize it as this by properties which affect the eyes, by its shape, its size, its way of moving or standing and so on. For me to have this recognitional capacity is for me to be a person who, if an object's eye-affecting qualities fall within a certain range, is aware of it straight off as a dog or chair.

We might be tempted to say that I infer from the object's shape or movement that it is a dog. But that cannot be right if the object is seen under standard conditions. If I inferred it was a dog I should have first to pick it out and identify it not as 'that dog' but in some other way, perhaps as 'that dark object' or 'that moving object'. But these cannot be standard ways of identifying objects. If I identify something as 'that s' I may be asked how many ses there are about, and whether 'that s' is the same s as one we identified earlier. But how can we say how many moving objects there are in the room, or whether this dark object is the same dark object? We can say only how many moving dogs or legs there are, or whether this is the same dark image or dark lump of clay; and in fact once we have learnt to recognize dogs or images of dogs by sight we are aware of things as 'that dog' or 'that image' from the start.

If I can recognize things as dogs by their shape, movements etc., could it be said that I conceive dogs as objects with a certain shape, a certain way of moving and, in general, certain visible characteristics? I think it is impossible to specify, at least in well-defined physico-mathematical terms, a set of visible characteristics such that anything which exhibits them will be a dog. If we are asked 'What shape do you conceive dogs as having? How do you conceive them as moving?' the only answer will be: 'The shape of a dog; a canine, as against a feline, way of moving.' Dogs come in many shapes and it would be beyond our linguistic resources to describe even one, say the shape of a Pekinese, without using some word like 'Pekinese'.

Objects of any sort will be practically significant in a variety of ways. Crocodiles are harmful to swimmers but when skinned provide a material useful for women's handbags. Patches of grass are useful for nourishing useful animals but damaging to books and cutting instruments left lying in them. Clouds obstruct climbers and motorists using mountain roads but bring the rain crops need and look pretty at sunset. Axes are useful for felling and splitting timber but wound children who play with them. Of a piece with thinking things useful for purposes is thinking they *become* more or less useful in various ways; horses become more useful through being broken in; young trees become useless through being eaten by deer. I suggest that we best say how A conceives ses by saying how A thinks they are practically significant.

The remark 'Arthur thinks that sharks bite bathers but yield materials for a delicious soup' attributes to Arthur not an actual piece of thinking but a kind of disposition. We might say that he believes these things about sharks dispositionally. But what does that mean? That if asked, 'How do you conceive sharks?,' he is disposed to say 'They bite bathers but make nice soup'? He might say that but not believe it, or believe it but (for fear of provoking conservationists) be disinclined to say it. The dispositional thought doubtless includes dispositions to say certain things but is primarily a disposition to behaviour. Arthur is the sort of person who, if he sees dorsal fins, refrains from bathing, or if he wants soup, goes shark-fishing.

If that is right we can suggest that whenever he acts in accordance with any of these beliefs he has about sharks, he applies the concept of a shark (unless there is some special reason to think the action is somehow coincidental). To put the matter formally: given that A can recognize $s$es readily as $s$es when he sees them under the conditions under which he sees B, and given that B has properties more or less within the range of properties by which A recognizes a thing as an s – given, that is, that B is s-like in appearance, then:

1 If A conceives an s as useful for ϕing,
   A thinks B is an s in using B for ϕing.
   (I think B is a spoon in using it to stir my tea.)
2 If A conceives an s as a source of harm h,
   A thinks B is an s when, for the reason that B is present, A acts to avert h.
   (I think B is a snail of a bad sort when seeing B in the water I take action to avoid bilharzia.)
3 If A conceives an s as a source of benefit b,
   A thinks B is an s when for the reason that B is present A acts to obtain b.
   (Odysseus thinks B is a siren if because B is on the beach he approaches to hear beautiful singing.)
4 If A conceives s_1s as rendered useless for ϕing by s_2s,
   A thinks that B is an s_1 and C an s_2 when for the reason that C is present A acts to prevent B from becoming useless for ϕing.

(Anstruther thinks that *B* is a slipper and *C* is a spaniel if for the reason that *C* is present, to prevent *B* from becoming useless for foot-protecting he moves it out of *C*'s reach.)

We apply sortal concepts in thinking things do not belong to sorts or wondering if they do, but it is easy to extend the account to cover these cases. Suppose that *B* is sharky in appearance but *A* does not, though *B* is present, hesitate to bathe: *A* thinks that *B* is not a shark. Or suppose that, though keen to bathe, *A* makes more careful observations of *B*: *A* wonders if *B* is a shark.

These are perhaps unrealistically simple cases but it would not be hard to construct subtler ones, and they suffice to illustrate the general point. A report of the form '*A* applies the concept of an *s*' does not specify a concept *A* applies in addition to concepts of properties; it describes or classifies or explains his applying of unspecified concepts. If I look for an object in order to carve the ham, remove it from the grass after the picnic lest it become rusty and prevent your young son from touching it lest he cut himself, I apply a variety of concepts to the object and to other things, but these bits of thinking have something in common. All are applications of my knowledge of knives, and we express this by saying that in each case I think the object is a knife. To have the concept of a sortal concept is to have the concept of a sort of concept-applying. (That is why sortal concepts have an interest for philosophers which concepts of properties lack.)

But surely, it might be objected (so C. Radford 1985), we could form a concept of a sort of object that is completely useless or completely harmless: a shy insect, perhaps, that lives in desert places. Might we not give it a name, say 'eremite-fly', and think to ourselves as we breast the summit of a sand-dune, 'That's an eremite-fly?'

To say '*A* thinks *s*es are useless' is no less to say how *A* thinks *s*es are practically significant than to say '*A* thinks *s*es are useful.' As we think, however, that objects are useful not in general but for specific purposes, so we think they are useless for specific purposes, and in the case of uselessness it will be a purpose for which there was some hope that the object might be useful. A spaniel may be useless for herding sheep but is hardly useless for boiling things in. Similarly we might think that Johnson crocodiles do not eat swimmers, but hardly that they do not cause lung cancer or damage aeroplane engines. If *A* thinks that eremite-flies do not eat or infect sandwiches, then *A* might think that this insect is an eremite-fly in not moving the sandwiches even though this insect is crawling near them.

But in these days when systematic natural science is a going concern and learning is admired living organisms have a special, artificial utility simply through belonging to particular species and having species names. Even if an eremite-fly is ill equipped to play a big part in the lives of ordinary human beings, it could revolutionize the life of a professional entomologist. Discovering one could make his reputation, besides gladdening his friends and disconcerting his rivals in the academic rat race. He will look a fool if when a specimen is produced he cannot say what it is. And even you or I could impress a fellow-traveller through the desert (or divert the conversation from a bad topic) by saying 'That's an eremite-fly.'

It is obvious that the account I am proposing can be extended to the more complex sortal concepts which embrace more than a species. Lambs, saplings, mares, and also dentists, dendrologists, lepers and even husbands are thought to be useful, beneficial, harmful and obstructive in various ways. We apply the concept of a policeman in approaching one for topographical directions, in driving more slowly because one is present and in many other ways. But when a sortal concept embraces a social relationship there is a further possibility. As I said in chapter 7, social relationships carry duties and rights. Sovereigns have duties to their subjects, dentists to their patients, employees to their employers, parsons to their parishioners, and vice versa. Suppose that I conceive the government of a country as having a duty to relieve famine among its subjects. Then I apply the concepts of government and subjects if, for the reason that some starving people are the subjects of a country to the government of which I belong, I send a grain ship; or if I feel slightly guilty at the thought of corpses piling up in the Punjab or Donegal.

Only human beings can be sovereigns, dentists or husbands but we can apply these concepts to other people without thinking of them as human beings or even as sentient; to think of them as sentient or intelligent involves teleological understanding. But before coming to that I wish to say something about causal understanding.

9.3   Causal understanding

Holmes thinks causally when he thinks (rightly or wrongly) that it is because the Sun is shining that the butter is becoming soft. Let us say that this thought is of the form $K\phi BfA$ or Kpq. What is it for him to think this? The chapter 7 account of belief might suggest that it is for him to act for the reason that because the Sun is shining the butter is becoming soft – $RKpq\phi A$.

Jonathan Bennett (1976, p. 107) does in fact try to explain what it is to think causally in this way. For him to do this, however, is extremely difficult. He holds that the behaviour of an agent who believes that p is caused either by the circumstance that p itself or by something else which affects the agent's brain in the same way. But while the shining of the Sun might cause a change in my brain the holding of a causal relationship between the sunshine and the melting of the butter can hardly cause anything.

Maintaining a teleological analysis of belief I do not face quite that difficulty, but it is still awkward for me to have a causal connection within an agent's reason for acting. For according to the general theory sketched in chapter 2 causal and teleological connections are not, strictly speaking, part of the content of our thoughts: it is not part of what we think about anything that it is the cause of anything or the reason for anything.

What I said about causal conditions indicates the analysis I favour. When Angus thinks that it is because the grass is dry that the fire is spreading, either for the reason that the grass is dry he acts to prevent the fire from spreading or for the same reason he refrains from acting in order to help it to spread.

We may extend this to causal explanation of all kinds. What appears as a causal explanandum will normally also be an object of desire or aversion. If it were not, if the thinker cared nothing about whether or not this object acquires this property, why should the change be thought about at all? If the explanandum is an object of desire the explanans will constitute a kind of technical reason rendering further causative action unnecessary; if the explanandum is an object of aversion, the explanans will be a practical reason requiring action that is preventive. To put the point formally:

A thinks that $K\phi BfC = R\phi B$ there is no ψing such that $TfC\psi A$ or $R\phi B$ there is some ψing such that $TNfC\psi A$.

This analysis may look complicated but it has several advantages. First, the causal connection is got out of the content of A's belief: this belief, A's reason, is now simply that ϕB. Secondly I redeem my promise in chapter 7 to argue that causal thinking can be understood only in terms of teleological. In this analysis the explanans of the causal judgement appears as a teleological explanans, a technical or practical reason. And a third merit of the account is that it lets us see how causal thinking arises. If for the reason that the Sun is shining on the step the cat lies there or is unwilling to move we do not attribute to the cat the judgement that the Sun is causing it to experience pleasant sensations. Its psychological state is rather sentience than intelligence. When, for the reason that the Sun is shining, lest the butter become liquid I move it into the shade, I surely do judge that the Sun is causing or may cause the butter to melt and my action is (mildly) intelligent. But there need be no sharp boundary between sentience and intelligence or non-causal and causal thinking. The two can merge into one another through what we call 'instinct' and 'experience'. We may think that it is because the roof is projecting over a certain place, and in order that it may not be rained on, that the swift builds its nest there. But that is consistent with thinking it builds instinctively; acting because of causally relevant circumstances need not be deliberate or an application of any piece of general causal knowledge.

This analysis will hold only for the causal thinking which is directly involved in purposive action. That is the commonest kind. The butter example, however, was suggested to me by a reference in Conan Doyle to some more theoretical thinking. Holmes thought something like 'The parsley has sunk 1.5 mm into the butter. So the butter must have been put out three hours ago.' It is not incorrect in this case to say that Holmes thought it was because the Sun shone on the butter for three hours that the parsley sank 1.5 mm. (Holmes may have muttered that to himself.) His thinking, however, is an application of some general causal law. There is some rate at which Holmes thinks sunshine causes butter to become soft, some function which he believes its softness to be of the time for which it has been exposed to sunshine. This general belief is dispositional. It could be applied in action or prediction but here it is applied in *a posteriori* inference. Holmes wishes for the purposes of his enquiry to know when the butter was put out. (He wants, in the language of chapter 5, to know before how many hours of getting softer it was put out.) The 1.5 mm change appears in his thought not as an object of desire or aversion but as a reason for thinking that there have been three hours of causal action by the Sun. To put it formally Holmes thinks that Kpq, in this case, in that Rq Holmes thinks that p. In chapter 8 I contrasted reasons for thinking with reasons for acting, but they can be fitted into the scheme of reasons for acting quite simply. A reason for thinking that p is a kind of reason, technical or logical in a broad sense of 'logical', for acting for the reason that p. Why does Holmes treat the witness who says the butter was put out 30 minutes ago as unreliable? Because the parsley has sunk a full 1.5 mm into it.

I return to more straightforward causal thinking. In chapter 6 I argued that in understanding changes causally we think that objects are composed of particular materials. I now suggest that in general to say a thinker applied the concept of a particular material is not to specify a concept applied in addition to concepts of properties but to describe an applying of property-concepts in causal thinking.

That suggestion needs to be qualified. Like sorts of object, materials are beneficial, useful, harmful etc., in various ways. When systematic natural science is a going concern oolite is useful in that using the word for it, saying 'That's oolite', impresses non-geologists. Gold can be exchanged for useful things but attracts violent men; wine gives drinkers pleasant sensations but impairs their efficiency as drivers. If I refrain from finishing the bottle lest I drive drunkenly it may be right to say I think it contains wine, and if Hobbes locks something up lest it be stolen by his servants or relatives he may well think it is made of gold. In these cases applying matter-concepts is not just analogous to applying sortal concepts: it is applying sortal concepts of a special kind, the concept of a bottle of wine or a chunk of gold.

But though materials can give practical significance to objects composed of them we conceive them primarily as differing in active and passive causal powers; or rather, as I said on pp. 113–15, we conceive them as that in objects by virtue of which objects have causal powers. That being so, there is a certain analogy between matter-concepts and sortal concepts. A report of the form 'A thinks B is an s' tells us A's notion of the practical significance of B, whereas 'A thinks B is composed of m' tells us A's notion of B as a causal agent or interagent. Both describe the applying of unspecified concepts, but the first describes this in so far as A is acting for reasons and purposes, and the second in so far as A is understanding causally. If for the reason that it is getting dark, Descartes lights an object, or if lest it should become useless for illumination he moves it further from the fire, we describe his application of concepts of darkness, distance etc., by saying, 'He thinks it's a candle.' If he thinks that it is because it is on top of the stove that it is ceasing to be cylindrical and opaque, we describe his applying of concepts of colour, shape and position by saying 'He thinks it's made of wax.'

But might he not simply think to himself 'This is made of wax'? Certainly he could simply say that; whether he could actually believe it without applying any more specific concept is less clear. If he says it, at least he applies the concept of the French or Latin word for the stuff. I suspect that a report of the form 'A thinks B is composed of m,' when it does not describe an applying of unspecified concepts, attributes A a disposition to think causally in a certain way; and 'This is made of wax,' when truthful, is an avowal of such a disposition. An analogous suggestion may be made about 'A thinks B is an s.'

9.4   Teleological thinking

We think that pretty well all animals are sentient and that as a species, if not as individuals, human beings are intelligent. What is it to think that something in one's vicinity is sentient or intelligent? Can the account of sortal concepts in 9.2 be extended to cover this?

That account will suffice for some remarks like 'Arion thought the animal was a dolphin', 'Tarquin thought the man was a dentist.' But Arion can think an animal harmless in a way dolphins are harmless without thinking it sentient; Tarquin can think a man useful in a way dentists are useful without thinking of him as notably different from a phial of oil of cloves. Can we say that the notion of a sentient being is the notion of something useful and beneficial in some ways, harmful or dangerous in others, and similarly with the notion of an intelligent being or person?

There are devices which we call 'electronic eyes' and we say they 'see' things or are 'sensitive' to light or heat. But thinking that an animal or baby is sentient is not just thinking of it in this way. Neither is thinking that an adult is intelligent or clever like thinking that a chess-playing computer is intelligent or thinking that a plastic card is 'smart'. An organism is sentient only if it moves in order to obtain or avoid things – things which affect its sense organs or the pleasant or unpleasant effects of these things. To say 'A thinks of B as sentient' is to say that A understands B's behaviour teleologically as action because of things perceived or action to obtain or avoid perceivable things. To say 'A thinks of B as intelligent' is to say that A understands B's behaviour as behaviour for more complicated reasons.

That being so the concepts of a sentient being and an intelligent being are not specific sortal concepts like those of a cat and a human being. They are at two removes from concepts of properties. 'A applied the concept of a cat' does not specify a concept A applied but it does give some indication of the kind of concepts applied or the purpose for which they were applied: A's purpose will have been to reap some benefit or to escape some evil associated with cats. To that extent the report is informative about the content of A's thought. But to say 'A applied the concept of a sentient being' is to describe merely the form of A's thinking: it is to say simply that A's thinking is or involves teleological understanding. I think of the baby as sentient if I act to prevent it from experiencing *painful* sensations. To give a report as specific as 'A thinks that B is a cat,' instead of 'A thinks B is sentient,' we need to say something like 'A thinks B hears a mouse'. Linguistic items on a level with 'cat' and 'mat' are such longer expressions as 'thing that thinks a cat is present', 'thing that is averse to moving off a mat'.

What, then is it to think teleologically? If causal connections should be analysed out of the content of beliefs, so should teleological. In chapter 8 I pointed out that a reason or purpose of one person can be adopted as a second-level reason or purpose by another. I can make your reasons and purposes my own. There are two ways of doing this. If there exists some circumstance which makes it good for you to ϕ I may act in order that you may be aware of this circumstance and ϕ because of it; or I may act in order that you may *not* be aware of it or may *not* ϕ in spite of it. We can adopt each other's reasons and purposes as friends or as enemies. I now suggest that doing one or the other is necessary for understanding teleologically. There is no such thing as purely detached teleological understanding. A thinks that $TfC\phi B$ only if there is some ψing such that either $TTfC\phi B\psi A$, or $TNTfC\phi B\psi A$. A thinks that $Rp\phi B$ only if there is some ψing such that $TRp\phi B\psi A$ or $TNRp\phi B\psi A$.

Why should that be? In the first place this account gets teleological connections out of our reasons. I see my friend moving in a certain direction and interpret his behaviour as walking for the reason that it is sunny and for the purpose of getting to the beach. On the proposed analysis it is sufficient for my thinking this that, for the reason that it is sunny, in order that he may get to the beach, I offer him a lift. A thinks that $RpTfB\phi B$ in that $RpTRp\phi B\psi A$. Here my purpose – that my friend should get to the beach because it is sunny or do what the weather renders it good to do – is complicated, but my reason is simple: my reason is that it is sunny. Anyone who thinks that there can be completely detached teleological understanding may be challenged to find another way of getting reasons and purposes out of the content of beliefs.

That challenge might be declined by someone who was un-convinced by the general theory of mental states proposed in chapter 7. Many philosophers still cling to the idea that think-ing that you think that p is thinking that you contain a repre-sentation of the circumstance that p, or that besides containing a representation you adopt an attitude towards it or experience one of Russell's non-localized bodily sensations. I challenge these philosophers to show how thinking that someone be-lieves something can be anything like this. A big merit I claim for my account is that it liberates us from the need to model our concepts of belief and desire on representations of physical properties.

But is it not altogether too paradoxical to say that thinking you believe that p is adopting an attitude of active benignity or malignity towards you? Certainly I can utter the words 'A thinks that p' ('The computer thinks I'm going to castle'; 'Those birds think I'm going to dig up some worms for them') without feeling any great warmth or hostility towards A. But I claim that the more we consider the matter the more we shall be forced to acknowledge that really believing that another agent believes something or desires something brings us into an interpersonal relationship with that agent. We cannot apply psychological concepts as isolated human atoms but only as friends or enemies. If that seems to detract from our existence as distinct individuals, so much the worse for individualism as a theory of human nature. I believe that in the end it forces us to deny the reality of sentience and intelligence.

What about people who are distant in space or time like Queen Anne or completely imaginary like Polyphemus? We can hardly be friends or enemies towards them; but surely we can attribute to them mental states? There are, in fact, several distinct possibilities. I can reason about the mental states of people around me as Holmes reasoned about the parsley in the butter. 'He did not pack his clothes so he cannot have intended to go away.' 'He will see me play the king so he must infer that the rest of the spades are with my partner.' These attributions of thoughts are often, I think, purely verbal. They are like attributions of thoughts to mechanical chess-players, or else the sentences are like tokens which we push about and operate upon without cashing them out into what they mean. The same may happen when a historian reasons about the remoter past. But it is also possible to like or dislike both historical and fictitious characters and to become emotionally caught up in their lives. As I said earlier, I think that this involvement takes the form of hypothetical wishes. If I feel sorry for Joan of Arc or Juliet Capulet I wish that, were there some real person in my sphere of influence who was in her predicament, I might act in definite ways to help her. If I like Odysseus I wish that, were there someone like him, he might be my friend; if I dislike Stalin I hope that no one like him will be my friend.

Agents are not just sentient but intelligent in so far as the reasons for which they act are of such a nature that acting for them is thinking causally or teleologically. Their actions are then classified as clever, stupid, honest, cowardly and so on. If you are trying to sell me a picture, offering you a sum because that is what it is worth, although you believe it is worth less, is honest. To adopt means to an end which are obviously insufficient when more effective alternatives are available is foolish. In general, classification of actions by technical reasons is classification of them as more or less skilful whereas classification of them by practical reasons is classification as more or less virtuous or vicious. People, as distinct from actions, are skilful in so far as they are able to act effectively, to bring about changes they want to bring about; they are virtuous or vicious in so far as they are disposed to do virtuous or vicious things.

This being so we apply the concepts of skill, virtue and vice primarily in understanding particular bits of behaviour. I apply the notion of cowardice when I think my companion averse to going to the side of a friend although the friend is being attacked by two youths for the reason that the youths have knives, and I also think that if he were to stand firm with his friend the youths would run away. It would normally be part of thinking in this way to want my companion to go to his friend's side and to realize that this is not in fact a suicidal policy. The spatial relations of the parties, the size of the youths, their mental states, the size and position of the knives, will all come into my thought and my diary entry after the incident ('I thought his behaviour cowardly') does not specify an additional concept I apply but summarizes my applying of many unspecified concepts in a complicated piece of teleological understanding.

Philosophers have sometimes used the sentence 'Socrates is wise' as if it expressed a very simple thought, the thought that the famous philosopher exemplifies the property of wisdom, rather as 'Mars is red' expresses the simple thought that the planet exemplifies the property of redness. I think it would be correct to say 'Plato thinks Socrates is acting wisely' if some complicated condition like the following is fulfilled: Plato thinks that Socrates prefers remaining in Athens, although he will be executed, to going to Megara, although he can continue philosophizing there; he thinks Socrates prefers this in order not to disobey the laws and because Megara is a foreign state with an unlovely political regime; and he thinks Socrates' estimation of the pros and cons is correct. If it is to be an accurate description to say, not just that Plato thinks Socrates is acting wisely, but that he thinks Socrates is wise, there are further conditions: Plato thinks that Socrates arrives at his decision fairly easily and with confidence, and Plato is not surprised at that. For in general 'Plato thinks Socrates is wise' rather attributes to Plato a disposition to understand Socrates' behaviour in a certain way than describes a particular bit of thinking.

To go deeply into how we apply concepts of qualities of mind and character would be a big undertaking, but I shall make a couple of points. First, as the examples show, thinking that you are behaving in a virtuous or vicious way involves not only fathoming your reasons and purposes but also judging the correctness of your thinking. In the mugging example I think that you overestimate the danger of standing by the attacked friend. Plato thinks Socrates was right that the reasons against escaping to Megara outweighed those in favour. We might at first imagine that this judging of the agent's thinking is gratuitous, that we could understand teleologically without it, and even that it might be better not to judge. If my general theory is correct, it is unavoidable. One person cannot understand another person's behaviour without wanting to benefit or harm that other person, and that involves considering whether the other person is assessing the situation correctly. I cannot really believe that you believe that your spouse is unfaithful while being indifferent to whether your belief is true; Sartre cannot have understood that his pupil thought his mother's plight a reason for not joining the Resistance without considering whether it deserved to be a decisive reason.

It follows that grasping the practical reasons of someone else's behaviour is an exercise of one's own knowledge of what is good and bad, of one's own ability to weigh one good or evil against another. It may be difficult or even impossible to understand the behaviour of a person whose moral character and order of practical priorities are completely alien: a vicious person may be unable to believe that anyone else is genuinely altruistic.

And as understanding your action as virtuous or vicious is an exercise of my own moral disposition, so understanding it as efficient or inefficient is an exercise of my own skill. I may believe on hearsay that you are a clever doctor or an incompetent angler; but I can understand the cleverness of your doctoring or the inefficiency of your angling only if I am versed in these matters myself.

10

Consciousness

10.1 Introspection

Many philosophers think that the most important thing about
us is not that we build spectacular temples to the gods, uncover
the laws of physical nature and behave in a friendly, understanding way to one another, but that we are conscious of
ourselves as intelligent beings. Of course we do not know any
artists, scientists or understanding friends who do not have this
awareness of themselves; but there are plenty of people with
self-awareness and no gifts for art, science or friendship, and
we still regard these dullards as belonging to the same kind as
ourselves and shrink from dealing with them as we deal with
nettles or lobsters. Recently there has been much discussion
among philosophers about the moral significance of this kind
of consciousness: if unwanted babies have not yet acquired it
or senile grandparents have lost it, does it follow that we can
put them painlessly out of the way? I shall not address any
such startling questions here. Rather I shall enquire how it is
that we are aware of ourselves and what this self-awareness
consists in.

There are two kinds of self-awareness to be considered. On
the one hand we are aware of our bodies or limbs; we normally
know whether we are standing or sitting and where our hands
and feet are; and we know this without having to look, much
less having to be told by other people. On the other we are
aware of our thoughts; we know what we are thinking or what

we want; and this too without having to be told by psychiatrists or having to infer it from things we notice ourselves saying and doing.

Until recently philosophers have not asked how we know the position of our limbs; but D. M. Armstrong (1984) has suggested that we know this by means of receptors in the joints and the Eustachian tubes in the head, organs which function in the same sort of way as sense organs. As to how we know what we are thinking, a traditional view is that we know this by introspection. If introspection were defined negatively as knowing, but not by hearsay or inference, that would be uncontroversial. But in practice it is conceived on the model of sight. We are thought to have a capacity which, as Locke puts it (*Essay* II i 4) 'though it be not sense, yet it is very like it,' and this enables us to look into our minds and see what thoughts there are there as we can look with our eyes into a tank and see what fish there are there. I think that both these views are wrong and I shall start with the view that we know what we are thinking by introspection.

Hobbes (*Leviathan* I 4) and Locke (*Essay* III ii 2) thought that language starts with words that signify feelings or types of feeling we know by introspection. Wittgenstein refutes this theory (*Philosophical Investigations* I 257–66) and some of his readers think his argument proves that there is no such thing as introspection and that we cannot, strictly speaking, be said to know the contents of our minds at all. It is clear, however, that we do know this and it seems to me that Wittgenstein himself relies on introspection as traditionally conceived to confirm the descriptions of our mental processes which occupy so much of the *Investigations*.

Believers in introspection describe it as a self-scanning process and Mellor says its 'mechanism' is 'in the brain. Whether it is in some definite part of the brain is a moot point, but a trifling one' (1977–8, p. 100). That suggests the following picture. There is an area A of the brain consisting of tiny electric lights like those screens of light bulbs sometimes used in advertising. When and only when a person has a thought a sentence expressing that thought lights up in A. There is also a bit of brain B on a flexible and retractable stalk. This moves over A in a manner partly, though not entirely, corresponding to our desires to know what we are thinking. There is a lens in *B* and light passing through it is projected onto a light-sensitive screen behind it, like the retina of the eye. We are aware of thoughts when and only when sentences expressing them are projected onto this screen in *B*. No one supposes, of course, that there is exactly this mechanism in the brain. But this would be a paradigmatic self-scanning mechanism, and reasons for thinking that it would be impossible to know our thoughts in this way are reasons for rejecting the traditional view that we know them by introspection.

We do know the thoughts of our friends in ways rather like this. My friend writes to me from Central Sulawesi: 'This morning I thought how beautiful the clouds are over the lake before the Sun causes them to disappear. I wished you were here with me.' I scan the letter, words like those written appear on my retina, and I think that my friend thought the clouds were beautiful and wished I was there. Or my friend says to me 'It's going to be a fine day. I'd like to climb Helvellyn'; similar sounds are produced in my inner ear, and I think my friend believes it will be fine and desires to climb Helvellyn. In these cases, however, no one would say that I know my friend's thought simply by the sense of sight or hearing. I know the words uttered by those senses but I have to interpret them. I have to understand what my friend means to say and I have to judge that my friend is speaking truthfully. Even, then, if I knew what I was thinking by the mechanism described, I should not know it by anything analogous to a sense. I should have to interpret the words in part *A*, and judge that they are an accurate expression of my thoughts. But it is absurd to suppose I do anything like that.

In defence of the self-scanning model it might be said that whereas the words in the letter or the sounds produced in the air are merely utterances of my friend's thoughts and the thoughts themselves are something different, the sentences in part *A* of my brain are identical with thoughts. To have a thought is to have appear in the brain something like a translation into a universal language of humanity of the English or German sentence that would normally be said to express that thought.

This is the theory Fodor advances in *The Language of*

Thought (1975) and it would allow for a copying process like xeroxing in the brain or the appearance of sentences like 'I believe that Mars is red.' My objections to it have been given in chapter 3. The cerebral formulae would have to be true or false (Fodor 1981, pp. 30, 195). But truth and falsity cannot attach to sentences any more than to pictures; they can attach only to linguistic acts and exercises of thought in purposive behaviour. And even if thinking did consist in the appearing of Fodorian formulae, that would not support the idea that we know what we are thinking by anything like a sense. As he concedes, the same physical formula in a human brain might translate the English 'It is now daylight' and in a Martian brain the English 'The marmalade is going mouldy' (so the famous 'Jam dies'). Which it means in a given case, and hence what the organism believes, depends either on how it causes the organism to behave (Fodor 1981, p. 202) or on what its biological function is (Fodor 1985, p. 99). Either way the organism will have to tell what it thinks by intelligence, not by sense.

10.2   Awareness of our bodies

Moving our limbs is a skill, a simple and basic one which we start to acquire, perhaps, before we are born: foetuses begin to move their arms and legs in the womb, and infants spend much of their first year developing elementary forms of muscular control. There is no such skill as the ability just to move a particular limb; we do not learn simply to move our hands; but we learn how to achieve a range of effects by moving our hands: holding or waving things, transferring food to the mouth, at a later stage modelling clay, sewing, writing, playing the violin and so forth.

Besides muscular we acquire perceptual skills. We learn to recongize objects of various sorts under ranges of conditions by sight, hearing, touch etc.; we also learn how to keep things under observation, noting changes which provide reasons for action or inaction. In general, perceptual and muscular skills are acquired together; we need both for achieving many of our objectives and both go to make up advanced skills like cooking, driving and carpentry. Such activities call for coordination of hand and eye or more generally of motor and perceptual capacities.

A skill is an ability to effect (or prevent) changes of a certain kind when or as you want. A cook can make edible substances digestible and delicious; a carpenter can make useful objects out of wood. It is part of exercising a skill to know whether or not you are achieving a desired result. Since we achieve our results by moving our limbs, that means that we must be aware of the limbs we are using and have some idea where they are. That is not a matter of having a series of discrete beliefs; the carpenter does not think 'Now my arm is straight, now it is bent at the elbow': the limbs move more or less continuously and our awareness of them is a more or less continuous monitoring. It is analogous to following a game or a piece of music. If you were asked at any moment 'What is the state of the game?' or 'What is happening in the music?' you could answer, but when you are not asked your attention is not divided into distinct thoughts like 'This is the second ball of the over' or 'This is the second variation.' Following a game and listening to music are in fact themselves skills, and the exercise of any skill is a continuous going on of various processes.

I suggest that the primary way in which we are aware of our bodies is in skilful making and doing. We sometimes speak of being aware of our bodies when we have bodily sensations: most often when they are unpleasant ones. But aches and pains are psychological states with no conceptual content. We can imagine that an animal or a baby experiences pain without having anything we would call 'awareness of its body'. Adults, on the other hand, not only experience pain but are aware of experiencing it: they are conscious of their mental state as such. Between the unselfconscious infant and the selfconscious adult there is the child (or animal) that has learnt how to effect a certain kind of change by moving limbs and exercises that ability. In doing so it must be aware of the limbs; my suggestion is that this is the basic way of being aware of one's body.

How does it come about? We distinguish between action which is merely instinctive and action which is skilful. Pouncing on prey or fleeing a predator seems instinctive. The presence of the predator or the prey is a practical reason and awareness of it takes the form of a desire to flee or pounce.

Action is skilful in so far as it can be explained by technical reasons, in so far as the agent is responsive to circumstances which bear on the effectiveness of its action. This is a matter of degree (as I indicated earlier I do not think that there is a firm line between instinct and skill) and so, therefore, is awareness of our limbs. It is part of exercising a skill like cooking or driving to keep certain things – the pans on the stove, other road-users – under continuous observation. Awareness of the condition of these things as rendering specific hand movements necessary in order to achieve our objectives (preparing the meal; reaching a destination without mishap) takes the form of wanting to make these movements. So these movements come into our minds. When I drive, the positions of my hands and feet need not be objects of awareness additional to the positions of swerving cyclists, parked lorries etc.; I am aware of my hands and feet in being aware of these external objects. At the same time exercising a manual skill involves some monitoring of one's hands if only to make sure they are not harmed or hampered. A violinist, batsman or cook may know partly by looking how he is holding his bow, bat or spoon.

This account is partly anticipated by G. E. M. Anscombe: in her monograph *Intention* (1963) she points out that we know the positions of our limbs 'without observation' and suggests that this is a kind of practical knowledge: I know how I am moving because I could offer a rational justification of my movements. Armstrong, in contrast, as I said earlier, says we know the position of our limbs by using special sense organs hidden in our joints and elsewhere like the closed-circuit television cameras that are sometimes watching us in shops. So when driving I know that there is a lorry emerging from a side-street by the sense of sight, and that my foot is descending on the brake by what Armstrong calls 'proprioception'.

If I am listening to an oboe concerto on my cassette player, the emergence of the lorry and the entry of the soloist are separate things I know by separate senses. But it is not like that with the lorry and the brake pedal. In driving we coordinate hands, feet and eyes; scanning the road and listening to tapes are not coordinate but merely parallel.

It may be that without receptors in my joints I should not

know the position of my limbs. But I do not learn to use these
receptors in the way I learn to use my eyes. If I did, I could
know where my limbs are and how they are moving independently of being able to use them skilfully. I could know the
position of my fingers as I know the position of fish in a tank.
But in fact this knowledge is bound up with skill. Touch-
typists know the positions of their fingers when typing without
looking; inexperienced typists do not. Nijinsky knows where
his feet are better than a clodhopper.

Armstrong's hardware is analogous neither to eyes and ears
nor to hands and feet but to muscles and tendons. We use these
in using our limbs, but in so far as we learn how to use them it
is in learning how to do things with our limbs. In learning to
play the violin I learn a new way of using the muscles in my
arm and also, if Armstrong is right, the receptors; but receptors
or no receptors, learning any new muscular skill is learning a
new way of knowing where the limbs involved are.

In so far as we exercise skill and know if our action is
successful we must know in a way what we are trying to do.
Swimming in a stream with a strong current I know what
position I want to reach or avoid; making white sauce I know
what consistency I wish the stuff in the pan to acquire. But this
point needs careful formulation. It is not part of my exercise of
skill to know *that I want* the sauce to acquire this texture or
that I am averse to coming within 50 yards of the waterfall. To
know that I have a desire or aversion is to be conscious not of
my physical but of my mental state, and it is surely possible to
act skilfully and judge causally without being aware of oneself
as a thinker at all. The most that can be claimed is that in
thinking causally we distinguish the properties which we want
objects to acquire (or which we want them not to acquire)
from the objects; whereas an animal need not do that in acting
instinctively.

10.3   Awareness of our minds

According to the action theory of mental states I think that
you think that *p* if I understand your behaviour as being for

the reason that p. It should follow that I think that I myself think that p if I understand my own behaviour as being for that reason. Similarly I think I desire fB if I think that it is TfB that I am acting. How, then, do I understand my own behaviour? Ryle says that the ways in which we know about our own mental states are pretty much the same as those by which we know about the mental states of others (1949, p. 156). That suggests that we observe our behaviour and interpret it, that we attribute beliefs and desires to ourselves as explanatory hypotheses; but a satisfactory account must show how our knowledge is more direct than this; it must find some way between inference on the one hand and introspection on the other.

Philosophers who believe in introspection often imagine that we first build up an idea of ourselves as conscious beings; we then notice that our environment contains a number of material objects that look like us and behave in a similar way; and we finally apply the notion of a conscious being to them too. This belief about the origins of our psychological concepts goes with beliefs, partly unconscious or unexamined, about the origins of the human race. It is supposed that (in line with the account in *Genesis* and the legend of Cadmus and the dragon's teeth) the first human beings popped up without parents or families but with pretty much the same intellectual equipment as we have today; they led solitary lives, the men grabbing the women and satisfying their lust when they got the chance, until a number of them thought it would be to their advantage to form a society and appoint policemen and priests.

Many animals live in societies and I cannot believe that we evolved out of animals which were not already social. It is part of belonging to a society to conceive certain relationships as carrying obligations and rights. These relationships will include the causal ones involved in family life. In chapter 8 I distinguished acting for social reasons from acting for altruistic ones. The altruist does not what is obligatory but what is friendly. But although there is a conceptual distinction here, the two ways of acting go together and reinforce each other. Friendship and altruism appear among social animals and it is hard to imagine a species recognizing obligations without having friendships. Parents and children, siblings and sexual partners almost inevitably feel concern for each other and think of each other as sentient.

Friends try to make each other aware of circumstances which are reasons for action. Suppose you act in order to make me aware of a dangerous serpent or a delicious fruit in my vicinity. In order to understand your behaviour I must realize that you want me to be aware of the serpent or fruit and act accordingly. That involves realizing that you think I am a sentient, purposive agent. This, I suggest, is how we first become conscious of ourselves as sentient beings or persons: we are aware of ourselves as objects of thought and concern, usually benign but occasionally malignant, to others. To understand the behaviour of someone else I must feel concern for that other person. Not only, then, do we apply the notion of a conscious purposive agent to others before applying it to ourselves; but our first application of it to ourselves is motivated by concern for others. (There is a suggestion of this in Adam Smith, *Moral Sentiments* III i 3, but it is not worked out).

I think that my friend wants me to be aware of the fruit as something it would be good to eat. I first think of eating it as an object of desire to *myself* in thinking my friend wants *me* to desire it, wants me to reach for it in order to eat it. If I want to please my friend I may do precisely that. I then understand my hand movement as movement in order to eat the fruit; I am conscious of eating the fruit as my purpose. But I am aware of it as my purpose because I have intentionally made it my purpose: I am acting not just in order to eat the fruit but in order to act for the purpose of eating it. To put it formally, A thinks that $TfB\phi A$ if $TTfB\phi A\phi A$.

Of course, there are other possibilities. I may think that, unknown to my friend, the fruit is poisonous. In that case I still recognize my friend's desire that I should take it, but instead of taking it I might act to inform my friend of its harmfulness. Or I may be quarrelling with my friend and sulkily refuse to eat the fruit. I am then aware of eating it as an object of aversion to myself, again because I have chosen to be averse to eating it.

On this showing we are conscious of our desires not because we perceive we have them by something like a sense nor because we infer we have them from our behaviour, but because we choose to have them in order to fulfil the desires of our friends or to frustrate the desires of our enemies. This account holds only for wanting to do something here and now; long-term dispositional desires like a desire to become a member of the European Parliament we probably discover partly by inference. Perhaps I thought I wanted to become a multi-millionaire but find I really wanted to have a life with my family. But the account will apply to beliefs. I will take a case which sounds complicated when analysed but which would easily be understood in practical life.

'Your uncle is in hospital,' says my friend, 'you should drive your aunt to visit him.' I cannot choose whether or not to believe that my uncle is in hospital. Neither, I think, can I choose here and now whether to think of this circumstance as making it friendly or obligatory for my aunt to visit him. But I can choose whether to be aware of this same circumstance of my uncle's plight as a reason for action by me in order that my aunt may act because of it. I could decide to be aware of it as a reason for inaction in order that she may not: it could be that for the reason that he is in hospital, in order that she may not visit him, I refrain from offering to drive her. And if I decide to be aware of the uncle's situation as a reason for driving the aunt I decide this partly in order to be the considerate nephew my friend wants me to be. Conversely if I decide to refrain from helping my aunt I decide not to be the sort of person my friend wants me to be – one to whom the situation of a friend's friend is a reason for benevolent action.

The account may be generalized to cover all beliefs about particulars. If A believes that p then, as we have seen, $Rp\phi A$. If A is conscious of believing that p A understands that $Rp\phi A$ and this involves assessing the circumstance that p as a reason for ϕing. In the examples we have considered it has been a practical reason but it could be a technical reason or even a reason for thinking. Suppose that for the reason that the rabbit is 100 yards away I do not, in order to kill it, blast off with my 12-bore. The rabbit's distance is a technical reason making it useless to fire. I am conscious of believing that the rabbit is this distance in considering whether it really does render it useless to fire. Or suppose that for the reason that there is a bulge in your pocket I think you are carrying a revolver. I am conscious of believing that there is a bulge in your pocket in considering whether this is an adequate reason for thinking that you (a philosopher from Texas) are carrying a revolver. Weighing up technical reasons and reasons for thinking is different from weighing up practical but the same account can be given of arriving at a decision: deciding that the circumstance that p is a good reason for ϕing or for believing that q is acting in order to be the sort of person who would ϕ or believe that q for this reason.

We attribute to ourselves not only simple beliefs like 'There is a bottle of wine in that cupboard' but more complicated beliefs like the following: (1) 'By going up in flames the wood on the hearth is making the room warm'; (2) 'The cat is approaching the bowl because goldfish are swimming in it'; (3) 'That statue weighs half a ton'; (4) 'Odysseus is crafty; (5) 'All ravens are black'; (6) 'Brothers ought to avenge insults to their sisters'; (7) 'Cornelius thinks human beings hate those whom they have injured.' We are conscious of beliefs like (1) and (2) in understanding our own behaviour as intelligent: the account in chapter 9 can be adjusted to self-understanding. Beliefs (3)–(7) though they can appear as reasons for thinking are rather dispositional than actual. I think all ravens are black if I am the sort of person to whom a bird's not being black is a reason for thinking it is not a raven (so Ramsey, 1990, p. 146, but the idea probably goes back to Aristotle). Hence we know that we have such beliefs rather by inference from how we think or act on particular occasions than directly.

Descartes argues that introspection gives us direct access to our thoughts and that being conscious of them we cannot doubt our existence as thinkers: according to him I can be more certain of my own existence as a conscious being than I can of the existence of anything else. Later philosophers have questioned whether we can be sure of the existence of thinkers as well as of thoughts. I cannot doubt the occurrence of certain beliefs and desires; but I can doubt the existence of a person who has these beliefs and desires since I have no insight into how they could be related to a thinker or what could be gained by postulating one. The relation of physical properties to material objects is no good as a model: it involves (they say) a dubious notion of matter. Besides, as Descartes himself points out, material objects are divisible, whereas the owner of a mental state cannot, as such, be conceived as divisible. We cannot think that half the mental state is exemplified by half the thinker.

To the non-philosopher these misgivings about the Cartesian view may seem irritatingly unrealistic. We not only believe we exist now as conscious beings but we have a grasp of our identity over time. I know who I am. I may not know for certain who my parents were or whether it was I that caused some particular change in the past, say who trod on the tomato; but there is a way in which I cannot fail to know who I am. It may be difficult to give a satisfactory analysis of this self-knowledge but the solution is not to deny it.

If the analysis offered here is correct our knowledge of ourselves as conscious beings consists in a teleological understanding of our behaviour. I know who I am in that I know for what reasons and purposes I am acting. This seems true both psychologically and philosophically. As a matter of experience our grasp of our identity as persons is indeed connected with knowing why we are behaving as we are. If I do not know why I am causing some change (say pushing a stranger off a train) I do not feel it is really I that is causing it. If I do not understand any of my behaviour my personality seems to disintegrate. And contrary to what Descartes imagined, it is quite easy for a philosopher to question his existence as anything but a material object. Many philosophers do that today. They question their existence as sentient, intelligent beings in questioning the validity of any kind of explanation except causal.

11
Thought and Philosophy

11.1 Two aspects of thinking

The conclusion of chapter 10 was that we are conscious of our thought in understanding our behaviour teleologically. This thought of which we are conscious has two aspects: it is an application of causal or otherwise technical knowledge, and it is purposive. We are conscious of the first aspect in grasping our technical reasons, and of the second in grasping our practical reasons.

The distinction between these aspects is of deep philosophical importance. Nearly all philosophers have felt that there is some useful distinction between form and content to be drawn in connection with thought; but it is debatable exactly how we should draw it and where it should fall. Most philosophers (including Kant, it seems to me) model it on the distinction between a shape or arrangement and the material that has that shape or arrangement. We impose certain structures, it is thought, on the materials supplied by experience, and a principal task of philosophy is to identify and describe these structures. I have preferred to distinguish between the things that enter into our thought and the ways in which they enter: that is how I would distinguish content and form. I now suggest that in grasping our technical reasons, in being conscious of the technical aspect of our thought, we know what things come into our thought, and that we are conscious of their entry, conscious of the forms our thinking takes, in being conscious

of its practical aspect. Hence if the general theory of philosophy outlined in chapter 2 is correct, the subject-matter of
philosophy is precisely what we are aware of in being conscious of this latter aspect of our thinking.

I think causally when I think of one object as causing
another to acquire a property, and this is to think of them as
composed of certain materials. It will hardly be contentious
that I know what properties I think objects acquire or fail to
acquire and what materials I think they are composed of in
being conscious of this aspect of my thought. But how is
knowing how objects and properties come into my thought,
how is knowing what forms my thinking takes, bound up with
consciousness of its practical aspect?

At the picnic I think that the Sun is melting the butter – that
is, causing it to lose its shape and texture – and I move it into
the shade of a tree. Many objects including the Sun, the tree
and the block of butter come into my thought, and many
properties including the shape I think the butter is losing and
the position of the Sun relatively to the tree, the horizon etc.

The shape the butter is losing comes in as a kind of teleological explanans, as something lest the butter lose which I act. It
is obvious that I know it plays this role in understanding my
behaviour teleologically: according to chapter 10, in judging
that it is worthwhile to act to prevent the melting. But the
shape also comes in as a causal explanandum, as one the Sun is
causing the butter to lose; and the sun appears as a causal
agent. Am I not aware of this in being conscious of the causal
aspect of my thought?

No, because causation does not, strictly speaking, enter into
thought. According to p. 170, when I think that the Sun is
causing the butter to melt, the Sun and its position in the sky
come into my thought, and for the reason that it is there I do
something, move the butter, lest it melt. I am conscious of
thinking that the Sun is *causing* the butter to melt in being
conscious of its presence as a reason making it necessary for me
to move the butter. (This, also, is how I am conscious of
thinking that the Sun rather *has* than *does not have* a certain
place relatively to the butter, the tree etc.) As to the tree, its
causal role is that of preventing the butter from losing its shape

or hardness; and I am aware of this in understanding that its presence is a reason for not moving the butter out of its shade: a reason that makes it unnecessary to move it, or necessary to refrain from moving it.

The Sun and the tree enter my thought as causal agents. At the end of chapter 6 I said that although objects *are* instances of properties no object enters our thought simply as such an instance. Objects enter our thought and are conceived as existing as causal agents and sometimes as purposive ones. I noted that this sounds arbitrary. If objects are instances of properties why should they not exist or enter our thought simply in that guise? The explanation, I now suggest, is that we are conscious of their entry into our thought in being conscious of the practical aspect of our thinking and to say how we conceive them as existing is to describe this aspect. Objects have practical significance as causal and purposive agents but not simply as instances of properties.

The point is a difficult one. Let me put it like this. Awareness of objects that come into our thought is not separate from awareness of their entry, and awareness of the things we take to exist is not separate from awareness of their existence. The distinction is not between two bits of thinking but between aspects of a single bit. In so far as I am conscious of the technical aspect of my thinking and grasp my technical reasons my thinking appears as awareness of instances of properties, awareness of objects which have or acquire these properties. In so far as I am conscious of the purposive aspect of my thinking and grasp my practical reasons, my thinking appears as awareness of causal and purposive agents, as awareness of objects that cause harm or benefit or that can themselves be benefited or harmed. So much, I hope, a little reflection will confirm. The further suggestion is that this second kind of awareness (or my thinking in this second aspect) is what we mean by 'awareness of the existence of objects' or 'awareness of their entry into our thought'.

Another example. Seeing a large snake near Alcmena's baby I say, 'There's a snake near little Hercules.' An utterance of the form '*A* thinks *B* is an *s*,' I have argued, describes the purposive aspect of *A*'s thinking; hence I know that *I* think the object

near the baby is a snake in understanding the purposive aspect
of my own thinking. I know this in realizing that for the
reason it is approaching the cradle I act to prevent the baby
from being squeezed. And I know that Alcmena enters my
thought as an intelligent, purposive agent in understanding that
I am speaking in order that she may be aware of the snake.

This is different from the example of the picnic not only
because I think of Alcmena as a person and of the presence of
the snake as a teleological explanans but because some of the
technical knowledge I apply is not causal but linguistic; knowledge not of physical nature but of human convention. I use a
word for a snake (perhaps the Greek word *ophis*) and a construction which is expressive of assertion and the existence of at
least one object of a certain sort. Is this linguistic knowledge
analogous to causal? I think our knowledge of words is, but
not our knowledge of constructions.

We can be aware both of the words and of the constructions
we use; but (except in so far as we choose it for its contribution
to 'tone') a construction is not something we use in addition to
words. Using it *is* using the words; or at least specifying it is
describing the using of the words. I use the word *ophis* for the
technical reason that it is a word for a snake, and I am aware of
it as a word I use in being aware of the technical aspect of my
thinking. If, like M. Jourdain, I have never been taught grammar, I may not know at all what grammatical construction I
use. But I use *ophis* in order that snakes may play a certain part
in Alcmena's thinking: in order that she may think that there is
one near her infant, and its proximity may function with her as
a reason. In grasping this purpose of mine I think that my
speech has the form: asserting that there is something of the
sort signified near the individual referred to. I need not know
grammar to think this. But this is just what it is to grasp the
meaning of my construction.

In chapter 3 I argued that words and constructions have
meaning in different ways. I can now suggest that the difference between causal powers and psychological qualities provides an analogue. The vocabulary of a language and especially
its range of words for properties and sorts determines its expressive power as our limbs determine our physical strength.
Its grammar enables speakers to express things as skill and

imagination enable us to do things. A lexicon without a grammar is like a body without a mind.

Many philosophers today doubt if there is such a thing as teleological understanding. If, as I claim, the topics philosophy is concerned with, from causation and existence to the expressing of things in words, are all things of which we are aware in grasping our practical reasons, these philosophers must be labouring under a severe handicap.

11.2 The physical and the psychological

In a fine and characteristic passage (*Treatise* II iii 10) Hume compares philosophy with shooting. He has in mind chiefly the shooting of small birds which the solitary sportsman can walk up with the aid of a good dog: the happy philosopher is like a man who 'is pleased to bring home half a dozen woodcocks or plovers after having employed several hours in hunting after them'. But philosophy can also offer the thrills of big game hunting. The speculations of its most daring exponents are dominated by two great apparent dualisms. One is usually referred to as that of 'mind' and 'matter' or 'soul' and 'body' though 'psychological' and 'physical' are the most accurate terms. The other is that of being and becoming or objects and changes. These are the elephants of the discipline. The satisfaction of gunning for them is that of 'going for the big ones'. In previous discussions we have been stalking them and they are now at close range and fairly in our sights.

Faced by an apparent dualism there are three courses we can take. We can accept the dualism: Descartes does that for mind and matter and Davidson inclines to it for objects and changes. We can do away with one of the members or reduce it to the other. Leibniz, Berkeley and Hume abolish matter and Russell reduces change or becoming to having different properties at different times. Or we can say that the physical and the psychological or objects and changes are irreducibly different aspects of a single reality. That is the kind of solution I find most satisfying and shall now spell out for each dualism in turn.

It is difficult to say exactly what the two components of the physical-psychological dualism are because the words in which we are accustomed to hear it expressed, 'body' and 'mind', are used in a bewildering variety of ways. When Archimedes dries himself after a bath drying his body contrasts with drying his face or his arms and legs: 'body' here means 'torso'. When Mark Antony harangues the Romans he may contrast Caesar's body with Caesar: by 'Caesar's body' he means not Caesar's torso but his corpse, the inanimate object into which he passed away or which the Liberators obtained by killing him. Physicists use 'body' as a variant for 'material object'. The Moon is a body in this sense and so am I. Bodies in the physicist's sense may be contrasted with gravitational fields, with institutional objects like business companies, with illusory objects like Macbeth's dagger, with non-material persons like the Judaeo-Christian God, and with properties, changes and states of affairs. All these contrasts are of some interest to philosophers and so is the contrast between Caesar and his corpse; but none of them constitutes a contrast between body and mind.

As for mind, I say 'I had it in mind to go,' meaning I intended or half-intended; 'I'll bear it in mind,' meaning I will not forget it; 'I wish you'd make up your mind,' expressing the wish that you would come to a decision; or 'My aunt may be as blind as a bat and as deaf as a post; but her mind is as sharp as a needle', where 'mind' means 'intellectual, as distinct from perceptual faculties'. None of these usages makes it clear what philosophers are asking about when they enquire into the relationship of mind and body.

We think that human beings interact causally with other objects and also that they sometimes act or refrain from acting for reasons; we think of them as causal and as purposive agents. I suggest that the contrast in which philosophers are interested is simply the contrast between these ways of thinking. The philosophically interesting concept of the human body is the concept of a human being as something which has changes caused in it and causes changes in other things. The concept of a soul or mind with which Plato and Descartes operated is the concept of a thing with desires and beliefs, and this is the concept of a purposive agent. Those powers we count as bodily are causal powers. Those we count as mental are not causal; they are skills, and skills are abilities to act for technical reasons. And other psychological qualities, qualities of character like loyalty and timidity, are dispositions (or indispositions) to act for practical reasons. Philosophers sometimes use the word 'disposition' for physical as well as for psychological attributes: they give brittleness or solubility as an example of a disposition. The same word ('levity', 'rigidity') may be used literally for a physical and metaphorically for a mental disposition. But there is no real analogy between physical and psychological dispositions because there is no real analogy between causal and teleological understanding.

Philosophers sometimes speak as if the difference between the physical and the psychological were simple, primitive and intuitively clear: we just *see* that shape and velocity are different from mental states and processes like joy and deliberation. I am not sure that the difference would be so plain to primitive people or even to Homer; and if I am right the concepts can be defined in terms of explanation. The physical is that which can play a role in causal explanation. The psychological is not, in general, that which plays a role in teleological explanation: it is rare for a mental state to be a reason and a mental state cannot, strictly speaking be a purpose because it cannot, strictly speaking, be caused or prevented. But the word 'psychological' signifies the character of teleological roles, the character of the relationship between teleological explananda and explanantia.

Aristotle explained the relation of body and soul as one of matter and form. He held that objects of any sort can be described in two ways; we can specify their matter and their form; and psychological words are words in which we describe the forms of living things whereas what may be called 'somatological' or 'body' words describe their matter. This account will be helpful only if we can understand what he means by 'matter' and 'form'. Unfortunately his readers disagree about this. Most of them say he wants to exploit the notion of a potentiality that can be actualized. The matter of an s is that which has the potentiality of becoming an s and the form is either the actualization of this potentiality or at least that, whatever it may be, which distinguishes an actual s from a potential one.

On this interpretation the matter–form distinction will not of itself illuminate the distinction between the physical and the psychological. For things have potentialities for physical properties and states just as much as for mental. Ice has the potentiality of becoming water, grape juice of becoming wine; and water differs from ice in temperature, wine from grape juice in alcoholic content. Not only is Aristotle's account unhelpful on this showing; it also seems to be incorrect. For what we reckon to be a potential member of the species *homo sapiens* is not a living person's body. It is either a human foetus (so Rosalind Hursthouse 1987, ch. 2) or human gametes.

I think Aristotle is trying to use the concept not of a potentiality which is actualized but of a possibility which is fulfilled. His idea is that the notion of a bodily property is the notion of a property we exemplify and a bodily process is a process which takes place in us; psychological notions, in contrast, are notions we have of ourselves as instances of properties or notions of goings on of processes. Perceiving, for example, is not a process which goes on in addition to the stimulation of the sense organs: the occurring of change in our sensory system in certain circumstances *is* perceiving. Socrates is not an instance of wisdom as well as of snubnosedness but a wise instance of snubnosedness, rather as billiard balls are not instances of spherical-shape-which-is-useful-for-a-certain-game but instances-which-are-useful-for-a-certain-game of spherical shape. On this interpretation Aristotle's theory is a forerunner of mine: not surprising, since my own ideas were evolved in the course of trying to make sense of his.

Perhaps the main difference between us is that Aristotle omits to say that the concept of the human body is the concept of a human being as a causal agent. And it might seem awkward for him to say that; for thinking of people as causal agents is not considering what properties they exemplify; the notion of a causal agent is not the notion of a thing of which there can be instances but a special sort of notion of an object as an actually existing individual. Aristotle, however, is the leading ancient exponent of the distinction between causal and teleological explanation. He would be delighted at any demonstration that the body–soul relation can be analysed in terms of it. And we have just seen that it is not unrelated to the distinction between properties and instances. It is in being conscious of our causal thinking that we know what properties we think objects have; whereas it is in being conscious of the purposive aspect, conscious of our thought as teleologically explainable, that we know what kind of instances of these properties – sentient or inanimate – we think these objects are.

To many people the crucial question about the physical and the psychological is whether we have immortal souls. If we have, practical consequences seem to follow. Happiness after death will be more important than happiness now; we should try to find out how to secure it; and it may be sensible to do things which would otherwise be foolish, such as establishing a costly and potentially repressive priesthood, and to refrain from things that would otherwise be sensible, such as killing human beings on the margins of life who are a burden. Philosophers can, of course, question whether consequences like this really follow; but the hope is sometimes that they will tell us whether any element in us really is immortal.

That might seem a tall order to execute from the armchair. But Plato and Descartes defend a dualism of the psychological and the physical, and many philosophers since the eighteenth century attack it, as though the doctrines of dualism and personal immortality were logically equivalent.

Philosophers would show it is unreasonable to believe in a life after death if they could show either of two things: (1) psychological concepts are analysable into physical ones without remainder; (2) psychological states are conceived as emergent from or otherwise dependent on physical. (The difference between these propositions is that the second allows us to have ideas of what it is like to perceive and experience sensations which are not definable in terms that belong to the exact sciences.) The more rigorous arguments used by twentieth-century philosophers in favour of either of these theses involve the premise that causal explanation is the only genuine kind of explanation, at least for matters of fact. This is something philosophers are fully qualified to discuss. We should be prepared, then, for them to proclaim a substantive conclusion: the belief that we might survive death is incoherent. But if what

I say in chapter 7 is sound we can relax: the vital (or lethal) premise is not established. We explain and understand teleologically as well as causally and we do not think that teleological explanation is reducible to causal.

But of course the failure of efforts to show that a belief is unreasonable does not prove it is reasonable. A number of philosophers led by Hume himself have thought that mental states are not conceived as dependent on anything material and yet held a view of human nature which makes immortality impossible or very, very unlikely. Plato and Descartes recognize that it is not self-evident, recognize that they need to argue, that dualism entails immortality. Their arguments are less than watertight. And if what I said just now is right and the notions of body and soul are notions of a single thing considered now as a causal and now as a purposive agent, their dualistic premise is false.

In my opinion philosophy shows neither that belief in immortality is unreasonable, not that it is reasonable: a conclusion in line with what I said about its scope on my first page.

11.3   Objects and changes

The issue over objects and changes has been less trumpeted by philosophers since Descartes than the issue over the physical and the psychological but its credentials are more ancient. Before the time of Plato there was little discussion of mind, but the Eleatics denied the reality of change whereas Heracleitus and his followers, according to Plato (*Theaetetus* 156), in effect denied the reality of material objects and maintained that everything is change. Plato gives most of his dialogue the *Parmenides* and Aristotle large parts of his *Physics* to conceptual analysis of change. And in modern times lack of explicit references to the object–change dualism has not meant lack of interest in it. We have seen that Russell reduces acquiring properties to having them after not having them. Philosophers since Descartes have regularly preferred being and having to becoming and changing. That is probably because they have been obsessed by the language and methods of mathematics, and there is no change in mathematics. But there are no kinds of material in mathematics either and philosophers since Descartes have had little place or work for the concept of a material object. Questioning the reality of mind goes with belief in the physical but not always in the material. Many thinkers have taken as the fundamental atoms of reality exemplifications of properties at moments, and these entities are as much event-like as thing-like.

The second of our dualisms, then, presents itself in at least three ways. (1) Do objects have properties and also acquire them? Is there becoming as well as being? (2) Does the world contain objects that are genuinely material? Are there material objects as well as momentary events? (3) Even if objects exist is the existence of objects anything over and above the occurrence of change?

In reply to (1) I have argued that the difference between being and becoming is a difference in the way in which properties appear in thought and speech. The difference between having a property and not having it is real and independent of us; and an object which is acquiring a property does not have it. But when an object's redness, say, comes into my thought as a reason I think of the object as being red (or having been, or being about to be); whereas when it comes in as an object of desire or aversion or as a causal explanandum I think of it as becoming red.

In reply to (2) I have tried to show that the notion of matter is bound up with causal thinking. We do not think that the various kinds of material are exemplified in the world in the way the various properties are. If to be real were to be exemplified we should not think that matter is real. But we think that objects are composed of materials in trying to understand their acquirings and losings of properties. If our explanations are correct they really do contain these materials; and it is idle scepticism to suppose that none of our explanations is correct. Philosophers since the seventeenth century have constantly failed to do justice to common-sense belief in matter because they have failed to achieve an adequate analysis of causal thinking or see how there can be any genuine understanding except for the sort of understanding we have of mathematical properties. Gilson says this of philosophers from Descartes to

Hume (1938, pt. 2); I think it is true of many philosophers to this day.

A negative answer to (3) is implicit in chapter 5. The existence of objects is measured in years or seconds, and strictly speaking it is only the going on of change that is measured in time units. We can suppose that one object remains unchanged throughout a period of change in another, but we cannot in general think of objects as existing away changelessly: as Austin put it, existence is not like breathing only quieter.

But if the existence of objects is nothing over and above the going on of change, does it follow that the dualism of objects and changes is one merely of aspects? In the way in which I have said that a human being is a single reality that is in one aspect a causal and in another a purposive agent, can we say that the world is in one aspect a lot of objects that exist and in another a lot of changes that go on?

That would be to overdramatize the situation. Words like 'reality' and 'actuality' are used in two ways: for the things that are real and for the reality, the being real, of these things. If we start from the first usage reality appears to be the totality of all objects that now exist. They are the things that are most obviously real. And reality in the sense of being real, accordingly, appears to be existence. If, on the other hand, we start from the second usage and take 'reality' to mean primarily the being real of what is real, reality is time or the going on of change. And then reality in the sense of that which is real must be changes that go on.

But what determines the usage from which we start? It is not just the accident of which we learnt first. We see-saw between the two views of reality, the geographer's and the historian's, the static and the dynamic, because they correspond to the two aspects I have been distinguishing of our mental life.

The thinking of which we are conscious is both causal and purposive. In being conscious of its causal aspect we know what materials we think objects contain and what properties we think they have or acquire. Hence so long as we consider this aspect of our thought what stand over against it as reality must be material objects which have or acquire these properties. Consciousness of this aspect of our thought is consciousness of thinking of reality as the totality of interacting bodies.

On the other hand consciousness of the purposive aspect of our thinking is consciousness of the ways in which objects and properties enter into our thought and of the forms our thinking takes. But our thinking takes the form of causal and teleological understanding. Objects come in as causal or purposive agents, as things which can benefit or harm in various ways or as things which can themselves be benefited and harmed. Properties come in as explanantia and explananda. But understanding is of change. So when we consider the purposive aspect of our thought what stands over against it as reality seems to be the going on of change.

The duality, then, of objects and changes is not independent of us in the same way as the duality of rotation and cooling or hydrogen and helium or even (paradoxical as it may sound) of sentient and inanimate agents. There are sentient agents if there is purposive behaviour. Whether or not behaviour is purposive does not depend on whether anyone thinks it is, neither does the difference between being purposive and not being purposive have to be explained in terms of elements in the experience of sentient or intelligent beings. But the difference, if I am right about it, between objects and changes does. Objects that exist are what reality seems to consist of when we consider the technical aspect of our thinking and the occurrence of change is what it seems to be when we consider the practical or purposive. That does not make the difference between objects and changes unreal because our experience really has these aspects.

11.4 Conclusion

If the difference between objects and changes cannot be explained without reference to our thought, and if philosophical problems generally are generated by misunderstanding of our thought, it may seem that philosophy is, after all, a trivial pursuit by comparison with those studies that are targeted upon reality. Why should we spend more than some of our idler moments, more than time which might otherwise be devoted to watching snooker on the television, to tracing the forms that ordinary thought takes?

In the first place there is no alternative way of studying the traditional topics such as goodness, consciousness and time. It is not as if we could cut out the identification of modes of thinking and speaking and tackle these things directly. They are the concern of philosophy because, as I said at the beginning, they are things the study of which is at the same time a study of language and thought. If we spurn linguistic and conceptual analysis we shall not discover what time is, or goodness, or consciousness, by other means.

Secondly, what is trivial about human thought or serious about seaweed, quasars or quarks? Is there anything more important than the vagaries of the human mind? Is there anything more fascinating? It is on the human mind above all that our happiness in life depends: on the intelligence and friendship of those around us, on the virtues of our fellow-citizens in society. Even civilization's ability to control the forces of nature depends on such practical conditions as peace, disinterestedness and delight in causal understanding. And the representation of the human mind is the supreme challenge to the artist.

Even the painter addresses the mind. It may seem that a Rubens or an Etty paints only the human body, that the Chinese artist paints not even that but bamboos or mountains; but even artists paint for sight in the service of reason: they show us material things as we have learnt or as we learn from their pictures to see them. But from the earliest times painters have aspired also to represent states of mind, whether of men or gods. And in literature the mind has always been not only the most challenging but almost the sole subject of description. The first word in European literature is a word for a complicated mental state traditionally though inadequately rendered in English by 'wrath': μῆνιν ἄειδε, Θεά, 'The wrath: sing, Goddess, of that.' From Homer onwards, poets, dramatists and novelists have explored again and again for their successive generations every aspect of the human mind, intellectual, emotional and sensual, except one.

There is one aspect of the mind which escapes the artist and remains for the philosopher. That is the way in which objects, properties and changes enter into ordinary thinking. This is no less important than how we feel about other people or about nature or art or science, or how we respond to danger or seek power or gain. It is more profound than any of these things and more universal. Anyone who is really interested in human nature must take some account of this inmost recess of it. For some, penetrating to it is pretty well the most exciting activity life has to offer; for some, though perhaps not for many people even with the highest intellectual gifts. For philosophy is concerned with the most abstract and bloodless end (as John of Salisbury complained) of the psychological spectrum. Some of the professional philosophers who say that philosophy as traditionally practised is now out of date might consider whether they have not themselves mistaken their vocation. Perhaps politics, journalism or the Church would have suited them better.

But it is not quite right to say that philosophy deals with an end of the spectrum of human life which eludes the artist, since that implies that philosophy is not an art, and as I said in chapter 1 I think it is. Some philosophers are willing to allow that philosophers *can* be artists (so R. Nozick 1981, pp. 645–7). But if philosophy is not of its essence a kind of art, what is it? Not a science, if science is conceived, as today it is, as systematic knowledge of the physical. If philosophy is indeed concerned with part of our existence as conscious, purposive beings it must be a kind of art. For the truth we most want about this side of our existence is the sort of truth aimed at by novelists, dramatists and representational painters. Giving a correct account of how things come into thought and speech is like representing love or hatred or ambition or fear as they do.

The difference is that the things treated by other artists – emotions, states of character etc. – can also be treated in a more frigid and analytical way by philosophers, whereas the central topics in philosophy cannot be treated by other artists. Shakespeare does not give an account of time; he shows how we feel about the going on of change. The nearest we come to a literary treatment of a central philosophical topic is in some of the writings of Borges.

But this difference does not suffice to prevent philosophy from being a genuine art. It has close affinities with the literary arts. Like orators, philosophers use rhetorical devices to brings others round to their point of view; like poets they think up illustrations; like novelists they put themselves inside other people's minds. And because they are concerned with things of which we are all aware in understanding the purposive aspect of our ordinary thinking, they must try to make themselves clear to educated people generally. The philosopher who writes primarily for professional philosophers in the way in which scientists write for other scientists is as misguided as those musicians who compose primarily for other musicians and professional music critics.

The motives which lead people to philosophize are the same as those which lead people to literature: an interest in the working of the human mind and in expressing in words things that are very hard to express. The work of philosophers and poets is important for the rest of society because how we lead our lives depends on how we understand our nature. In the case of philosophy this is hard to see, partly because many philosophical topics do not initially present themselves as bearing on human nature at all – topics like time, causation and existence – and partly because it is not immediately obvious how views on any philosophical topic will affect the way in which we live.

The influence on practical life of metaphysical ideas can be documented historically but even when this has been done (I shall not set about the task here) it remains contentious. We are tempted to oversimplify positions, to polarize them and at worst to attribute base motives to philosophers with whom we disagree. In point of fact it would probably be impossible to construct a metaphysical picture from motives of personal or sectional interest; but there never was a philosopher who did not have a social background from which he or she must have drawn certain pretheoretical ideas about the human situation and certain tastes in thinking.

If I may give way for a moment to the temptation to oversimplify and polarize I would distinguish two types of metaphysical picture. One is atomistic and mathematical. It shows a world in which the things that exist approximate to points or mathematical solids, and patterns of regularity take the place of causation and purpose. On the physical side it is a world without colour, heat or mass. On the psychological there is an abundance of feelings and mental images, but these psychological phenomena occur in bundles that are only loosely connected, and each bundle (corresponding to each human person) exists on its own, logically and psychologically independent of every other. This metaphysical vision fits a liberal, republican and mainly urban society in which power, influence and wealth are distributed (or believed to be distributed) largely in proportion to talent and effort: the sort of society, in fact, that we now have in most of Europe and in English-speaking countries elsewhere.

In this book I have argued, on the whole, against these metaphysical doctrines and in favour of others. My world consists of material objects with causal powers mutually interacting. Sentience and intelligence are objectively real islands in a sea of inanimate nature. Feelings are shot through with thought; picturing is subordinated to understanding. And we are unable to apply the concepts of belief and desire either to others or to ourselves without engaging in friendly or hostile interpersonal transactions: to that extent we are psychologically and in a way logically dependent on one another. This vision fits a practical philosophy in which obligations to relatives and neighbours count high; in which the individual may be called on to make big sacrifices for family or society; in which social life and the peaceful pursuit of the arts are the ends by which political activity and social change are evaluated; and in which there is space for religion.

The two practical philosophies have been in competition at least since the sixteenth century and in the past supporters of each have extended their animosity to the other's metaphysical authorities. Hume has seemed a monster to traditionalists and Aristotle to liberals. I do not think that such partisanship contributes much either to human felicity or to philosophical insight. On the one hand, as I hope this book has shown, analytical philosophers are not committed by their methods to either side of the debate. In the earlier part of this century many of them thought they had no choice but to subscribe to some kind of liberal humanism. Most of my generation think we have other options; and we can find something to imitate both in Aristotle and in Hume. On the other hand the whole enterprise of academic philosophy is an urban phenomenon. Primitive people do not have a reactionary metaphysics: they have no metaphysics at all; neither have modern landowners who remain on their country estates, however abreast they may keep of the latest agricultural technology. The philosophers of ancient Athens were among the begetters of our urban civilization and philosophical criticism of its institutions comes from within.

Conservatives should not be troubled by that. It is not by chance that country people tend to drift to the town while urban intellectuals seek country cottages. After all, it is the traditionalist picture which emphasizes the dependence of the individual on society and the liberal picture which stresses individual autonomy. The most intransigent critics of liberalism do not wish to destroy the city altogether: at most they wish to replace the city of Mammon by that of some other deity.

Technical Terms and
Symbols

atomistic theory, account: one which postulates things that are indivisible or unanalysable, and represents all other things as constructions out of these.

believe: I use this word widely to cover knowing and perceiving as well as being of an opinion.

category: I say that different parts of speech, e.g. 'not' and 'nut', belong to different grammatical categories, and things about which we think and speak in different ways, like a mile and a motorcar, belong to different logical categories.

change: an object's acquiring or losing a property: becoming black, leaving London.

conceptual: a conceptual question or truth is a question or truth about how we conceive things.

construction (grammatical):   something specified in a grammatical rule for constructing sentences: orders of words, mood-inflections, insertions of particles.

continuum: an object, change or time-stretch is a continuum in so far as the end of one of its parts is the beginning of another. A single playing-card is (or looks like) a continuum, a pack not.

counterfactual: what is contrary to fact. In 'If my father had believed Cassandra he would still be alive' the condition under which the speaker's father would still be alive – believing Cassandra – is expressed as unfulfilled or contrary to fact, and the whole sentence is a closed or counterfactual conditional.

declarative: a declarative utterance is one which is affirmative or negative, or in which the speaker says something true or false: contrasts with interrogative, imperative and optative utterances.

disposition: an object has a disposition or dispositional property when it is the case that should a certain condition be fulfilled it will behave in a certain way. Brittleness is a dispositional physical property: if struck in a certain way brittle things break. Cowardice is a disposition of character: when it is right but dangerous to do something a cowardly person does not do it.

dispositional belief: A person who holds a belief but is not considering it believes it dispositionally: most of the time we believe only dispositionally that 2 + 2 = 4 or that Queen Anne is dead.

epistemological: to do with how we know or conceive something: it is an epistemological question how I form an idea of time or how my idea of it differs from my idea of thyme.

explanandum: something which is explained or calls for explanation.

explanans: something which explains. The Earth's coming between the Moon and the Sun could be given as a causal explanans of a lunar eclipse.

first-order: see *order*.

force: when a speaker makes a statement, announcement or promise his utterance is said to have the force of a statement, announcement or promise.

indexical: an indexical word is one which is demonstrative or which otherwise indicates a particular individual, place or time, e.g. 'those', 'here', 'tomorrow'.

isomorphic: of the same shape or form. Language is isomorphic with thought in so far as forms of speech correspond to forms of thought.

linguistic item: a word or construction.

material, matter: I use these words to cover not only solid substances but also liquids and gases like milk and air.

object: any living organism, artifact or inanimate object and anything else (if there is anything else) we think about and talk about in the same way.

ontological: to do with what exists or is real. It is an ontological question whether there are properties as well as objects.

order, first-order, second-order: First-order thought and speech concern things (the ontological level); second-order thought and speech concern thought and speech.

predicating: the act of relating properties to objects in speech. In 'Theaetetus is seated' I predicate a limb position of Theaetetus.

predicate: a thing predicated like a shape or a spatial relation. A linguistic item like 'spherical' or 'to the left of' I call a 'predicate-expression'.

property: something which can be had or exemplified, whether by a single object on its own or by an ordered set of objects.

purpose: an explanation in terms of purpose is an explanation of action (or inaction) in terms of a change which is an object of desire or aversion to the agent.

quantifier: a word like 'all', 'some' or 'no'.

reason: a reason is an object of belief which accounts for the believer's behaving in some way or having some further thought.

symmetrical: a relation is symmetrical if from the fact that one object stands in it to a second, it follows that the second stands in it to the first, e.g. being different from, being simultaneous with.

teleological explanation: explanation in terms of a reason or purpose.

truthfunction: if the truth of one proposition depends solely upon (is some function of) the truth of another or of others, the first is a truthfunction of that other or those others. 'If blood is green, grass is red' and 'Blood is green and grass is red' express different truthfunctions of the propositions that blood is green and that grass is red. Linguistic items which determine what truthfunction a speaker expresses, e.g. 'not', 'if', 'and', are called 'truthfunctional operators' or 'connectives'.

Symbols

I often wish to refer to forms of thought or linguistic expression or to say something about all thoughts or utterances of a given form. For these purposes I use letters according to the following conventions:

p and *q* stand for propositions. 'If blood is green, grass is red' is of the form: if *p* then *q*. 'Polonius thinks Hamlet is mad' is of the form: Polonius thinks that *p*.

A, *B* and *C* stand for individual objects and *f* and *g* for properties. 'Mars is red', 'The tomato became red' and 'Napoleon was under a tree' are all of the form: *A* is (was) *f* (or: *fA*).

s and *m* stand for sorts of object and for materials respectively. 'Caliban thinks the flask contains wine' is of the form: *A* thinks the *s* contains *m*.

φ and *ψ* stand for modes of causal action. 'Hamlet pulled' and 'Hamlet moved Polonius' are of the form: *A* *φs* (or: *φA*)

N stands for 'not', *K* for 'because' (introducing a causal explanation) *R* for 'for the reason that' (introducing a tele-ological explanation), *T* for 'in order that'. 'Icarus is not spherical' is of the form: *NfA*. 'Because the Sun shone the plum became sweet' is of the form: *KφAfB* (or *Kpq*). 'For the reason that the Sun was shining, in order that his body might become brown, Adonis did not leave the beach' is of the form *RφATfBNψC* (or, more simply, and taking Adonis' purpose to be that *he* should become brown, *RpTfANφA*).

Bibliography

Books not written in English are cited in translation.

Abbott, E., 1926 (1884): *Flatland*. Oxford, Basil Blackwell.

Anscombe, G. E. M., 1963 (1957): *Intention*. Oxford, Basil Blackwell.

Aquinas, Thomas, 1963–75 (1267–74): *Summa Theologiae*, ed. T. Gilbey and T. O'Brien. London, Eyre and Spottiswode.

Aristotle, 1984: *Complete Works*, Oxford translation, ed. J. Barnes. Princeton University Press.

Armstrong, D. M., 1984: *Consciousness and Causality* (with N. Malcolm) Oxford, Basil Blackwell.

Austin, J. L., 1961 (1956): Performative utterances, in *Philosophical Papers*. Oxford, Clarendon Press.

—— 1962: *How to Do Things with Words*. Oxford, Clarendon Press.

Bennett, J., 1976: *Linguistic Behaviour*. Cambridge University Press.

Braithwaite, R. B., 1932/3: The nature of believing. *Aristotelian Society Proceedings*, 33, 129–46.

Charlton, W., 1989: Aristotle and the uses of actuality. *Boston Area Colloquium in Ancient Philosophy*, 5, 1–22.

Churchland, Paul, 1984: *Matter and Consciousness*. Cambridge, Ma., Bradford Books.

Cohen, L. J., 1986: *The Dialogue of Reason*. Oxford, Clarendon Press.

Davidson, D., 1980 (1963–78): *Essays on Action and Events*. Oxford, Clarendon Press.

—— 1984 (1968/9): On saying that, in *Inquiries into Truth and Interpretation*. Oxford, Clarendon Press.

—— 1987 (1977): The method of truth in metaphysics, in *After Philosophy*, ed. K. Baynes, J. Bohman and T. McCarthy. Cambridge, Ma., M.I.T. Press.

Dennett, D. C., 1989: *The Intentional Stance*. Cambridge, Ma., Bradford Books.

Descartes, R., 1984 (1628–44): *Philosophical Writings*, tr. J. Cottingham, R. Stoothof and D. Murdoch. Cambridge University Press.

Dewey, John, 1917: The need for a recovery of philosophy, in *Creative Intelligence*, J. Dewey and others. New York, Henry Holt.

Dordillon, R., 1931: *Grammaire et Dictionnaire de la Langue des Iles Marquises*. Paris, Institute d'ethnologie.

Dummett, M., 1973: *Frege, Philosophy of Language*. London, Duckworth.

—— 1987 (1975): Can analytical philosophy be systematic, and ought it to be? in *After Philosophy*, ed. K. Baynes, J. Bohman and T. McCarthy. Cambridge, Ma., M.I.T. Press.

Einstein, A., 1962 (1920): *Relativity, a Popular Exposition*, tr. W. Lawson. London, Methuen.

Fodor, J., 1975: *The Language of Thought*. New York, Thomas Crowell.

—— 1981 (1965–80): *Representations*. Brighton, Harvester.

—— 1985: Fodor's guide to mental representation. *Mind*, 94, 76–100.

Frege, G., 1952 (1879–1919): *Frege, Translations*, tr. P. Geach and M. Black. Oxford, Basil Blackwell.

—— 1956 (1918): The thought, tr. A. and M. Quinton. *Mind*, 65, 289–311.

Gale, R., 1968: *The Language of Time*. London, Routledge and Kegan Paul.

Gilson, E., 1938: *The Unity of Philosophical Experience*. London, Sheed and Ward.

Goldman, A., 1971: The individuation of action. *Journal of Philosophy*, 68, 761–774.

Hare, R. M., 1952: *The Language of Morals*. Oxford, Clarendon Press.

Harré, R., 1970: *The Principles of Scientific Thinking*. London, Macmillan.

Harrison, J., 1971: Doctor Who and the philosophers. *Aristotelian Society*, Suppl. 45, 1–14.

Hegel, G. W. F., 1929 (1812–16): *The Science of Logic*, tr. W. H. Johnston and L. G. Struthers. London, Allen and Unwin.

Heidegger, M., 1967 (1927): *Being and Time*, tr. J. Macquarrie and E. Robinson. Oxford, Basil Blackwell.

—— 1975 (1961): *The End of Philosophy*, ed. and tr. J. Stambaugh. London, Souvenir Press.

Hobbes, T., 1946 (1651): *Leviathan*, ed. M. Oakeshott. Oxford, Basil Blackwell.

Hornsby, J., 1980: *Actions*. London, Routledge and Kegan Paul.

Hospers, J., 1967: *An Introduction to Philosophical Analysis*. London, Routledge and Kegan Paul.

Hume, D., 1888 (1739): *A Treatise of Human Nature*, ed. L. A. Selby-Bigge, Oxford, Clarendon Press.

—— 1902A (1748): *An Enquiry into the Human Understanding*, ed. L. A. Selby-Bigge. Oxford, Clarendon Press.

—— 1902B (1751): *An Enquiry Concerning the Principles of Morals*, ed. L. A. Selby-Bigge. Oxford, Clarendon Press.

Hursthouse, R., 1987: *Beginning Lives*. Oxford, Basil Blackwell.

Isocrates, 1929 (354/3 BC) Antidosis, in *Isocrates*, tr. G. Norlin, vol. 2. London, Heinemann.

John of Salisbury, 1982 (1159): *Metalogicon*, tr. D. McGarry. Berkeley, University of California Press.

Kant, I., 1929 (1781): *Critique of Pure Reason*, tr. N. Kemp Smith. London, Macmillan.

—— 1952 (1790): *Critique of Judgement*, tr. J. C. Meredith. Oxford, Clarendon Press.

Kekes, J., 1980: *The Nature of Philosophy*. Oxford, Basil Blackwell.

Kripke, S., 1980 (1972): *Naming and Necessity*. Oxford, Basil Blackwell.

Lewis, D., 1986: *On the Plurality of Worlds*. Oxford, Basil Blackwell.

Locke, J., 1975 (1689): *An Essay concerning Human Understanding*, ed. P. Nidditch. Oxford, Clarendon Press.

McGinn, C., 1989: *Mental Content*. Oxford, Basil Blackwell.

Mackie, J. L., 1974: *The Cement of the Universe*. Oxford, Clarendon Press.

McTaggart, J., 1927: *The Nature of Existence*, vol. 2. Cambridge University Press.

Madell, G., 1988: *Mind and Materialism*. Edinburgh University Press.

Malcolm, N., 1984: *Consciousness and Causality* (with D. M. Armstrong). Oxford, Basil Blackwell.

Mellor, D. H., 1977/8: Conscious belief. *Aristotelian Society Proceedings*, 78, 87–101.

—— 1981: *Real Time*. Cambridge University Press.

—— 1986: Tense's tenseless truth conditions. *Analysis*, 46, 167–72.

Merleau-Ponty, M., 1962 (1945): *Phenomenology of Perception*, tr. C. Smith. London, Routledge and Kegan Paul.

Mill, J. S., 1973–4 (1843): *A System of Logic*, ed. J. M. Robson. University of Toronto Press.

Moore, G. E., 1903: *Principia Ethica*. Cambridge University Press.
—— 1936: Is existence a predicate? *Aristotelian Society*, Suppl. 15, 175–88.
Nagel, T., 1970: *The Possibility of Altruism*. Oxford, Clarendon Press.
—— 1986: *The View from Nowhere*. New York, Oxford University Press.
Newton, I., 1934 (1686): *Principia Mathematica*, tr. A. Motte. Berkeley, University of California Press.
Newton-Smith, W., 1980: *The Structure of Time*. London, Routledge and Kegan Paul.
Nozick, R., 1981: *Philosophical Explanations*. Oxford, Clarendon.
Plato, 1961: *Collected Dialogues*, ed. E. Hamilton and H. Cairns. New York, Bollingen.
Putnam, H., 1962: It ain't necessarily so. *Journal of Philosophy*, 59, 658–71.
—— 1975: The meaning of 'meaning', in *Philosophical Papers*, vol. 2. Cambridge University Press.
—— 1988: *Representation and Reality*. Cambridge, Ma., M.I.T. Press.
Quine, W. V. O., 1961 (1952): *From a Logical Point of View*. Cambridge, Ma., Harvard University Press.
Radford, C., 1985: Charlton's feelings about the fictitious. *British Journal of Aesthetics*, 25, 380–3.
Ramsey, F. P., 1990 (1925–9) *Philosophical Papers*, ed. D. H. Mellor. Cambridge University Press.
Rorty, R., 1980: *Philosophy and the Mirror of Nature*. Oxford, Basil Blackwell.
Russell, Bertrand, 1900: *The Philosophy of Leibniz*. London, Allen and Unwin.
—— 1903: *The Principles of Mathematics*. London, Allen and Unwin.
—— 1918–19: The philosophy of logical atomism. *Monist*, 28–9.
—— 1921: *The Analysis of Mind*. London, Allen and Unwin.
Ryle, G., 1949: *The Concept of Mind*. London, Hutchinson.
Sartre, J,-P., 1989 (1945): *Existentialism and Humanism*, tr. P. Mairet. London, Methuen.
Searle, J., 1969: *Speech Acts*. Cambridge University Press.
—— 1979: *Expression and Meaning*. Cambridge University Press.
Shoemaker, S., 1969: Time without change. *Journal of Philosophy*, 66, 363–81.
Smith, Adam, 1976 (1759): *The Theory of the Moral Sentiments*, ed. D. Raphael and A. Macfie. Oxford, Clarendon Press.

Spinoza, B., 1985: *Collected Works*, ed. and tr. E. Curley, vol 1. Princeton University Press.

Stebbing, S., 1932/3: The method of analysis in metaphysics. *Aristotelian Society Proceedings*, 33, 65–94.

Stevenson, C. L., 1937: The emotive meaning of ethical terms. *Mind*, 46, 14–33.

Strang, C., 1974: Plato and the instant. *Aristotelian Society*, Suppl. 48, 63–79.

Strawson, P. F., 1959: *Individuals*. London, Methuen.

Unger, P., 1975: *Ignorance*. Oxford, Clarendon Press.

—— 1984: *Philosophical Relativity*. Oxford, Clarendon Press.

Urmson, J. O., 1956: *Philosophical Analysis*. Oxford, Clarendon Press.

—— 1967: Memory and imagination. *Mind*, 76, 83–91.

Vendler, Z., 1957: Verbs and times. *Philosophical Review*, 66, 143–60.

Wilkes, K. W., 1978: *Physicalism*. London, Routledge and Kegan Paul.

Wilkinson, G. S., 1990: Food sharing in vampire bats. *Scientific American*, 262, 64–70.

Wittgenstein, L., 1958 (1953): *Philosophical Investigations*, tr. G. E. M. Anscombe. Oxford, Basil Blackwell.

—— 1972 (1922): *Tractatus Logico-Philosophicus*, tr. D. F. Pears and B. F. McGuinness. London, Routledge and Kegan Paul.

—— 1979 (1951): *On Certainty*, tr. D. Paul and G. E. M. Anscombe. Oxford, Basil Blackwell,

Wright, L., 1973: Functions. *Philosophical Review*, 82, 139–68.

Xenophon, 1923 (?385–354 BC) *Memorabilia*, tr. E. C. Marchant. London, Heinemann.

Index